Northern Ire
Good Friday

Victims, Grievance

Mike Morrissey and Marie Smyth

Pluto  Press

LONDON • STERLING, VIRGINIA

C000100785

First published 2002 by Pluto Press
345 Archway Road, London N6 5AA
and 22883 Quicksilver Drive, Sterling, VA 20166–2012, USA

www.plutobooks.com

British Library Cataloguing in Publication Data
A catalogue record for this book is available from the British Library

ISBN 0 7453 1674 3 hardback
ISBN 0 7453 1673 5 paperback

Library of Congress Cataloging in Publication Data
Morrissey, Mike, 1946–
   Northern Ireland after the Good Friday agreement : victims, grievance,
and blame / Mike Morrissey and Marie Smyth.
      p. cm
Includes bibliographical references.
   ISBN 0–7453–1674–3 — ISBN 0–7453–1673–5 (pbk.)
   1. Northern Ireland—History—1994– 2. Social conflict—Northern
Ireland—History—20th century. 3. Protestants—Northern Ireland—
History—20th century. 4. Catholics—Northern Ireland—History—20th
century. I. Smyth, Marie, 1953– II. Title.
   DA990.U46 M68 2001
   941.60824—dc21
                                                                2001002160

11   10   09   08   07   06   05   04   03   02
10   9   8   7   6   5   4   3   2   1

Designed and produced for Pluto Press by
Chase Publishing Services, Fortescue, Sidmouth EX10 9QG
Typeset from disk by Stanford DTP Services, Towcester
Printed in the European Union by TJ International, Padstow, England

Contents

List of Tables and Figures

FIGURES

Acknowledgements

We thank Roger van Zwanenberg, Robert Webb and the other staff at Pluto Press for another seamless production process. We particularly wish to thank Chrissie Steenkamp for her work on the manuscript, and for her time and thoroughness in the tedious job of sorting out references. Once again, thanks to our spouses, Frances Connolly and Alan Breen for tolerating all that this book has entailed. We thank those who funded the research on which this book is based: the Central Community Relations Unit of the Central Secretariat; Making Belfast Work, North and West teams; the Special Support Programme for Peace and Reconciliation through the Northern Ireland Voluntary Trust; a private donation; the Cultural Diversity Group of the Community Relations Council; the Belfast European Partnership Board and the Community Relations Council.

We also wish to acknowledge the help of the following people: Yvonne Murray, Linenhall Library; Professor John Darby; Gillian Robinson; Brandon Hamber, Centre for the Study of Violence and Reconciliation, Cape Town; Professor Arlene Avakian of the University of Massachusetts at Amherst; Arlene Healey from the Young People's Centre; and Maurice Meehan from Barnardo's Northern Ireland. Our thanks to all the young people from various communities in North and West Belfast, Derry and elsewhere who contributed enormously to our understanding of the impact of the Troubles; and to 85 adult interviewees and over 1000 survey respondents who participated in our enquiries.

Finally, and by no means least, our thanks to our current and former colleagues, Siobhan McGrath, Marie-Therese Fay, Dr Jennifer Hamilton, Aishlene Campbell, Jan Keenan, Kirsten Thomson and Chrissie Steenkamp at the Institute for Conflict Research, Belfast; and to our chairperson, Chris O'Halloran, for providing gentleness and sanity at all times, even if it was only pretend!

Preface

In *Northern Ireland's Troubles: The Human Costs* we described the patterns of deaths that had resulted from the political conflict from the late 1960s to the early 1990s. The project was undertaken in the belief that the process of reconciliation in Northern Ireland would benefit from an understanding of who had died, where they had lived and what organisations were responsible.

The core assumption was that our narratives of the Troubles are essentially partisan so that we tend to attribute blame and responsibility to the 'other side'. Thus, some of those who died are seen as innocent victims while others got no more than they deserved. This tendency crosses the political divide – Unionists focusing on a Republican conspiracy against the security forces in particular and the Protestant population in general – Nationalists pointing to bias and repression amidst the security forces and the widespread murder of Catholics by Loyalist paramilitaries. An understanding that no side has a monopoly of grief derived from an objective account of political deaths might enable one to see the conflict from the perspective of the 'other side', illustrating that no one has a monopoly on grief or grievance. Thus we took the view that those who died could not be divided into 'real' and 'bogus' victims. The concept has to be inclusive and comprehensive although some individuals had a greater degree of choice about participating in the events that caused their deaths than others.

Since then, events have moved on. The peace process remains fraught with difficulty, but a new programme for government that makes reference to the victims issue has been produced. There are different sets of victims' organisations with differing definitions of victimhood, each making claims to legitimacy and to sources of funding. Reconciliation is still a priority within what remains a divided society. Moreover, The Cost of the Troubles Study, which gave rise to the first book, undertook a survey of the Northern Ireland population to investigate the impact of the Troubles on those who have lived through them. This piece of work facilitates a broader and deeper understanding of the everyday impact of the Troubles on people's lives than a database of fatalities.

Moreover, the organisation became Community Conflict Impact on Children (CCIC). Thus from researching the impact of the Troubles in general, it has come to focus on the particular problems of young people. This organisational realignment occurred partly because a key test for any society is how it treats its own and others' children and partly because embedding peace in Northern Ireland will be a long-term process. There is therefore a need to understand and work with children at this point. In this guise, the new organisation assisted with a survey of young people to assess their experiences of the Troubles and to capture their attitudes to the peace process.

The purpose of the present book is to address these new issues:

- How has the victims issue developed within the peace process?
- How do we understand the partial, indeed partisan, narratives of the Troubles that are shaping the politics of victimhood?
- Are there special categories of victims? Here we wish to explore sectarian assassination where victims were chosen solely on the basis of their religion
- What was the experience of those who lived through the Troubles?
- What impact did it have on their lives?
- How can this be understood in terms of the areas in which people lived, their religion and their gender?
- How have children experienced the Troubles?
- Do their opinions augur well for a peaceful society?

Thus the purpose of the book is to contribute to our understanding of the situation of victims in Northern by presenting new analysis drawn from all the data sets generated by The Cost of the Troubles project. It addresses issues that were not dealt with in previous work and for the first time presents new evidence drawn from a region-wide survey.

The material is organised in four parts:

- Part I comprises Chapter 1 which presents a contextual overview of the victims issue that has arisen during the peace process
- Part II examines particular sets of victims. Chapter 2 points to the very different kinds of experiences of the Troubles that arose from living in different places. It suggests that this

diversity of experience may be a factor contributing to different understandings of the Troubles and to the construction of different versions of victimhood. Chapter 3 looks at the particular phenomenon of sectarian assassination (the killing of victims simply because of their religion), offers some explanation of why this occurred and compares it with hate crime in the US. Chapter 4 re-examines the contentious issue of children as victims supplemented by responses from children themselves on their experiences of the Troubles

• Part III presents the results of two surveys. The first was conducted across Northern Ireland with adult respondents (The Cost of the Troubles Study survey). Chapter 5 explains how the survey was carried out and re-emphasises the importance of place and other variables in one's experience of political violence. Chapter 6 looks at particularly severe experiences and effects of political violence and offers some analysis for interpreting the effects of the Troubles. Chapter 7 reports on a second survey (the YouthQuest 2000 survey) conducted with 1000 children. This survey covered a wide range of topics relating to the Northern Ireland peace process, but here the concentration is on experience of political violence. The effects of the Troubles on children thus occupy a major segment of the book. However, since the peace process will of necessity be long term in delivering a peaceful and stable society, the condition of children at this point in time is of unparalleled importance

• Part IV (Chapter 8) concludes the book by commenting on truth, justice and closure of the victims issue.

Part I: Overview

1 Putting the Past in its Place: Issues of Victimhood and Reconciliation in the Northern Ireland Peace Process

Any serious attempt at assessing the human impact of the Troubles was deemed premature until the beginning of the peace process of the 1990s. Until then, such assessments had been confined to statements about the total number of bombs and shooting incidents, fatal casualties and the estimated damage to the economy. Any examination of humanitarian damage due to the Troubles whilst the conflict was ongoing was likely to underestimate it, since for the most part, the society functioned on the basis of denial of the conflict and its consequences. Perhaps it is true in all violently divided societies that auditing the harm caused by that conflict must be a task associated with the end of such conflict. Such work cannot, it seems, be undertaken whilst the conflict is ongoing and survival the main goal.

The ceasefires of 1994 created a new atmosphere in Northern Ireland in which an appraisal of the impact of the Troubles became more possible. None the less, such appraisals are fraught with difficulties. So complete is the division of Northern Ireland society that the identifications of the assessor with one or other side of the conflict will tend to blind him or her to aspects of the total picture. Nor are academic researchers above these processes. The challenge of arriving at a comprehensive overview of the humanitarian costs of the Troubles in Northern Ireland is the challenge of overcoming the effects of one's identification with one or other side of the conflict, and the challenge of being able to set aside some of the most intense personal experiences of most of our adult lives (in the case of the authors). The reader must judge how successfully that challenge has been met.

Since the late 1960s, over 3500 people out of a population of 1.5 million have been killed in the conflict in Northern Ireland. Official statistics for this period show over 40,000 people injured, although the real figure is likely to be higher since not all injuries were officially recorded. By March 1995, the British government had paid £814.219 million in personal injuries compensation, and a further £300.516 million for damages to property (Bloomfield, 1998: p. 4). Yet in comparison to location in the world experiencing conflicts, Northern Ireland's Troubles are relatively small scale, or 'low intensity' with an overall death rate of 2.25 per 1000 population. This is about the same level of conflict as the Middle East or South Africa, and worse than Turkey (0.57 per 1000) and Argentina (0.32 per 1000). However, Salvador (20.25 per 1000) had almost ten times the death rate, and Cambodia (237.02 per 1000), where about a quarter of the population died, had a death rate approximately 100 times that of Northern Ireland (Fay et al., 1997: p. 44).

Suffering, however is a difficult commodity in which to draw comparisons. As Frankl (1959: p. 64) points out, 'suffering completely fills the human soul and conscious mind, no matter whether the suffering is great or little. Therefore the "size" of human suffering is absolutely relative.' This 'filling of the human soul and conscious mind' with the pain of its past is the challenge that Northern Ireland, poised as it is on the edge of peace, must address itself. In this first chapter, issues of definition and contested views of victimhood (see Smyth, 2000) will be described. The prospects for finding successful strategies to manage the past and for the emergence of an agreed account of that past will also be assessed. The chapter will also examine definitions of victimhood in the context of arguments for and against *universalistic* and *inclusive* definitions and their implications for politics and for targeting humanitarian resources. Finally, the role of those bereaved and injured in achieving reconciliation, and in assisting the society with the task of managing the past will be addressed.

DEFINITIONS OF VICTIMHOOD

Definitions of victimhood in Northern Ireland's Troubles are characterised by two main trends, namely *universalism* and *inclusion*. Universalistic definitions of victimhood tend to emphasise that all residents of Northern Ireland – and those who live beyond Northern Ireland – have all been affected by the cumulative effects of three decades of violence. Many people who have lived through Northern Ireland's Troubles would describe themselves as having been harmed by the events of the last 30 years. There are many who nurse a festering anger at various politicians or public institutions. Many others are fearful of a return to violence and find it hard to trust the possibility of a peaceful future. Many are acutely aware of the harm done to others through death, injury and human rights violations. Consciousness of the harm done to a member of one's own community is very high, since in divided societies such harm takes on a wider significance. A harm done to one is perceived as harm to every member of that community. Feelings of anger, fear and grievance are expressed publicly and communally, with much long-term grieving and most forms of remorse relegated to the private sphere.

The idea of universal victimhood within Northern Ireland is central to politics in Northern Ireland and is compounded by the political cultures of both Loyalism and Republicanism. The cultures of contemporary Loyalism and Republicanism (Smyth, 1998) in Northern Ireland are cultures of victimhood. Both Loyalist and Republican paramilitaries make reference to their status as victims as a context that justifies their respective recourse to armed conflict. Loyalists see themselves as victimised by the Irish Republican Army (IRA), whereas Republicans describe themselves as victims of British Imperialism and Loyalist sectarianism. By claiming the status of victim, they each depict their position as deserving of sympathy, support, outside help and intervention by allies in order to dispatch the victimiser.

Furthermore, since all victims by definition are vulnerable, the violence of the victims is seen in the context of their victimisation. This can render the victims' actions, including their violent actions, the responsibility of the victimiser. It is increasingly common to see ageing war criminals portrayed as old, infirm and vulnerable. Claims to senility, infirmity and vulnerability are then used to argue the pointlessness of prosecution or extradition, as in the case of Augusto Pinochet, the former president of Chile. Those who have participated in the violence of the past, particularly those who have killed and injured others, may themselves lay claim to victimhood in the new dispensation, since without such a moral fig leaf their violence becomes too naked, politically inexplicable and morally indefensible. Claiming the status of victim is an attempt at escaping guilt, shame or responsibility. Universalistic definitions of victimhood, by including everyone as a victim, tend to facilitate this escape, and therefore tend to promote a political culture of powerlessness and undifferentiated chaos.

The effects of political violence are not limited to those injured or killed. The effects are pervasive. Within Northern Ireland, social and political institutions have been shaped by the history of division. They have been formed and have adjusted themselves to ongoing violent conflict. During the conflict, cultures of denial and silence (for example, Healey, 1996) prevailed within such institutions and remain virtually intact to this day. Therefore, these institutions, too, can be regarded as 'victims' of the conflict, shaped as they have been by the operational and cultural constraints of the Troubles. Yet most of the attention to the impact of the Troubles has focused elsewhere – on the human impact, on those who have been bereaved or injured.

The ending of the institutional silence on such issues began in 1997. The British government appointed a Victims Commissioner, Sir Kenneth Bloomfield, to investigate the situation of victims and make a report to the government. A unit within the Northern Ireland office, the Victims Liaison Unit, was to co-ordinate the affairs of victims, and a Minister for Victims, Adam Ingram, was appointed. However, it posed a difficulty, particularly for those in the Nationalist community, that he was also simultaneously Minister for Security. Mo Mowlam, then Secretary of State when welcoming the Belfast Agreement in the House of Commons, indicated the government's intention in relation to the appointment of Bloomfield:

> It is important when we are talking about all these positive devel-opments that we do not lose sight of the terrible price that has been paid by the victims of violence and their families. No amount of progress in the search for lasting peace will bring back those loved ones who have been lost. But I hope that Ken Bloomfield's Victims' Commission will soon be in a position to provide us with some practical suggestions as to how we can best recognise the suffering endured by the victims of violence and their families. I cannot say better than the words in the agreement itself. 'The achievement of a peaceful and just society would be the true memorial to the victims of violence.' (Northern Ireland Office, 1998)

Bloomfield published his report in May 1998, noting in his intro-duction the demands that this role had placed on him:

> In more than twenty-five years of public service I have never been asked to undertake a task of such human sensitivity. The letters I have read and the stories I have heard in carrying out the work of

the Commission will be burned in my memory forever. (Bloomfield, 1998: p. 6)

The Good Friday Agreement, signed on 10 April 1998, contains two paragraphs – 11 and 12 on page 18 – on the issue of victims. Bloomfield's report to the government examined the definition of victim and found 'some substance in the argument that no one living in Northern Ireland through this most unhappy period will have escaped some degree of damage' (ibid.: p. 14).

Whilst Bloomfield recognised that the experience of grievance may be widespread, it was clear to him that universalistic definitions of victimhood would neither aid the targeting of humanitarian resources at those in most need nor assist the development of social policy in the field. Practical concerns such as the targeting of resources moved to the foreground as political agreement was achieved and the prospect of social provision for victims became a real prospect. The Bloomfield Report refers to the need of the Victims Commission 'to aim its effort at a coherent and manageable target group' (ibid.). The difficulties with universalistic (or over-inclusive) definitions were not only practical and resource driven. It was also clear that in moral terms, such definitions failed to differentiate between the enormous loss and suffering of some and the lesser suffering of others, thereby creating further grievance.

CONTESTED NATURE OF VICTIMHOOD: INCLUSIVE DEFINITIONS

The contested nature of victimhood had emerged from early on in the Northern Ireland peace process. The difficulty for some in recognising the suffering of the 'other side' precluded them from allowing victim status to the 'enemy'. Therefore definitions that permitted a bilateral approach to the conflict were bound to problematic for those with these kinds of difficulty. To begin with, inclusive definitions relying on human suffering as the qualification for victim status were operationalised, notably by Bloomfield, whose brief from the government was 'To lead the Commission to examine the feasibility of providing greater recognition for those who have become victims in the last thirty years as a consequence of events in Northern Ireland … .'

The Secretary of State in announcing the Commission had referred to 'The pain and suffering felt by victims of violence arising from the troubles of the last 30 years, including those who have died or been injured in the service of the community.'

Bloomfield's brief was therefore permissive of an inclusive approach. He settled on 'the surviving injured and those who care for them, together with those close relatives who mourn their dead' as his 'coherent and manageable target group' (ibid.). No exclusions of paramilitaries or their families, nor of victims of state violence was contained in the wording of the final document, although some later complained about *de facto* exclusion from the process of consultation and insufficient emphasis on victims of state violence in the final report. These complaints notwithstanding, Bloomfield's approach did not categorically exclude those who had been, up until then, excluded elsewhere by reason of their affiliations, their previous actions or, in the case of victims of state violence, the identity of those who bereaved or injured them.

This inclusive approach posed challenges to those who had been victimised by those on the other side of the conflict, who had to countenance the inclusion of those from the community that had harmed them in the same 'victim' category as themselves. A great deal of anger was expressed, often by former members of the security forces, about their being considered in the same category as 'terrorists'. The politics of victimhood was being defined in response to Bloomfield's inclusive approach.

On the other hand, tentative and eventually more confident alliances* that crossed the sectarian divide were formed between those who had suffered. Self-help groups, and groups focusing on delivering services to those who had been bereaved and injured operationalised an inclusive approach. Indeed, it is difficult to anticipate how, ethically, anything other than inclusive approaches can be used in the delivery of human services. Yet although unity within the population of those bereaved and injured in the Troubles was an unlikely project from the outset, it was attitudes to the Good Friday Agreement that in the end composed the main fault-line within that population. Whether the victim constituency polarised on the issue of the early release of prisoners or whether this issue merely crystallised existing division is an imponderable. Whatever came first, lobbying to disqualify certain categories of people from legitimate victimhood intensified alongside the activities of the anti-Agreement

---

* The Cost of the Troubles Study was formed as an organisation by the author working with those injured or bereaved by Loyalist, Republican or security forces from both of the two main traditions in Northern Ireland. WAVE, the largest voluntary organisation offering services to those affected by the Troubles operates on an explicitly cross-community basis.

lobby. The use of the terms 'innocent' or 'real' as qualifications for victimhood began to appear.

New groups began to spring up, representing various interest groups in the field. FAIR (Families Acting for Innocent Relatives) and HURT (Homes United by Republican Terror, later changed to 'Homes United by Recurring Terror') are two examples of groups formed from mid-1998 onwards who adopted an exclusivist approach, describing themselves as 'victims of terrorism', 'innocent victims', or 'victims of Nationalist terror'. These groups were largely concentrated in the border regions, in regions where death rates of the local security forces had been highest. Their energies in the initial phase of their operation were concentrated on lobbying, meeting politicians and voicing opposition to developments such as early prisoner releases. Attempts to include them in the broader rage of activities in the field continued but did not always meet with success. FAIR, for example, was invited to join the Touchstone Group, an advisory group to government established at Bloomfield's recommendation, but did not take up its seats. Early prisoner releases as part of the Good Friday Agreement was a difficult issue for many who had suffered at the hands of paramilitaries. The difficulty posed by early prisoner releases was recognised by the government in the timing of announcements of such releases alongside announcements of measures designed to help victims. Some of these measures were hastily designed and were later much criticised, such as the location of a Family Trauma Centre in South Belfast, rather than in North or West Belfast, where the effects of the Troubles had been most marked.

The reliance of both Loyalist and Republican politics on notions of victimhood has already been noted, and therefore it was, perhaps inevitable that bids for the admission of ex-prisoners to the category of victim would be made. However, perhaps one of the effects of continuing pressure from groups such as FAIR was to ensure that lobbying to include prisoners under the victims remit became increasingly less likely to succeed.

TOWARDS A COMMON VIEW OF THE PAST

In humanitarian terms, it is necessary to define priorities and allocate resources amongst those who have suffered most. The emotive and subjective nature of such decision-making, together with competing claims for priority must properly be informed by some universally agreed knowledge of the differential effects of the Troubles on the population of Northern Ireland and beyond. Universalist definitions of victims also serve to conceal the way in which damage and loss has been concentrated in certain locations, communities and populations. No analyst can rely on his or her ability to objectively assess the damage that has been done in Northern Ireland, since all, even supposed outsiders, are subjectively identified with one or other side. Therefore, it is necessary to find a way of providing an overview, delineated in more or less universally agreed terms. Such knowledge can more closely define the way in which such damage is differentiated by age, location, gender and significantly by religion and nationality. Elsewhere (Smyth et al., 2001) we have argued the need for and value of adopting a transparent set of indicators of the effects of the Troubles.

An assessment of the impact of the Troubles can be provided by the use of the distribution of death due to the conflict as an indicator. Death is a relatively unequivocal measure, although there are some definitional issues (Fay et al., 1999a: pp. 126–32). None the less, death appears to be the least problematic of the available concepts in definitional terms. It also serves as a reasonably good surrogate for other effects of the Troubles, such as injury (ibid.: p. 136), and the death rate of specific geographical locations is positively correlated with other conflict related factors, such as reported exposure to Troubles-related violence and its psycho-social consequences (Fay et al., 1999b). Annual deaths figures show a correlation coefficient of 0.93 when compared with the annual number of injuries associated with the Troubles. Deaths and injuries can be seen as the primary human cost of the Troubles, and although injuries outnumber deaths by approximately ten to one, they follow the same patterns of distribution in the population. Therefore, the distribution of deaths can be used as an indicator for targeting intervention and associated resources.

At a political level, however, the use of any overarching indicator challenges preconceptions about victimhood in general. The use of data on deaths due to the Troubles challenges both Loyalists' and Republicans' sense of their own victimhood. Most obviously, it challenges Republicans by showing their predominant role in causing deaths, and it challenges Loyalists by showing that Catholics have suffered more than Protestants in terms of deaths and injuries. Such challenges may prove important in the development of an agreed – or at least a more reconciled and comprehensive – account of the suffering in Northern Ireland since 1969.

THE ROLE OF VICTIMS IN RECONCILIATION

Throughout Northern Ireland's Troubles, a number of those who have been bereaved in the Troubles have campaigned for reconciliation and peace. Gordon Wilson whose daughter was killed in the Enniskillen bomb, and Mairead Corrigan whose sister's children were killed are two well-known examples. Others, too, have been put in the spotlight at key moments to pronounce on new political developments or initiatives. Media representations of those bereaved and injured in Northern Ireland's Troubles have sometimes probed in a rather crude and insensitive manner. In interviews with the newly bereaved, broadcasters have asked immediate family members if they forgave the perpetrator, or if they wanted revenge – often within hours or days of the death. The bereaved person's response is held up as a moral benchmark by which others could gauge their degree of entitlement to desire revenge or retaliation. If those closest to the loss, those most entitled to blame and revenge, respond with magnanimity, then who could respond otherwise? In this way victims can be put in a position of a kind of moral leadership. Thomas (1999) describes how those who have endured great suffering, such as Holocaust survivors, are popularly cast in the role of what he describes as potential or actual 'moral beacons'. Thomas articulates a widespread assumption that 'great suffering carries in its wake deep moral knowledge' (ibid.: p. 204) – an assumption he refers to as the 'Principle of Job', whereby those who have endured extremes of suffering may be appointed or act as 'moral beacons' for a larger population.

Such figures are often used as examples of moral behaviour or some accomplishment of self-governance of which they set an example. If, in spite of their great suffering, they can forgive, then the rest of us can also forgive. Gordon Wilson and Mairead Corrigan were recent examples of such 'moral beacons'. Conciliatory in political attitude and forgiving of those who cause bereavement, injury or hurt, the moral beacon is a de-escalator of conflict, a proponent of the New Testament doctrine of 'turn the other cheek'. On a global scale, Nelson Mandela is an example of a 'moral beacon', through his response to the rulers under Apartheid and his political magnanimity on gaining power in South Africa.

However, Thomas argues that suffering in itself is not a sufficient qualification for the role of 'moral beacon'. He points out that in the US, although African Americans historically endured the suffering of slavery they tend not to be regarded as 'moral beacons', whilst Jews, particularly Holocaust survivors, are frequently regarded in this light. Other factors, such as race, class, religion and ethnicity affected the likelihood of becoming a 'moral beacon'.

In Northern Ireland, this tendency to qualify some and not others is manifest. The victim of punishment beatings, the widow of the alleged informer or the partner of a prisoner are unlikely to qualify as 'moral beacons', in spite of their undoubted suffering. Rather, the suffering must be recognised as 'undeserved' according to dominant values. In societies divided by racism, sectarianism or ethnic conflict, ambivalent attitudes towards the suffering of certain categories of 'other' people, and processes of victim blaming are commonplace. One party to the conflict does not necessarily regard the suffering of the other party as problematic; one side's suffering can be a source of the other side's triumph. The 'moral beacon' must be congruent with the dominant political values. In a society in which, in spite of the peace process, violent political division persists dominant political values may be difficult to determine. The battle of domination of one set of values over another is ongoing. Manifestation of this in Northern Ireland has been the attempts, referred to earlier, to qualify victimhood with concepts such as 'innocent' or 'real', which have coincided with the increased political role of certain victims groups.

The popular assumption behind Thomas's 'Principle of Job' is highly questionable. Does suffering necessarily result in enhanced moral development? Does suffering necessarily increase suitability for roles of moral leadership? Frankl's (1959) observation of life in the death camps of the Second World War would indicate that in some cases, where some prisoners collaborated, jeopardising others' lives in order to save themselves, suffering in fact can diminish rather than increase moral integrity. Experience of suffering is also commonly used to explain subsequent violent or abusive behaviour. Adults who are abusive often cite 'difficult childhoods' as explanatory factors in their abusive or violent behaviour. In the context of Northern Ireland politics, for example, Crawford's (1999, p. 132) study of Loyalist prisoners found that 30 per cent of those he interviewed had 'members of their family' killed by the IRA/Republicans (he does not specify the closeness of relationship in his definition of 'family'). By implication, previous experience of bereavement explains why these prisoners subsequently took up arms.

Perhaps due to this 'moral beacon' function, virtually unassailable moral authority can be acquired by reference to or by association with victims in Northern Ireland. Some politicians have sought to exploit this from time to time. The campaign for 'Protestant civil rights' which took the form of a 'Long March' in 1999 incorporated many of the newly formed victims groups under the umbrella organisation Northern Ireland Terrorist Victims Together (NITVT), alongside anti-Agreement politicians from the Democratic Unionist Party (DUP) and the anti-Agreement side of the Ulster Unionist Party (UUP). The overtly political demands of the campaign included a declaration by the IRA that the war is over; decommissioning including ballistic testing of weapons; destruction of paramilitary weapons; disbandment of terrorist groups; and an international tribunal to investigate the role of the Irish government in the development of the Provisional IRA.

At another point the mainstream UUP, faced with the prospect of going into government with Sinn Féin, supported Michelle Williamson, whose parents were killed in the Shankill Road bomb in 1993, to take a court action seeking a judicial review of the Secretary of State's ruling on the status of the IRA ceasefire. David Trimble personally accompanied her to court. The goal was to have the Secretary of State's ruling overturned to that Sinn Féin would be excluded from the political process.

However, some politicians began to have doubts about the ethics of such strategies. Fraser Agnew, United Unionist Assembly Party member resigned in September 1999 from the Long March campaign, stating: 'I believe innocent victims are being manipulated and exploited for political ends. It's almost like emotional blackmail' (cited in Pauley, 1999).

Northern Ireland has yet to resolve its response to the public voice of those who have suffered. In the absence of any institutionalised acknowledgement of their suffering, the understandable anger of those who have suffered at this lack of acknowledgement has been channelled and expressed in many diverse ways, some constructive and some less so. Arguably, it is the duty of the public to listen respectfully and to afford public acknowledgement of loss and pain to those who have suffered. The guilt and powerlessness that such listening and acknowledgement can elicit could easily lead to confusion of the duty to listen with a non-existent duty to act on the wishes of victims. As is argued above, there are dangers in regarding those who have suffered as moral authorities simply by virtue of their suffering.

The way in which politics on the victims issue developed was to be even more radically shifted by one major event. A massive explosion in Omagh town centre on 20 August 1998 killed 28 people. Another died later, and two unborn children also died. The Real IRA had planted the bomb. Omagh became the focus of attention on the issue of victims for a considerable period. Ministerial visits to Omagh, visits by the then US President Bill Clinton and other dignitaries were followed by announcements of various public investments in the town and surrounding area over subsequent months. Fund-raising for the Omagh Fund was widespread. The scale of the devastation caused by the Omagh bomb and the timing of the carnage within the peace process provided, for once, a clear and agreed focus for concern about victims. There was an unprecedented political unity in condemnation of the bomb, so humanitarian efforts were unequivocal and concern was universal. It was clear what Omagh needed. Omagh provided for government and other public figures the opportunity to demonstrate that, given the opportunity, they could do something positive for victims. Caring for the victims of Omagh was almost caring by proxy for the thousands of others who had been left in isolation and without support. The scale and recency of the suffering of the people in the Omagh bomb served to temporarily sideline all other victims concerns. In the longer term, it remains to be seen whether the lot of those bereaved and injured yet neglected in the past has been much improved by recent fund-raising and developments in provision. Even amongst those bereaved and injured in Omagh, some discontent has been expressed about the way money from the Omagh Fund has been handled.

A further effect of the Omagh bomb was to focus the attention of those concerned with so-called 'victim issues' on one event – albeit understandable, at least in the short term. It was no longer – if it ever had been – a central matter of public concern that it is generally the poorest people that have suffered most in the Troubles. It was no longer a concern that they continued to live in communities blighted by militarism and deprivation, and that the overall amount of humanitarian assistance that had been given to them was paltry. The Omagh bombers inadvertently provided a clearly defined opportunity for an outpouring of humanitarian aid, an occasion which allowed the expression of the universal concern about those bereaved or injured, a group of people that could unequivocally be regarded as 'real' and 'innocent' victims. The Omagh bombers also diverted an emerging debate about the nature and extent of Troubles related need away from a large-scale problem located in militarised communities towards a smaller and more easily defined target group, the victims of Omagh. It would take years to move beyond that focus, and perhaps the opportunity that existed at that stage of the peace process to examine the impact of the Troubles in a comprehensive way may never be entirely recovered.

The opportunity to establish an overall transparent and fair system for identifying and prioritising amongst the needs of those who have suffered in the Troubles has been dogged by continued attempts at political hijacking of the victims issue. Furthermore, progress on this, as with progress on many other issues in Northern Ireland, is at the mercy of the political process. The rift that divided Unionists and Nationalists and that now increasingly divides those who support the Good Friday Agreement and those who do not, dictates the amount of attention and priority given to victim issues.

MANAGING THE PAST

The transition to peace in Northern Ireland, should it succeed, will not entail a change in dispensation in the near future such as that which took place in South Africa. In Northern Ireland, the nature of the Good Friday Agreement and protocol within the Northern Ireland Assembly ensures bilateral involvement in decision-making on a permanent and ongoing basis. It is as if the transitional Government of National Unity became the permanent government in South African terms. This arrangement, where no unilateral decisions can be taken, has implications for how the victims issue, the management of the past and the process of reconciliation will be handled – or avoided – in Northern Ireland.

The culture of suffering and grievance within the society creates a series of practical and moral challenges to the prospect of peace building. Within the voluntary sector in Northern Ireland there was a sudden proliferation of interest in the provision of services to victims and their families. Sir Kenneth Bloomfield was a governor of the BBC whilst he was Victims Commissioner. The BBC began broadcasting a short daily morning radio slot in which someone described the impact the Troubles had had on him or her. Some called for a South African-style truth commission; others, such as the Bloody Sunday families succeeded in obtaining public inquiries into various deaths, and yet others, notably those bereaved where collusion between paramilitaries and security forces was alleged, continue to call for more public inquiries. Families called for the return of the bodies of the 'disappeared', and several bodies were indeed found and returned after a painful period of excavation that left other families worn out and empty-handed. Unfinished business, all relating to the legacy of the last 30 years began to be re-examined, this time with the heightened expectation of resolution. Now that the Troubles were supposedly over, these things ought to be sorted out. The loose ends of the past needed to be tied down before moving to a new chapter in Northern Irish history became possible. 'Justice', 'truth', 'healing' and 'closure' were terms that recurred in these discussions. It was usually outsiders or professional observers rather than local people who raised issues of reconciliation and forgiveness. Those living in communities worst affected by the Troubles had their aspirations modified by the fact that they were often still living with the continued threat of violence.

By re-conceptualising the damage of the Troubles as belonging to the past and by redefining the divisions amongst people (pro- versus anti-Agreement compared with Catholic versus Protestant) it was possible for people in the new Northern Ireland to come together, albeit tentatively at first, on a newly defined basis. Conferences to discuss 'managing the past' or 'burying the past' began to occur, thus reconstructing the difficulties and suffering caused by political upheaval as now belonging primarily to the past. The existence of two cohorts of people challenges the long-term viability of such discourses: the bereaved, those with maimed bodies, those who live with the chronic pain of physical disablement and lost livelihoods who continue to live in the present and will continue to suffer in the future; and those who live with the reality of ongoing violence in a time of supposed peace. Only if this range of experiences can be genuinely included in such discourse can the discourse itself be broadened and deepened. Only the inclusion of these range of experiences will shift the discourse of 'managing the past' from the realms of the aspirational to the territory of the possible.

In Orwell's *Nineteen Eighty-Four* (1949), the Party slogan was 'Who controls the past ... controls the future; who controls the present controls the past.' No one agreed version of the past might ever emerge in Northern Ireland, given the nature of settlement. In South Africa, the Truth and Reconciliation Commission's version of the past was the version compatible with the overall orientation of the ruling African National Congress. At least in the foreseeable future, no one side will hold the power to determine the way the past is managed in Northern Ireland. Yet the past must be at least contained if not entirely resolved. The new Northern Ireland Assembly must struggle, implicitly or explicitly, with the impact of the past on the present and ultimately on the future. The nature of that Assembly, and decision-making therein, would indicate that a less clear-cut, more inconclusive process than that which occurred in South Africa will take place in Northern Ireland. The contents of that process have yet to be determined. The new dispensation in Northern Ireland must, to borrow a concept from Fanon, make the road as they walk. There is no ready-made home-assembly solution that can be imported from elsewhere. The terrain means that the foundations on which such a road will be built will require special techniques, and it must weave between various camps leaving no one without access to it. Should it be successfully built, it will be a triumph of political engineering.

Part II: Victims

2 Disaggregating the Troubles: The Importance of Place

If the war in Northern Ireland is over, violence is far from ended. Indeed, the process of moving from a violent conflict to a post-conflict situation seems to involve a messy period of low-level violence. During 1999 and 2000, attempts to burn Catholic churches, schools and Orange halls, the intimidation of individuals from their homes and the continuing disputes over territory – along interfaces or contested marching routes – continued unabated. All of this contributed to a continuing sense of fear and suspicion in those areas that suffered most from political violence and a general uneasiness in the wider society. Several factors contributed to this period of uncertainty.

First, there were ongoing problems about implementing the Good Friday Agreement. Many Unionists were convinced that Republican difficulties over arms decommissioning represented no more than the continuity of the 'ballot box and armalite' strategy for Irish unity – the IRA would maintain its arms in order to continue the military struggle if the political strategy failed. Other Unionists were opposed in principle to sharing power with Republicans who, in their view, had been engaged in a violent paramilitary conspiracy against the Northern Ireland state for over 30 years. Even the Official Unionist Party, which signed up to the Good Friday Agreement, vacillated between power-sharing and a boycott of the new political institutions.

Whilst Republicans condemned this 'prevarication' as a simple inability to countenance militant Nationalists in any power-sharing arrangement, it was certainly more complex than that. The referendum that endorsed the Agreement was only won by dint of providing Unionists with assurances that decommissioning of paramilitary arms would take place. Opinion polls taken at a later date indicated a fall-off in Unionist support of the Agreement. This fall-off occurred when it became clear that the IRA was incapable of handing over arms. The fear within the Republican movement of a serious split if the leadership consented to decommissioning was real but hardly consoling to Unionists who faced the prospect of allowing their historic enemy into government. Indeed, evidence that Republicans were continuing to attempt to acquire more weapons in the US was provided by arrests made by the FBI. For Unionists, this was less than reassuring. Mounting uncertainty within the political process contributed to ongoing tensions within civil society.

That the peace process itself was essentially driven by elites was one of the problems facing the process of reconciliation, a process that required the involvement of the wider civil society. The Hume–Adams initiative, regarded in some quarters as the opening initiative in the peace process, was attributable to only two individuals. Subsequently, all of those engaged in political negotiations (political parties, paramilitary organisations and the British and Irish governments) account for only a tiny fraction of the Northern Ireland population. The mass of the population was outside the political arena, waiting nervously, fearful of the signals emerging from within. In the period of waiting, many were predisposed to settle scores or 'cleanse' territory whilst the political vacuum lasted. That the newly devolved administration in Northern Ireland lasted only eight weeks in its first phase was indicative of the tensions and contradictions of the period.

Paramilitary rivalry, too, exacerbated political difficulty. As political prisoners were released in the implementation of Good Friday Agreement, new antagonisms emerged amongst Loyalist paramilitaries on the outside. To begin with, the Loyalist Volunteer Force (LVF) resumed its hostilities with the Ulster Volunteer Force (UVF) from which it had originally split. This hostility, first manifest in Portadown, soon spread to Belfast as sections of the Ulster Freedom Fighters (UFF) lent support given to the LVF. Six died and several were injured in the ensuing clashes. Meanwhile, the UFF threatened to break its ceasefire because of what it termed the 'ethnic cleansing' of Protestants in North Belfast. Certainly, the Northern Ireland Housing Executive reported housing intimidation in North Belfast, but, in the overwhelming majority of cases, the families were Catholic. However, subsequent feuding between Loyalist paramilitaries (the Ulster Defence Association (UDA) and the UVF) came to a head in the late summer of 2000. This internecine conflict, which was concentrated in the Shankill area, forced over 200 Protestant families to move house.

On the Republican side, splinter organisations were attempting to undermine the peace process. They continued to recruit the disaffected from the IRA and mounted a fresh series of incidents including an attempt to bomb Hammersmith Bridge in London. The desire to undermine the peace process was driven by their belief that Sinn Féin and the IRA had 'sold out' the core historic mission of the Republican movement – the war to drive the British out of Ireland. They remained unimpressed by indications that successive British governments showed little wish to remain in control of Northern Ireland, seen as an area fraught with political minefields; the underwriting of whose public sector cost the British Exchequer almost £4 billion each year. For Republican splinter organisations, the 'holy grail' of Irish unity had not been achieved, so the war had to go on.

Moreover, disputes over marching routes continued. The unresolved 'Drumcree dispute' entered its sixth year without resolution. Yet Drumcree was merely the most visible signal of spatial contests that were being waged between communities right across the region. Expert mediators brought in from Britain and South Africa soon ran into the brick wall of the Orange Order's absolute determination to march and the equally absolute resolution of the Gervaghy Road residents to prevent their marching. Across Northern Ireland, disputes of a similar kind left grievance, distrust and hatred in their wake. Interventions and rulings by the Parades Commission were only accepted to the degree that they endorsed one or other communities' position. The Orange Order decided not to negotiate with the Parades Commission, while the Portadown Orange Lodge, from its position of centrality as the Lodge involved in the Drumcree dispute, campaigned for its dissolution.

Yet another factor underlies these divisions and disputes. The views and positions taken by those involved in such disputes are at least partially determined by their experiences and memories of more than 30 years of political violence. In the year 2000, only those in their fifties had any mature experience of life in Northern Ireland without political violence. For many in the population, living with political conflict has been the totality of their life experience. Contrary to various perceptions, there is no single, defining experience of Northern Ireland's Troubles. Various locations and subgroups within the population were subjected to very different kinds and levels of violence. Accordingly, the accumulation of experiences and memories was radically different for people living in these various locations and sub-groups. Whilst it would be grossly reductionist to suggest that political attitudes are entirely the result of such experience, it would be equally foolish to suggest that what happened to individuals, their families, friends and neighbours played no part in their formation of their assessments and viewpoints. The evidence generated by The Cost of the Troubles Study points to different, indeed contradictory, experiences of political violence across Northern Ireland and the sub-populations therein.

Accordingly, the purpose of this chapter is to explore the variety of experience of the Troubles in selected locations. This will illustrate the wide variation in experience of the Troubles that contributes to the formation of widely differing perceptions and assessments of the Troubles in general, and the motivations of parties to Troubles-related disputes in particular. This process of forming an overall 'picture' of the Troubles is particularly important in the social construction of victimhood. To take an example, a constant theme of Loyalist politics is that the Protestant community has been the primary victim of the Troubles – the main object of the IRA's terrorist campaign. Certainly, Republican paramilitaries were responsible for the majority of deaths. However, those deaths caused by Republicans include almost 600 members of the British Army of whom only a tiny fraction came from Northern Ireland. The view of the Protestant community as the primary victim does not square with the general evidence of Troubles-related deaths, even when members of the local security forces are treated as overwhelmingly Protestant. In both absolute and relative terms, Catholics were a majority of fatal victims. This remains the case even if Catholics who were killed by Republican paramilitaries (almost a quarter of the total) are excluded from consideration. (For more information on relative death rates, see Fay et al., 1999a.)

Conversely, Nationalist antagonism towards the security forces is based on the perception that the security forces are engaged in ongoing repression directed primarily at Nationalists. Nationalist resistance to any alteration to plans for police reform following the Patten Report on the reform of the Royal Ulster Constabulary (RUC) is based on a depth of feeling related to this perception of the security forces. The evidence, however, indicates that Republican paramilitaries, originating from within the Nationalist community, were responsible for more Catholic deaths than all of the security forces combined, whilst the RUC accounted for less than 1 per cent of the 3700 people who died in the Troubles. Ideology does not have a direct relationship to evidence.

Thus, deep-seated beliefs and attitudes persist even contrary to the factual evidence of the distribution and perpetration of political violence. One explanation is that perceptions of victimhood are simply a reflection of the bifurcation and deep divisions that are both cause and effect of the Troubles themselves. According to this perspective, the only genuine victims are those killed by the 'other side'. Thus, it might be said (by anti-Nationalists) that Republican victims, and by extension Catholics, paid the price for their insurrection. Or conversely, Protestants who joined the local security forces and were prepared to act oppressively towards Catholics were 'legitimate targets' (according to anti-Unionists). This complete polarisation is an essential part of the make-up of the contending ideologies involved in the Northern Ireland conflict.

This, however, is likely to be a partial explanation: other factors may be at work. One of these factors is the localised nature of experience and thence of perception. In general, people were perceptually unable to encompass the entirety of the Troubles as they dragged on for three decades. Instead, they related to a local, personal or community version, a version that may have varied significantly from the overall pattern of Troubles-related violence. This local version supported and augmented their particular beliefs about the Troubles and the nature of the conflict, and, since there were many different local versions, different and contradictory, belief systems emerged. This assertion is explored in greater depth later in the book, by studying survey results from respondents who were asked about their actual experiences of the Troubles. In this chapter, however, the evidence supporting the statement that different areas have different Troubles-related experiences is examined.

Political deaths are used as a surrogate for political violence generally. We have argued elsewhere that there is a good correlation between deaths and injuries and this is true across both time and space (Fay et al., 1999a). To illustrate the importance of place we have chosen three case studies: Belfast, as the largest city and where the number of political deaths is disproportionately large relative to its population share; Derry Londonderry, where the single most celebrated incident of the Troubles – Bloody Sunday – took place; and Dungannon, the site of the first civil rights march in 1968 and which also illustrates the experience of rural Protestants.

Any analysis of political deaths in particular places must resolve the problem of whether to analyse the number of fatalities that took place within the location or the number of local residents who died. The distinction is important mainly because members of the security forces were not killed in the areas where they lived. This is obvious in the case of members of the British Army, but was also true for members of the RUC and Ulster Defence Regiment (UDR). Thus, areas that apparently saw very little violence nevertheless had significant numbers of local residents who were killed. Conversely, some areas with substantial numbers of violent incidents had far fewer deaths of local residents. The Castlereagh district was an example of the former, while South Armagh exemplified the latter.

In order to explore this further, sub-samples were abstracted from a database of all political deaths consisting of 3700 cases between 1969 and 1998. These contained records of both fatal incidents and deaths of local residents, and both are analysed. The sub-samples were obtained by translating into wards the postcode of the fatal incident location or home address of the deceased. Wards were then aggregated to district or city-sector level. 'Outsiders' were also identified. However, when the focus of analysis is fatal incident, 'outsiders' were those from outside the area who died there. When the focus is on local residents, 'outsiders' were individuals who died in the area but lived elsewhere. Some caution is due to the fact that the postcode translation exercise was unsuccessful in about 10 per cent of cases. In the case of Belfast, the missing postcodes were ignored since there were good data on over 1600 cases. However, the distribution of missing cases may not have been uniform across other sectors and may thus have introduced some bias into the results. With Derry Londonderry, non-translated postcodes were included as a 'not known' category because of the smaller number of cases involved. The second case study was analysed at district council level so the translation problem did not arise.

THE TROUBLES IN BELFAST

Demographic and Social Background

Between 1971 and 1991, the population of Belfast City Council area decreased by a third – from 416,700 to 279,230. During this period, Belfast City Council area's share of the Belfast Urban area population fell from 70 per cent to 59 per cent. The largest decline occurred in the 1970s: between 1971 and 1981, there was a 25 per cent drop in the population followed by an 11 per cent drop in the succeeding decade. The decline in the population in the 1970s was accompanied by a decline of 18 per cent in the number of households. However, in the following decade, between 1981 and 1991, there was an increase of 4 per cent in the number of households. Single-person households almost doubled in number between 1971 and

1991. Since 1991, there has been a gradual population increase in Belfast of just over 1 per cent, reflecting a halt in the population haemorrhage of the previous two decades (Gaffikin and Morrissey, 1996).

The principal decline in Belfast's population was in the inner city. Between 1971 and 1991, inner-city residence decreased by 55 per cent, with a 39 per cent decline in the number of households. This pattern is typical of industrial cities elsewhere, such as Liverpool and Glasgow. However, Belfast is distinctive in that the degree of change is not the same for the two principal religions within the city. Although both Catholics and Protestants have left the city between 1971 and 1981, there was only a 16 per cent decline in the city's Catholic population, yet there was a 41 per cent decline in the Protestant population. The result was that Catholics, who comprised 34 per cent of the city's population in 1971, had increased to 42 per cent of the population by 1991. The pattern of dispersal has also differed, with the Protestant population dispersal spread over a wide area in the east of the province, whereas Catholic movement has been clustered, and to areas close to the city's boundaries.

The age profile of the population of Belfast in 1991 shows a preponderance of elderly residents compared to the rest of Northern Ireland: 16 per cent of Belfast residents and 12 per cent of residents within the rest of Northern Ireland were aged 65 or over. The age distribution of the population is not uniform within Belfast, with a substantially higher percentage of residents in the South and East Belfast being aged 65 or over compared to North and West Belfast. West Belfast has a particularly young population with 44.2 per cent of its population aged under 25, compared to 33.6 per cent and 32.4 per cent in the South and East sectors. Indeed, just under a fifth of the population in West Belfast is aged nine or less (1991 Census).

The age structure of the population varies in different parts of the city. Figure 2.1 depicts the age distribution of population in percentage terms for North, South, East and West Belfast compared to Belfast as a whole.

In 1971 Catholics made up 31.4 per cent of Northern Ireland's population; Presbyterians, 26.7 per cent; Church of Ireland, 22.0 per cent; Methodists, 4.7 per cent; and other denominations, 5.8 per cent. By 1991, the proportion of Catholics had risen to 38.4 per cent, Presbyterians had fallen to 21.3 per cent, Church of Ireland had fallen to 17.7 per cent, Methodists had fallen to 3.8 per cent and other denominations had risen to 7.8 per cent. These changes

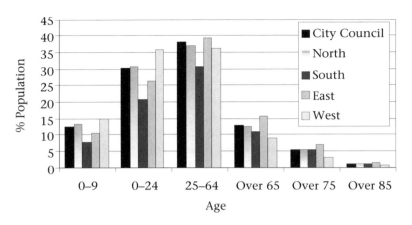

Figure 2.1   Population Segments in Belfast

occurred with the context of population growth of only 38,198. The most dramatic change was the increasing Catholic proportion of the population. Belfast saw a similar change in the religious composition of its population, although the pattern was highly uneven with North and South Belfast experiencing the most significant growth in the Catholic proportion of their populations.

Wards containing a high proportion of Catholics are located principally in the West of the city while wards in the East of the city are principally Protestant. The South and North of the city demonstrate much more heterogeneity in the religious composition of their residents than the other sectors. In 1991, the precentages of residents who were Catholic within the North, South, East and West sectors were 38.9 per cent, 30.7 per cent, 5.4 per cent and 78.5 per cent, respectively.

The distribution of deprivation, as measured by both the Townsend deprivation index and the Robson deprivation index are shown in Table 2.1. Townsend utilises a four-variable deprivation index, whereas Robson et al. (1994) used 14 variables at ward level. On both measures, deprivation is concentrated in the North and particularly the West of the city. North and West Belfast had 63 per cent and 83 per cent of their wards respectively with deprivation scores greater than the Northern Ireland average. Since these measures are derived from census data, they therefore reflect the situation in Belfast in 1991.

Table 2.1   Deprivation by sector within Belfast (Townsend Index
and Robson Index)

Area/sector	Townsend deprivation index			Robson Deprivation index	
	No. wards	No. (%) wards deprived	No. (%) wards with significant levels of deprivation	No. wards	No. (%) wards with a Robson index greater than zero[1]
City Council	51	31 (61)	22 (43)	51	28 (55)
North	16	12 (75)	8 (50)	16	10 (63)
South	11	3 (27)	3 (27)	11	3 (27)
East	12	4 (33)	3 (25)	12	5 (42)
West	12	12 (100)	8 (67)	12	10 (83)

[1] Zero = Northern Ireland average.

In summary, while Belfast lost population over the past three
decades, it nevertheless became a more Catholic city. Catholics were
concentrated in the North and West of the City, both of which had
relatively young populations. Moreover, these sectors had disproportionate concentrations of deprived wards.

Political Violence

The Troubles were concentrated in Belfast. Over 40 per cent of deaths
resulting from political violence happened there even though the
city contains about a fifth of the regional population. As will be seen
later, certain kinds of violence were even more concentrated – almost
half of all sectarian deaths took place in Belfast. Yet different parts
of the city had very different experiences of political violence.

The pattern of deaths over time can be seen in Table 2.2.

The concentration of deaths in the early period is apparent. More
than half of all deaths occurred in the first seven years of the
Troubles and very few took place after the ceasefires. This was true
of both the city as a whole and of each sector of the city. Violence
was also spatially concentrated, with just over 60 per cent of deaths
of local residents located in the North and West of the city. Indeed,
if the non-Belfast deaths in this section of the table are excluded
(these consist mainly of members of the security forces), the share of
local resident deaths from North and West is even greater – over 75
per cent. Just over 10 per cent of all resident deaths happened in
South Belfast and just under 10 per cent in East Belfast. North and

West Belfast's share of fatal incidents was even greater – 68 per cent of the total.

Table 2.2   Political Deaths in Belfast, 1969–99

	West	North	East	South	Non-Belfast	Total
Deaths of local residents						
1969–75	255	233	68	94	179	829
1976–80	104	118	21	17	65	325
1981–85	39	32	9	21	31	132
1986–90	43	42	11	15	31	142
1991–95	49	45	16	25	24	159
1996–99	10	11	0	1	4	26
Total	500	481	125	173	334	1613
Fatal incidents						
1969–75	286	297	61	114	71	829
1976–80	105	127	40	38	16	326
1981–85	51	31	11	23	16	132
1986–90	44	53	20	15	10	142
1991–95	46	46	19	40	8	159
1996–99	7	8	2	5	4	26
Total	539	562	153	235	125	1614

Given that the number of residents killed in the Troubles in North and West Belfast was almost three times that in South and East Belfast, it is likely that the perception of the Troubles was very different in these different parts of the city. This differential experience of violence is also likely to be compounded by the different religious (and therefore political) composition of each sector and by different levels of deprivation. This is depicted in Figure 2.2. The area percentage of fatal incidents and deaths of local residents are placed alongside two other factors: the religious composition of the sector and the percentage of the sector's wards with deprivation scores above the Northern Ireland average on the Robson index. On the measures of political violence used here, North and West Belfast have higher shares than elsewhere; both had higher percentages of Catholics in their populations and both had higher percentages of deprived wards.

Elsewhere, no significant correlation between political deaths and area deprivation for the whole of Northern Ireland was found (Fay et al., 1999a). It may be hypothesised that the presence of large numbers of security force members in the total of deaths reduces the correlation coefficient.

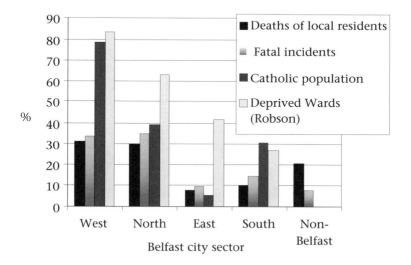

Figure 2.2   Area Deaths and Other Characteristics

However, in the case of Belfast, the association between all four variables is apparent.

Some differences were also apparent in the gender composition of deaths within each sector of the city. Based on the deaths of local residents, men in North and West Belfast account for 60 per cent of all male deaths, whereas women in these two sectors made up 75 per cent of all of the city's female deaths. The death risk for women was thus higher in these two parts of the city. The age distribution of victims also varied across the city. For example, just over 22 per cent of West Belfast victims were 20 years of age or less compared to 13 per cent in East and South. Of West Belfast victims, 8 per cent were over 50 compared to 13 per cent in East Belfast and 20 per cent in South Belfast. Therefore the death risk for younger people was higher in West Belfast than for those in the South or East sectors of the city.

In three of the four city sectors, Catholics comprised the majority of local residents' deaths (West Belfast, 78.4 per cent; North Belfast, 59.7 per cent; East Belfast, 44.0 per cent; South Belfast, 52.6 per cent). However, in interpreting these figures it is necessary to take into account the proportion of Catholics in the general population of each sector, which differs between sectors. Accordingly, the risk of dying in a Troubles-related incident should be calculated according to the religious composition of each sector. The risk is calculated with the data on residents' deaths and with the religious composition data for 1991. However these data do not compare like with like, since the deaths data represent an aggregation of 30 years of violence, whereas the population data are for a single year. However, it is not possible to produce ward population averages across the three censuses because ward designations changed over the period. None the less, it is known that the Catholic share of Belfast's population increased between 1971 and 1991. Thus, the deaths' data are compared with population data in which the proportion of Catholics was greater than over the entire period. The calculation of a 'death risk' for Catholics therefore has to be regarded as a minimum figure. It should be recognised that the concept of risk here simply denotes the relationship between a particular religion's share of all deaths and its share of the area population. This calculation takes no account of the absolute numbers who died. This risk factor is shown for both religions in Figure 2.3.

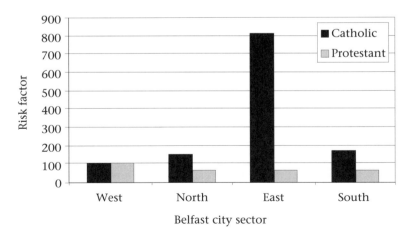

Figure 2.3   Death Risk by Religion

The place where the greatest number of Catholics died (West Belfast, 392) had almost equal risks for Catholics and Protestants, that is, the victim share of each religion corresponded with the population share of each. In North Belfast, the risk for Catholics was about twice that for Protestants. In South Belfast, it was two and a half times greater. However, in East Belfast, it was more than ten times greater. If the actual numbers of deaths are examined, this amounted to 55 individuals compared to almost 300 in North Belfast and almost 400 in West Belfast. However, the rate is high even though the numbers are lower, since Catholics comprise a very small proportion of the overall population of East Belfast.

The majority of those who died in each sector were civilians. Table 2.3 shows a composite of local resident deaths with fatal incidents in order to include members of the British Army. To that extent, the total is false since it represents an aggregation of components from two different tables. However, it does serve to illustrate the differing character of the Troubles in each location.

Table 2.3   Political Status of Victims by Belfast Sector

Political status	West	North	East	South
Civilians	349	369	70	126
Political activists	15	6	2	1
Republican paramilitaries	89	45	13	13
Loyalist paramilitaries	24	28	16	9
Local security forces	20	21	19	16
British Army	87	41	3	10
Total	584	510	123	175

In West Belfast, the deaths of members of paramilitary organisations were close in number to the deaths of members of the security forces, 113 and 107 respectively. Together, these made up almost 40 per cent of all victims. Republicans made up the majority of paramilitary victims, whilst members of the British Army accounted for the majority of security forces' victims. Of some significance was the number of political activists who died, associated in the main with Sinn Féin. In the next chapter, we discuss how, in the early 1990s, Loyalist paramilitaries deliberately targeted Sinn Féin members as acceptable surrogates for the IRA. In West Belfast, the degree of conflict between security forces and Republican paramilitaries and the level of activity amongst Loyalist paramilitaries is reflected in the data on composition of deaths. However, even here, civilians – those without attachment to paramilitaries, security forces or the political parties associated with paramilitaries – accounted for almost 60 per cent of the deaths.

Civilians from North Belfast made up the highest single number of civilian deaths and comprised 72 per cent of the area total. The security forces made up about one-eighth of all victims in North Belfast, with members of the British Army accounting for two-thirds of all security force victims in that sector. In East Belfast, members of the local security forces (the RUC and UDR/Royal Irish Regiment (RIR)) made up almost one in six victims – a higher proportion of the total than elsewhere. These data refer to those who were killed and who were resident in East Belfast, and a high proportion of RUC and UDR members with home addresses in East Belfast were killed elsewhere. There were only four fatal incidents in East Belfast involving members of local security forces, and only three British army fatalities. Moreover, almost a quarter of all victims in East Belfast had been members of paramilitary organisations. South Belfast had the highest percentage of civilian victims at over 70 per cent.

Crucial to the construction of a particularised version of the Troubles is the perception of who was most responsible for deaths. This is central to an understanding of the Troubles in terms of who should be 'blamed' most. Table 2.4 shows the number of fatal incidents in each sector by the main organisations responsible. The total number of deaths in this category exceeds the number of resident deaths, since it includes victims from outside each area. However, these two figures are added since this provides the best indicator of the overall level of violence for which each organisation was responsible.

Table 2.4   Fatal Incidents in Belfast by Organisation Responsible

	West	North	East	South
British Army	91	56	9	6
Local security forces	17	6	1	2
Republican paramilitaries	347	226	39	108
Loyalist paramilitaries	120	301	102	98
Total	575	589	151	214

Using deaths as a yardstick, it can be seen that the activities of the security forces were overwhelmingly concentrated in West and North – 90 per cent of all fatalities for which the security forces were responsible. Amongst this total were 105 civilians. Almost 80 per cent of deaths for which Republicans were responsible also took place in these two areas. Of these, 126 were members of the British Army and 65 were RUC members. A total of 81 people killed were Republicans, the result of internal feuds or operations that went wrong, such as the Shankill bombing. A total of 134 victims of Republican paramilitaries were Catholic, of which 50 were non-Republican paramilitaries, that is, civilians. There may have been members of the security forces who were Catholic, but in general the religion of the security force victims was recorded as 'not known' in the database. There were over 400 victims of Loyalist paramilitaries in West and North Belfast, the vast majority of whom were Catholic civilians.

The picture in East and South Belfast contrasts with that in West and North. In the first place, the security forces were responsible for a substantial minority of victims. Unlike North and West Belfast, Loyalist paramilitaries were responsible for a greater number of victims than Republicans in the South and East areas of the city.

It can be seen from the diverse patterns of violence in various sectors of the city that people's experience of the Troubles in Belfast depended on which city sector they inhabited. In the North and West, the security forces were most active and a significant component of the overall violence was the 'war' between the security forces and Republicans, and the role of Loyalist paramilitaries was mainly in killing Catholic civilians rather than Republicans or members of the security forces. Loyalist paramilitaries were particularly active in this domain in North Belfast. It is evident that, amid speculation that the security forces covertly supported Loyalist paramilitaries, the material experience of living in North and West Belfast with relatively high levels of security force and Loyalist paramilitary activity, could lead to the development of an analysis of the Troubles as primarily 'state repression'.

In the East and South, however, where violence was almost entirely carried out by paramilitaries, a different experience of the Troubles would tend to lead to a different analysis. Even though the data show that Loyalist paramilitaries were responsible for the majority of deaths in East Belfast, this was directed primarily at the minority Catholic population and could be seen as retaliation for local residents and local members of the security forces killed elsewhere. The general militarisation of both sectors by the security forces did not attain the same intensity that it did in West and North Belfast. Representations of the Troubles were based on media accounts or on visits to the city centre where the threat was largely from Republican bombs. Furthermore, Loyalist activity, although high, was not perceived to be threatening to a largely Protestant local population, therefore the major problem in the Troubles would be perceived to be Republican paramilitaries.

These data on deaths fail to represent the full complexity of the situation. The concentration of violence within city sectors in particular places, such as along interfaces between the two communities, is not apparent from a scrutiny of these data. Nor is it clear that many sub-areas were relatively untouched. The risk of injury or death from political violence was distributed unevenly within these city sectors. Accordingly, certain sections of the populations of West and North Belfast, where violence was concentrated, suffered even more disproportionately and such areas also tended to be characterised by deprivation and community segregation. These three factors – violence, deprivation and segregation – interrelate to form and shape the integral experience of the Troubles.

Experience of the Troubles was also acquired in areas of Northern Ireland other than residential areas. As mentioned above, shopping and recreation involved some of the population travelling outside their communities. If we examine deaths due to explosion, which mostly occurred in the city centre, it emerges that very different proportions of the victims from each sector of the city died in explosions. For example, a quarter of all the victims residing in East Belfast died in explosions compared to around 15 per cent in West and North Belfast and 18 per cent in South Belfast. Explosions often caused multiple deaths, and city- or town-centre incidents invariably attracted a high level of media attention not always directed at events in local areas. Although deaths by explosion did not take place frequently in local areas, they had an impact on local attitudes. It is not hard to see how people living in East Belfast came to see a bombing campaign ostensibly directed against 'economic' targets as being directed against their community. From this perspective, the Troubles were viewed as a Republican conspiracy.

This exploration is aimed at elucidating how particular kinds of experience may have led to very different perceptions and analyses of the Troubles. Of course, direct personal experience is mediated by various other factors such as information and messages emanating from the media. However, one of the striking aspects of locality in Belfast during the Troubles was the way in which local communities supported and maintained their own analysis of events. This was achieved through the production of local media – ballads, bands, graffiti, murals, humour, community or paramilitary newspapers, and on occasions pirate radio – which served to document, express and reinforce the local experience and versions of the Troubles. Meanwhile, the dominant discourse and the establishment's version of the Troubles was, with very few exceptions, maintained by local and national mainstream media in similar ways.

DERRY LONDONDERRY

Background

The city known as Derry by Catholics and Londonderry by Protestants has been a long-term symbol of the Irish conflict. For over 300 years it has remained a symbol of Loyalist resistance, based on its refusal to submit to the forces of James II during the Williamite wars. These events are commemorated by an annual march around its city walls by the Apprentice Boys, a loyal order dating back to that time. Following the partition of the island of Ireland, the city was located on the northwest border of Northern Ireland, less than five miles from Donegal. The majority of its population has always been Catholic, and whose numbers have steadily increased over the past three decades. By 1991, Catholics made up three quarters of Derry's population. By then, the River Foyle that bisects the city became the boundary of segregation with the majority of Protestants living on the eastern side of the river, and, more recently, some Protestants leaving the city altogether in favour of the more Protestant hinterlands of Limavady and Coleraine.

In the 1960s, charges of gerrymandering in the local authority elections and of discrimination in the city were a powerful impulse to the creation of the civil rights movement. Indeed, a Londonderry Commission was put in charge of local services when the locally elected authority was judged incapable of impartiality. One of the first civil rights marches, in October 1968, was halted with considerable violence and massive publicity by the RUC. Many regard this incident as the starting point of the Troubles. This was compounded by an attack on a civil rights march from Belfast to Derry at Burntollet in 1969. The violence of August 1969, which brought the

British Army on to the streets of Northern Ireland, started in Derry Londonderry as an attempt to halt the annual Apprentice Boys' march. In February 1972, in the most notorious action by British troops in Northern Ireland, a section of the Parachute Regiment killed 13 individuals during the rioting following a civil rights demonstration. Local residents have steadfastly maintained that those killed were unarmed. The British Army, and most Loyalists, claimed they were Republican paramilitaries intent on 'taking on' the Parachute Regiment. The shadow of this event, known as 'Bloody Sunday', remained with the city, making a substantial contribution to the shape of victim politics in Northern Ireland and eventually precipitating, in 2000, the most expensive public inquiry in British judicial history.

Despite the city's symbolic significance in the Troubles, Derry City Council – its local authority – was the first to adopt power-sharing between Unionists and Nationalists following the reform of local government in Northern Ireland. Even though disputes continued, for example, over Loyalist marches in what had become a predominantly Catholic city centre, the city also saw the first direct talks between Loyalists and local Nationalist residents in an effort to resolve differences. It was the first Irish city to elect a Sinn Féin mayor since Terence McSweeney was elected Lord Mayor of Cork.

In 1997, the population of the Derry District Council area was 104,000 persons, of whom almost 30 per cent were aged less than 16 years compared to 25 per cent in the region as a whole. Only one in ten of its population were of pensionable age (the comparable figures were 15 per cent for Northern Ireland and 18 per cent for the UK). In April 1999 there were 5200 unemployed in the district with just less than half in the long-term category. In 1996, GDP per head in Northern Ireland was 81 per cent of the UK average. In the North of the Region (which includes the city) the figure was 75 per cent (CSO, 1999: pp. 213–15). Although Derry Londonderry city contains just over 5 per cent of all wards in Northern Ireland, it accounts for one-tenth of the 50 most deprived wards in the region based the Robson index. Within the city, deprivation is distributed unevenly. All of the Census Enumeration Districts have deprivation scores above the Northern Ireland average in wards such as Brandywell, Creggan and Shantallow, whereas others like Altnagelvin and Bally-nashallog are all below the average deprivation score.

For purposes of the analysing the variety of experience of the Troubles, Derry Londonderry was divided into two parts, the west and east banks of the River Foyle. Locally, these are known as the Cityside and the Waterside. The bulk of the population is concentrated in the former, which is almost entirely Catholic. The 1991 distribution of the religion in the two sectors is shown in Figure 2.4.

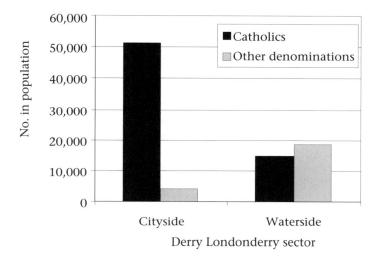

Figure 2.4   Religious Distribution in Derry Londonderry

While almost the entire Protestant population is concentrated in the Waterside, there are still substantial numbers of Catholics living there. The Cityside is both larger and overwhelmingly Catholic.

Political Violence

Derry Londonderry deaths recorded on the database amount to less than a sixth of the deaths recorded for Belfast although the population of Derry is about a third that of Belfast. Of the 252 deaths recorded as occurring within the district, 20 had postcodes that did not translate into wards. Among residents' deaths, 68 had postcodes that would not translate. Of the latter, 58 were recorded as 'non-Northern Ireland' on the religion variable. This code was used mainly to record members of the British Army although some other individuals, for example, from the Irish Republic are also included. In the other ten cases, it is likely that the original postcodes were replaced as the result of redevelopment. Both sets of missing locations were a significant percentage of the total and, for that reason, have been analysed alongside the sector analysis.

As elsewhere, political violence in Derry Londonderry was concentrated in the early years of the Troubles. However, the concentration in the early years is even more marked in the city: 50 per cent of all fatal incidents had already happened by 1976; 88 per cent by 1986. Over the entire period, there were 165 fatal incidents in the Cityside, 44 in the Waterside, and 24 outside the city that involved residents. About 6 per cent of those who died were women with similar percentages in each of the two city sectors. Less than half of all victims were Catholic (44 per cent) although this figure changes dramatically when non-Northern Ireland victims are excluded (78 per cent). Again, if non-Northern Ireland victims are excluded, 72 per cent of victims in the Waterside and 40 per cent on the Cityside were Catholic.

Security force victims represented a significant percentage of all the Derry Londonderry deaths: 22 per cent (56) were members of the British Army, 11 per cent (28) were members of the RUC and just under 6 per cent (14) were members of the UDR. Altogether, members of the security forces made up almost 40 per cent of all those who died. Civilians made up a further 40 per cent. The only other significant group consisted of members of Republican paramilitaries – 17 per cent. Loyalist paramilitaries hardly appeared amongst these victims. The relative size of the security force component of the dead is at considerable variance with the data for Northern Ireland where security force members made up just over a quarter of all victims. Security force deaths in the city are a much bigger share of all deaths than for the whole of Northern Ireland. Over 70 per cent of security force members were killed in the Cityside sector and comprised almost 45 per cent of all the deaths in the Cityside. Interestingly, two of the British Army deaths were of Cityside residents.

Republican paramilitaries were responsible for two-thirds of all deaths and this was consistent across both Cityside and Waterside sectors. The security forces were responsible for just over 20 per cent of all deaths, but their share of deaths was higher – 30 per cent – in the Cityside. Of the 44 fatal incidents that took place in the Waterside, the security forces were responsible for only two. Almost 70 per cent of all the deaths for which the British Army was responsible happened between 1971 and 1973, the largest number being in 1972 (25 deaths) that included Bloody Sunday. In contrast, just over 30 per cent of deaths for which Republican paramilitaries were responsible occurred in the same period.

The Derry Londonderry experience of the Troubles was not only different from the pattern in Northern Ireland as a whole, but the two city sectors also had very different patterns of violence. This reflects not just the higher number of victims and incidents on the Cityside, but also the different roles of the central organisations involved. Certainly, Bloody Sunday was a highly traumatic event, seared into the consciousness of the city's Nationalists but thereafter the security forces killed very few in this city. Moreover, the city has a higher proportion of security force victims than Northern Ireland as a whole.

DUNGANNON

Background

Dungannon is virtually in the middle of Northern Ireland on the eastern edge of Lough Neagh. It was in this area that civil rights grievances were first voiced in the 1960s focusing on inequities in the allocation of public sector houses and jobs. One of the first civil rights incidents involved the occupation of a local authority house (which had been allocated to a single person) by a large Catholic family. The first civil rights march in Northern Ireland occurred there in August 1968.

In 1997 it had a population of 48,000 of which 27.2 per cent were aged less than 16 years. The population had increased by just over 8 per cent since 1991 (CSO, 1999). The district contains 22 wards of which 17 had deprivation scores greater than the Northern Ireland average. Deprivation was predominantly concentrated in the Altmore and Coalisland wards whose population in the 1991 Census was mainly Catholic. In 1997, 19 per cent of the adult population were dependent on income support. The number unemployed in April 1999 was 1500 with just less than half being jobless for more than a year.

Political Violence

Like elsewhere in Northern Ireland, political violence in Dungannon was concentrated in particular periods of the Troubles. In Northern Ireland generally, the most intense period of political violence was 1971–77, sparked off by the introduction of internment. This pattern was also observable in the Dungannon data. Other periods in which death rates were high in Dungannon were 1983–85 and 1990–94. The former could be explained by the political agitation following the IRA hunger strike; the latter corresponds to an upsurge in violence in the years before the first IRA ceasefire.

Almost 94 per cent of the victims in Dungannon were men, a slighter higher rate than for Northern Ireland as a whole. The age patterning of deaths shows similarities with the rest of Northern Ireland. Victims were concentrated in younger age groups – 54 per cent were aged 30 or younger, just less than a quarter were aged 20 or under.

In Dungannon, Catholics accounted for 45 per cent of victims compared to 39 per cent Protestant. If 'non-Northern Ireland' and 'not known' categories are ignored, then 52 per cent of victims were Catholics and 48 per cent Protestant. If only local residents are analysed, then Protestants represent 45 per cent and Catholics 55 per cent of victims. It seems that Protestants appear disproportionately among the victims in Dungannon compared to the rest of Northern Ireland in light of their relative share of the population. In the 1991 Census, the religious breakdown of the Dungannon District was 56 per cent Catholic and 38 per cent Protestant. Moreover, since the cases in the database where religion is recorded as 'not known' are mainly members of the Northern Ireland security forces, at least 90 per cent of these can be assumed to have been Protestant. These deaths can be redistributed accordingly into the two religious categories. When this is done, Protestants and Catholics were almost equally numbered as victims whether the consideration is all deaths or the deaths of local residents only.

Dungannon is also unusual in terms of the distribution of the status of the victims. Within Northern Ireland as a whole, victims were composed of roughly 2000 civilians, 1000 members of the security forces and 600 members of paramilitary organisations. More than half of all victims were thus associated with neither the security forces nor paramilitaries. In Dungannon, however, only 42 per cent of victims were civilian, and a larger proportion – 46 per cent – had an association with the security forces. Of these, 20.4 per cent were members of the UDR. Unlike the regional pattern, the security forces thus contributed the largest single percentage of those who died in Dungannon. However, members of Republican paramilitaries make up the remaining share – 12 per cent – of the Dungannon victims. There does not appear to be a single member of a Loyalist paramilitary organisation among the victims.

Essentially, the British Army and Republican and Loyalist para-militaries were responsible for all deaths in Dungannon. Neither the RUC nor the UDR was responsible for any deaths. The IRA was responsible for almost two-thirds of all deaths, the British Army just over one-tenth and Loyalist paramilitaries around one-fifth. The central role of Republican organisations is consonant with the high proportion of security force members among the victims.

Given the nature of the Dungannon experience, a local version of the Troubles would tend to highlight the role of Republican para-militaries, particularly with respect to their role in killing local security forces. Given the religious composition of these forces, the Troubles can be represented as an anti-Protestant insurrection.

CONCLUSION

The assignation of blame and the passing of moral judgement is part and parcel of the formation of a perspective on the Troubles. What this chapter has illustrated is that the location of blame, the type of moral judgement made and the assessment of who the enemy is in Northern Ireland depend not only on religious or political identity but also on where one lives. Across Northern Ireland, whilst no section of the community has had a monopoly of grief or grievance, none the less, the experience of loss, anger and grief due to the Troubles can lead some to feel that they are entitled to such a monopoly. What is presented here is a rational statistical analysis of diverse forms of experience of the Troubles in various locations. Yet experience of the Troubles is rarely rational or statistical. More often it provokes strong emotions and forms strong views about what is right and wrong, who is enemy and who is friend. Experience of the Troubles produces and influences attitudes to violence, politics and the 'other'. These attitudes in turn play a part in the way the conflict itself develops. Attitudes inform voting behaviour, and other more active and aggressive participation in the political life of the country.

Individual experience is mainly a reflection of what happened in local areas in which there were diverse forms of political violence and disparate victim compositions. There can be no single version of the Troubles, no single 'correct' interpretation because of the diversity of local community experience. People reflect on their own particular experience and seize on other incidents that reinforce the view they develop. Furthermore, real material differences between the experience of different locations means that even without this tendency, substantial differences exist between locations, leading even the most open-minded and intellectually rigorous of observers into contentious debate if the view they form is based simply on their own experience of the Troubles. The move to a post-conflict society will entail the recognition of the validity of diverse accounts, a tolerance of this diversity. And if reconciliation is ever to be achieved, a crucial component of it will be the capacity to see the Troubles through the eyes of those previously regarded as enemies.

3 A Special Kind of Victim: Sectarian Killing

The victims of sectarian assassination were chosen simply because they belonged to a particular religion rather than some connection to the security forces or to paramilitary organisations. Sectarian assassination has been a central feature of the Troubles over the past 30 years. It has been associated principally with paramilitary organisations. However, some argue that local security forces have also been in incidents claimed by paramilitaries. While apparently peripheral to the major contest between republicans and the security forces, it has nevertheless been a significant feature of the overall pattern of violence, accounting for just under a quarter of all deaths. Moreover, it epitomises the savagery of political violence where individuals are killed, not because of what they have done, but because of who they are. Indeed, the Troubles were first signalled in 1966 by the sectarian murders of two Catholic civilians in Belfast. The founder of the modern UVF, Gusty Spence, was charged with both killings and was convicted of one of the two (Taylor, 1999: pp. 41–4).

The chapter is in four parts:

- The first provides some background on the nature of sectarian killing
- The second looks at the characteristics of its victims in terms of gender, religion, and so on. In addition, it examines the organisations responsible and looks, in particular, at Belfast which saw the brunt of sectarian killing
- The third examines the motivation behind sectarian killing
- Finally, the chapter broadens the debate by offering some general observations by way of conclusion.

THE BACKGROUND TO SECTARIAN KILLING

Compared to the war between the security forces and republican paramilitaries, intercommunal conflict has been an entirely different order of violence. Conflict approaches (McGinty, 1998) distinguish between vertical and horizontal violence in contested and divided societies. The term 'vertical' refers to the conflict between the security forces of the state and those who wish to overthrow it – in the case of Northern Ireland, the battle between, on one hand, the British Army, the RUC – Northern Ireland's police force, and the UDR – the locally recruited regiment of the British Army; and, on the other, Republican paramilitaries. However, in a divided society like Northern Ireland, one section of the population opposed to the 'insurrection', provides local members of the security forces and creates its own paramilitary apparatus to conduct a war against the rebels. Repeated allegations of collusion between the latter and the formal security forces have led some to suggest the term 'private, coercive apparatuses' of the state. In Northern Ireland, these forces have been manifest in the various Loyalist paramilitary organisations. These have defined their role as the defence of Northern Ireland reflecting a concern that the formal security forces have been either unable or unwilling to conduct an effective war against their Republican opponents. It has been this dual dimensional conflict that has resulted in the deaths of so many civilians unattached to either security forces or paramilitary organisations, either as the byproduct of the vertical or the direct targets of the horizontal conflict.

Moreover, residential segregation in Northern Ireland has steadily increased during the period of the conflict (Poole and Doherty, 1996; Murtagh, 1999). In certain cases, the degree of physical separation has been substantial – the River Foyle largely divides the Catholic and Protestant populations of Derry/Londonderry (Smyth, 1995c) – in Belfast, east of the River Lagan has a Catholic population of only 12 per cent whereas west of the river has 55 per cent. This separation of populations has been seen as moderating the capacity for inter-communal violence – people live in enclaves for greater safety (Smyth, 1996). However, in other instances only a few streets, frequently intersected by 'peace walls', separate the different religions. North Belfast is the primary example containing 14 out of Belfast's 17 peace walls. This proximity factor has often been associated with extreme intercommunal violence.

In addition, the necessity to move outside an area for work or leisure can carry a high risk. Indeed, demographic change, particularly the increasing proportion of the Northern Ireland population who are Catholics, has had spatial implications – Catholics are now the majority in places where previously they were a minority. Some such places have been associated with 'traditional' Loyalist marching routes and thus become contested spaces, flash points of confrontation and violence during the 'marching' season. During periods of tension, minority populations, predominantly Catholics, have been frequently intimidated where they live or work. Thus, patterns of contiguous territories give rise to particular forms of violence and specific categories of victims.

Republicans legitimate their actions with reference to the 'anti-imperialist struggle'. The legitimate targets of this struggle are those involved in or associated with the British state. However, the definition of legitimate targets has been highly elastic – construction workers rebuilding police stations, those providing catering for the British Army or those long retired from the RUC reserves. The specific history of Northern Ireland has meant that those associated in some way with the state have been overwhelmingly Protestant. Accordingly, Protestants perceive Republican intentions as being directed primarily at them in an attempt to intimidate or evict them from Northern Ireland altogether.

Conversely, Loyalist paramilitaries had no 'obvious target' for their activities – the IRA, by definition, has been a covert organisation. Nevertheless, it employed classic counterinsurgency tactics by attempting to terrorise the Catholic population that gave rise to and 'hid' the Republican guerrillas. Thus, particularly in the 1970s, all Catholics were regarded as 'legitimate' targets for Loyalist paramilitaries (Cadwallader and Wilson, 1991: p. 6). The motivation was either revenge for the 'Republican terror campaign' or an effort to pressurise the IRA to desist – or, in some cases, the realisation of sadistic fantasy. Shirlow and McGovern (1997) allude to further economic motivation for sectarian attacks on Catholics in predominantly Loyalist workplaces.

> You have to blame the IRA. If they didn't fight a war and intimidate our people, we wouldn't mind them working here. But if they don't stop, then targeting Catholics is part of our war. Anyhow, they get the jobs and are helped and we are simply left behind by a Government that doesn't care. (Interview in ibid.: p. 196)

It has been argued (McGinty, 1998) that paramilitaries in Northern Ireland tend to monopolise the conduct of violence, and by their very nature and *modus operandi* they both control the direction of violence and minimise acts that would threaten their long-term legitimacy. According to this analysis, the paramilitary monopoly and regulation of violence explains the allegedly low levels of 'hate violence' in Northern Ireland. However, to see such violence as individual acts may understate both the extent and the complexity of such violence in Northern Ireland. Three main features of sectarian killing in Northern Ireland are noteworthy.

First, on each side there has been a set of different paramilitary organisations in rivalry with each other, each determined to demonstrate that it is the authentic defender of its own community. Such authenticity has frequently been manifest in a more vigorous pursuit of violence. This organisational fission tends to throw up organisations whose impulse is to continue to conduct military missions while the mainstream paramilitaries limit or even cease their operations. For example, the Real IRA continued to pursue a bombing campaign after the IRA ceasefire of 1996, resulting in 29 civilian deaths. The LVF continued its campaign of violence long after the ceasefires of the UDA and the UFF. Indeed, there was suspicion that members of the latter two assisted in some of this violence under the cloak of a *nom de guerre*.

Second, during periods when the security forces appeared least able to contain the Republican paramilitaries, their opponents, the Loyalist paramilitaries, were most active. Loyalist reaction took as its primary target the Catholic population, legitimated by reference to the Catholic population shielding the terrorists within it. However, a reading of personal accounts by Loyalist paramilitaries also suggests that such actions were underpinned by a supremacist ideology:

> The construction of the Catholic community as the 'Other' of Loyalist ideology must be seen in this vein. Ethnicity, in terms of an Ulster Protestant identity, within the framework of Loyalist ideology, is inevitably predicated upon the negative categorisation of Catholics. This in turn acts as a means to sanction the procedure of sectarianised power relations at the level not only of 'ideas' and 'individual action' but also in terms of social structure. Sectarianism therefore emanates as a pivotal mode of domination and boundary demarcation. (Shirlow and McGovern, 1997: p. 178)

Others suggest that this is a one-sided view of Loyalist paramilitaries:

> They are concerned to establish their particular perspective as one universally applicable to the whole of Loyalism. This is their ideological struggle and they are not especially interested in

establishing ideological hegemony over the Catholic or nationalist population. (Finlayson, 1999: p. 54)

Instead, responsibility for Loyalist sectarian violence lies with those
who misled the young, who were 'past masters at incitement from
the comfort and safety of their armchairs, but drew back when it
came to action themselves ... forgotten by those who urged them
onto the streets and afterwards condemned them for the actions
they took in defence of Ulster' (Combat, in ibid.). Finlayson describes
this explanation of Loyalist violence, largely advanced by former
Loyalist combatants, as 'a narrative of sin and redemption in which
the devil is Paisley' (ibid.: p. 68).

Legitimation for Loyalist participation in sectarian killing focuses
on the operations of the IRA and the lack of containment by the traditional security forces. For example, the selection of UDR targets by
the IRA in border areas has been construed as an attack on local
farmers who formed the backbone of this force in the rural environment. Such attacks frequently took place at their homes with
obvious effects on wives and children and were perceived to be a key
component of the 'ethnic cleansing' of the local Protestant
population. McAuley (1994: pp. 129–36) described Protestants' perceptions that they were being pushed out of their areas and
workplaces; that they were under seige, under genocidal attack and
were left with no option but to retaliate. A speaker at an Independent
Orange Order rally in Ballycastle on 12 July 1997 described the IRA
as 'the Beast of Roman fascism', and went on to claim that eight out
of ten Protestants in the South had been eliminated, and that
Northern Protestants could expect the same from resident groups
(Brewer, 1998: p. 125).

Third, paramilitary organisations simply did not have the capacity
to control and monopolise violence. There were too many such
organisations on the ground, no single organisation ever exercised
complete hegemony within its own area and they had neither the
personnel nor resources. The multidimensional, multilocational
nature of political violence in Northern Ireland is signalled by the
status of the casualties – 2000 civilian deaths, 1000 members of the
security forces and around 700 members of paramilitary organisations. In Northern Ireland, the fact that more civilians were killed
than the aggregate of the other two groups suggests that, for some,
civilians were the primary targets. (See Appendix 1 for the methods
used in constructing the database of sectarian deaths.)

VICTIMS OF SECTARIAN ASSASSINATION AND THE
ORGANISATIONS RESPONSIBLE

As in the general Northern Ireland conflict, the victims of sectarian
killing have been predominantly male and Catholic – 91 per cent
male and 71 per cent Catholic respectively. The respective responsibility for the deaths between the two sets of paramilitaries exactly
paralleled their religious distribution, that is, 71 per cent Loyalist
and 29 per cent Republican. This is almost tautological since the
term 'sectarian' signifies killing across the religious divide. Both sets
of paramilitaries killed members of their own religions. Equally,
Republicans killed large numbers of security forces and, via bombing
campaigns, equally large numbers of civilians. However, the focus
here is exclusively on the intentional deaths of civilians who were
'on the other side'.

Of the 809 such deaths, the means of death was identified in 806.
Unsurprisingly, the vast majority of victims were shot (748), the
remainder being assaulted or stabbed with three victims dying in a
house fire. The last occurred in 1998 during the Drumcree crisis (an
ongoing dispute about the routing of an Orange march through a
Catholic area in Portadown) when three young children died as a
result of a petrol-bomb attack on a house in Ballymoney (*Independent*, 13 July 1998).

The majority of victims were in the younger age categories (see
Figure 3.1).

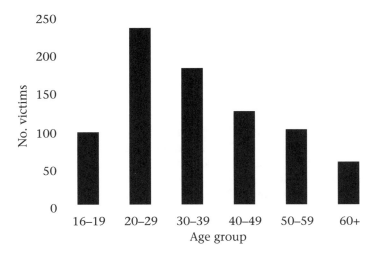

Figure 3.1   Sectarian Deaths by Age Group

Almost 40 per cent were aged between 16 and 29 years and nearly two-thirds were under 40. Northern Ireland has a relatively young population. However, in 1991 only 23.9 per cent of the population was aged between 16 and 29 and 37.4 per cent were aged 16–39 (NISRA, 1997). Nevertheless, almost a fifth of the victims of sectarian killing were over 50, while 56 victims were over 60.

Again, like the Troubles generally, there were different periods of intensity of sectarian violence (see Figure 3.2).

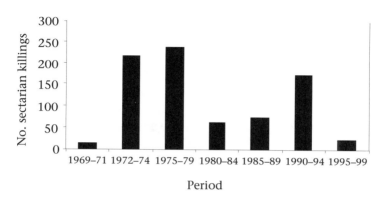

Figure 3.2   Intensity of Sectarian Violence by Period

The most intensive period of the Troubles was between 1972 and 1979 when there were over 450 sectarian killings. During this period, the activity of Republican paramilitaries was at its most intense. The primary response of Loyalist paramilitaries was sectarian killing. However, the next peak occurred between 1990 and 1994 just before the declaration of the first IRA ceasefire – leading some to suggest that a factor in the IRA's ceasefire decision was the increasing capacity of Loyalist paramilitaries to target members of Sinn Féin. It is interesting, moreover, that 24 killings that occurred after the ceasefire were concentrated particularly in the period during which the ceasefire broke down. A particularly intense cycle of violence followed the killing of the leader of the LVF, Billy Wright, in the Maze prison. This organisation responded by killing Catholics. The temporal patterning of the deaths does appear to be associated with the particular organisations responsible.

Figure 3.3 depicts sectarian deaths over time divided between Loyalist and Republican paramilitaries.

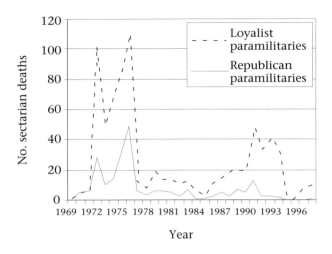

Figure 3.3   Sectarian Deaths by Year by Organisation Responsible

The practice only really gained currency after 1971. Before 1972, there were only 12 deaths in this category. However, in that year alone, there were 102 deaths of which Loyalists were responsible for 74. The killings dropped to around 50 in 1973 and 1974 and then rose again to around 100 in 1975 and 1976. In all four years, Loyalist organisations accounted for 60–80 per cent of sectarian deaths. Thereafter, the killings fell to around 20 per year until 1990. Many such deaths were particularly barbarous – the infamous 'Shankill Butchers' kidnapped and tortured their victims. Many were almost decapitated, had their throats cut, and were mutilated beyond recognition (Taylor, 1999: pp. 151–5).

However, after 1990, sectarian killings were again on the increase. Between 1990 and 1994, Loyalist paramilitaries accounted for 144 sectarian deaths compared to 29 by Republican paramilitaries. During this period, Loyalist paramilitaries also killed 12 civilian political activists (associated with membership of Sinn Féin), about half of all the political activists they killed over the entire period. There is some evidence that Loyalist organisations believe that in the early 1990s they were more able to effectively pursue the 'war against Republicans' by specifically targeting Sinn Féin members (ibid.: p. 156).

Of all political deaths resulting from the Northern Ireland Troubles, 46 per cent occurred in Belfast, yet 62 per cent of all sectarian killing took place within the city. Whilst Belfast had the highest number of violent incidents over 30 years of conflict, it saw a particular concentration of sectarian deaths. Part of the explanation lies in the complex mosaic of different religious territories within the city. Heartlands of Nationalism and Loyalism, like the Falls and the Shankill are literally side by side. North Belfast, in particular, has a complex set of small segregated spaces amongst which tension is frequently high. Certain 'traditionally Protestant' spaces found they were under pressure from Catholic expansion. In a normal situation, such demographic changes would have little impact on social life within the city. However, in a situation of Republican challenge to the state and intercommunal conflict, they were a recipe for violence. The geographic proximity of people with different religions and contesting political views meant that the civilian population was easy prey, particularly since people had to cut across 'other' territories as they moved about the city. It is thus worth looking at the characteristics of sectarian killing within this city.

Some patterns of this kind of violence within Belfast mirrored what happening in the region. The victims were predominantly male (91 per cent) and the principal method was shooting (92 per cent). Equally, the victims were concentrated in the younger age groups – 45 per cent between 16 and 29 years of age and more than two-thirds aged 16–39. However, the proportion of Protestants among the victims was higher than in the region generally, at 25.1 per cent. Correspondingly, Republican paramilitaries accounted for a similar proportion of the victims.

This review suggests that, at one level, sectarian killing manifested the same characteristics of all deaths in Northern Ireland but in an exaggerated form. Thus they were disproportionately male, young, Catholic and spatially concentrated compared to the more general database. However, in one respect there was a marked difference: Republican paramilitaries were responsible for just over 50 per cent of all deaths in Northern Ireland, but Loyalist paramilitaries were overwhelmingly responsible for sectarian killing. It might be argued that this feature is simply an artefact of the methods used to filter such deaths from the database; for example, that in many instances Republicans killing members of the local security forces was sectarianism disguised as anti-imperialist struggle. It can also be argued that Loyalist paramilitaries were simply employing classic counter-insurgency tactics – 'poisoning the water in which the fish swim', but neither is sufficient explanation for what happened or for how their activities are constructed by Loyalists.

MOTIVATION AND SECTARIAN KILLING

There are distinctions between the two populations in Northern Ireland in terms of their recourse to sectarian killing. The figures presented here show that over 70 per cent of such killings were carried out by Loyalists. Two questions arise:

1. How do we explain the disproportionate involvement of Loyalists in the sectarian killing, and their espousal of sectarian killing as an effective military strategy?
2. How does the involvement of Republicans in sectarian killing square with their disavowal of this strategy and their condemnation of its use by Loyalists?

The answer to the first question lies in the nature of militant Loyalist politics, which gives rise to and provides the rationale for sectarian killing. There are five aspects of this politics that together provide a context in which the espousal of sectarian killing can be understood. The first set of factors is related to the religious origins of Loyalism and its connection to Protestant religious fundamentalism. This fundamentalism provides an important set of moral and psychological cardinal points for Loyalist thinking, notwithstanding the substantial secular nature of some sections of Loyalist involvement. The textual references for such religious orientation, which in turn shapes the political orientation, lie almost exclusively in the Old Testament, which is often interpreted literally. This authoritative use of the Old Testament has a number of consequences.

First, it contributes to the overall siege mentality of Loyalists, with its numerous biblical references to persecution.

And He said unto Abraham, know of a surety that thy seed shall be a stranger in a land which is not theirs, and they will make them serve, and they will afflict them for four hundred years. (Genesis 15:13)

Lo, it is a people that shall dwell alone and among the nations it shall not be reckoned. (Numbers 23:9)

Many are my persecutors and my assailants yet from they testimonies did I not turn away. (Psalms 119:157)

Brewer (1998) points out that Ian Paisley uses this formulation to dismiss criticism, taking 'comfort in the self-appellation that he is a persecuted prophet' (ibid.: p. 112). The idea of righteousness in the face of persecution – indeed, one's righteousness being enhanced by persecution – lies at the heart of the so-called 'siege mentality' of the Loyalist community in Northern Ireland. This siege mentality is reinforced historically by actual sieges which are held as highly significant events in Loyalist history (for example, the siege of Derry) and the sense of besiegement that many in the Loyalist community feel as a result of the IRA campaign against the (predominantly Protestant) security forces.

Second, the idea that persecution is the explanation for suffering presupposes a persecutor who is bent on the destruction of the 'chosen people'. Indeed, identification with the chosen people in biblical terms has always been a feature of modern Loyalism. Elements of the Loyalist movement, for example the paramilitary group Tara, formally identified with the British Israelite Movement. This movement believes that they, as God's chosen people, must resist threats to their purity and ascendancy from other populations such as Jews, Catholics, people of colour and other 'pretenders'. A statement in the *Loyalist News* of August 1971 illustrates this:

The Protestant way of life was under open siege. The Loyal institutions ... had not responded. The appropriate response was paramilitary, extra-constitutional, local and defensive. This was the fundamental response, traditional, only novel in that trustworthy leadership seemed to be lacking. So the people of God must act for themselves.

And again, a UFF statement in 1973 said:

We are fighting for our very survival; our backs are against the wall. We have more in common with the state of Israel ... like the Jewish people, each time an act of aggression is committed against our people, we shall retaliate in a way that only the animals of the IRA can understand. (Brewer, 1998: p. 154)

This vision of the political arena circumscribes the political task in terms of preventing the realisation of the supposed goals of these populations to 'take over' – the country, the government, or the economy. This ideological tendency to see 'outsiders' as persecutors and part of a conspiracy against one's own people is again supported by an external reality in Northern Ireland with the existence of the military campaign of the Republican paramilitaries against the (predominantly Protestant) security forces.

Third, the message lacks any sense of relativity and is replete with concepts such as 'truth' which are deemed to be absolute. The world is black and white, and you are either for us or against us. Notions of retribution and fit punishment are fundamentalist and stark also: 'An eye for an eye, and a tooth for a tooth' (Exodus: 21.24). Furthermore, God speaks directly to his chosen people and not, as the (abhorred) Catholic belief, through intermediaries. There is less room for negotiation, fewer intermediate steps and greater individual autonomy when God speaks to each person individually. And in the Old Testament, the news is frequently bad. God's chosen people are shown to be universally and perpetually persecuted.

In the eyes of those carrying out the killings, this perceived persecution provides the justification for their actions, as illustrated in an interview with John White, a founder of the UFF, speaking to Peter Taylor:

But most of the killings that the UFF carried out were not against the IRA, they were against innocent Catholics.

I think at the start of the campaign the vision was that the IRA had full support within their communities and therefore it was felt that in order to put pressure on the IRA, the same effect would be achieved by conducting a campaign against the communities where the IRA found its support.

So the nationalist Roman Catholic community was regarded as a legitimate target by the UFF, was it?

Well, in the end, it was felt that the IRA gained very popular support within their communities and it was seen as a strategy that if pressure could be put on the IRA by their communities, then that would have an effect and that they would consider desisting from the attacks on Loyalist communities. So there was a clear strategy and methodology behind UFF activities.

It was as simple and brutal as that, was it?

Well, it was simple and it was brutal, you know, but it was a tactic of retaliatory action against a community who was inflicting great pain in our community. (Taylor, 1999: p. 116)

John White was himself convicted of killing Senator Paddy Wilson and his companion, a Protestant woman, Irene Andrews, on 23 June 1973. Senator Wilson had been election agent for Gerry Fitt, and a senator in the upper house of Stormont. He had refused to carry a gun for personal protection on the grounds that he would not want to use it. Senator Wilson had been stabbed 30 times and his throat had been cut; Irene Andrews had been stabbed 20 times. It was one of the first sectarian killings of the current Northern Ireland Troubles. John White received two life sentences, and 23 years later was a member of the Loyalist delegation to Downing Street to meet John Major (ibid.: p. 118).

Fourth, accusations made by Catholics against Protestants of persecution at their hands gives rise to an anticipation of revenge being taken at some point in the future. Whether or not the accusations are accepted as justified, some anticipate that the accusing population of Catholics may well be moved to seek retribution for the past. Evidence to support the anticipation that Catholics in power will behave in discriminatory or oppressive ways is vigorously sought in order to support the thesis of their malevolence and to justify their continued exclusion. This thesis has the further advantageous effect of retrospectively justifying any acknowledged ill-treatment of this population in the past. That a newly powerful Catholic elite might employ tactics identical to those they accuse their Unionist predecessors of employing defuses any doubt that past behaviour should be a source of guilt or even responsibility. Yet the Catholic reiteration of accusations of past Unionist persecutory behaviour serves to rekindle the suspicion that revenge or malevolence – and not, as is claimed, justice – is the motivator for Catholic criticism and attacks on Protestants.

Fifth, the way in which Unionist politics in general, and Loyalist politics in particular, are gendered may provide additional insight into the tendency towards paranoid constructions of politics. Female participation in formal politics in Northern Ireland is low: none of the 18 Westminster MPs are female, 3 of the 26 District Councils in Northern Ireland have no women members, 9 have only a single female member, and only 12.4 per cent of all local councillors in Northern Ireland are female (Roulston, 1999). Since substantial differences between males and females exist in terms of their behaviour, emotional management, attributional styles and behaviour in groups (see for example, Kanter, 1976, 1977; Burstein et al., 1980; Tannen, 1990; Brody and Hall, 1993), then one would expect corresponding differences in attribution within organisations that contain a critical mass of female members who can exert influence on the organisation's thinking. However, within Unionism in general, female participation has been at consistently low levels, and within Loyalism in particular, some believe (Pollak and Moloney, 1986: p. 243) that female participation at any central level is debarred for particular historical and perhaps religious reasons. This is in contrast to political organisations within the Nationalist body politic and within Republicanism in particular. Sinn Féin, as a result of feminist pressure in the 1970s, established a Women's Department and subsequently its manifestos contain explicit commitments on issues of gender equality and women's participation. These commitments are manifest in the gender composition of their party negotiation teams and selection of spokespersons for Sinn Féin.

A comparison of the involvement of Republican and Loyalist paramilitaries in sectarian assassination points clearly to the predominant use of this strategy by Loyalist paramilitaries. We have argued that such involvement is ideologically consistent. The history of mainstream Unionism, certainly in an earlier period, also shows evidence of supporting sectarian attacks on Catholics. Brewer (1998) points out that Craig told Protestants driving Catholics out of the shipyards in the 1920s that he agreed with the course of action 'you boys had taken in the past'. This led, Brewer argues, to a situation in 1922 where Protestant workers 'therefore felt morally sanctioned to violence ...' (ibid.: p. 95). That it was this same Craig who was valorised in the naming of a new town after him, Craigavon, in the 1960s demonstrates the widespread acceptability of anti-Catholicism. It was sanctioned, understood and understandable. This, in itself, contributed to its growth and validated its enactment.

The answer to the second question – how does the involvement of Republicans in sectarian killing square with their disavowal of the Loyalist strategy and their condemnation of it? – is as follows.

The albeit lesser involvement of Republican paramilitaries in sectarian assassinations of Protestant civilians is less easy to locate within Republican ideology, a fact which may indeed go some way towards explaining the lesser involvement itself. Ruane and Todd (1996), relying on Hutchinson (1987), describe the roots of modern nationalism and Republicanism thus: 'Much of the intellectual impetus came from Protestants seeking to reconcile Catholic and Protestant, settle and native; their important legacy was the concept of a single, inclusive Irish nation.'

A more contemporary description of Catholic attitudes towards Protestants and the Unionist community suggests that changes have taken place:

> Catholic attitudes towards Protestants, once shaped by the inferiority born of economic disadvantage and political repression have become less focussed, more confused – where once they tended to be an uncomfortable mixture of inferiority and superiority, the superiority built largely on a conviction that the Nationalist identity was much more secure than the precarious Brutishness of Protestant unionists ... Republicans still use the language of victimhood to justify the IRA, but have to strain to align it with their theme of a risen people, freed by their own struggle. (O'Connor, 1993: pp. 150–1)

O'Connor also explains that an aspect of the superiority felt by Catholics relates to sectarianism itself:

> As a West Belfast teacher said, describing how his republican pupils wanted badly to believe IRA 'explanations' that Protestants are never targeted because of their religion, it was 'deeply distasteful for them to believe they are sectarian – because that's what Protestants are – and, by definition, we are not'. (ibid.: p. 17)

Attitudes to violence in the Catholic community may also be shaped by the experience of violence. The Catholic community has borne relatively more of the violence than the Protestant community over the three decades of the current Troubles (Fay et al., 1999a). More Catholics have been killed and approximately 80 per cent of the estimated 30,000–60,000 people forced out of their homes in the early 1970s were Catholic. Catholics report more experience of the Troubles than Protestants (ibid.). A frequent comment made by those with direct experience of the Troubles is that they would not wish their suffering on anyone, even or especially for purposes of retaliation. It may be the case that more direct knowledge of the consequences of violence tempers the appetite for sectarian or retaliatory violence, and, coupled with the declamatory press coverage of Republican violence and the Republicans' overwhelming share of responsibility for the total violence of the Troubles, this may lead to a more selective and conditional underwriting of violence by the Catholic community.

Certainly data presented here confirms earlier findings that sectarian killing is predominantly a Loyalist phenomenon and strategy. McGarry and O'Leary (1995) found that sectarian killings comprised 6 per cent of all Republican killings, whilst they comprised 78 per cent of all Loyalist killings after 1969. That Republicans did in fact carry out sectarian killings is undeniable, and this too requires explanation. It is necessary to look beyond the strict ideological framework of Republicanism, to the more sociological or lived experience of Republicans to find motivation for these killings. The reality of segregation, increased polarisation and ongoing violence across the sectarian divide has created and maintained mutual antipathy and demonisation that composes sectarianism. Republicans as well as Loyalists are part of that dynamic which facilitates and therefore maintains and supports sectarian violence and killing. That the share of involvement between the two communities varies reflects differences in their ideological frameworks and military goals.

Understanding of sectarian killing as part of the Northern Ireland conflict has not been served by a pervasive tendency to omit such killings from consideration or to minimise their impact. The tendency to ignore such killings might be seen in the context of an overall tendency to ignore or minimise Loyalist violence, illustrated by persistent demands for Republican decommissioning, in the context of ongoing Loyalist violence against Catholics in late 1999. However, the omission of its consideration from scholarly analyses requires closer analysis. O'Connor points out that one book (Flackes and Elliott, 1989) used as a standard reference on the Troubles 'makes no mention of forced migrations of the early seventies, and includes no loyalist murders of Catholics in the events of 1972'. O'Connor also recalls:

By 1973, twenty-three of the thirty Catholic-owned bars in North Belfast had been bombed by loyalists. But what preoccupied the media was IRA car bombs and the killings of soldiers and civilians. Except for the *Irish News*, the Catholic-owned Belfast paper, the local press and broadcasters took their line from the police. *The Belfast Telegraph*, intent on supporting Terence O'Neill and later Brian Faulkner as reforming Unionists in their struggle with their own hard-liners, steadily played down loyalist violence and focused on the IRA. *Belfast Telegraph* reports talked of 'random' shootings and frequently omitted the religion of the victim as the BBC did for some time. The explanation was that giving the religion of the victim 'fed sectarianism'. There is, in other words, a period of recent history that is unrecorded and all but hidden – except in the memories of whole districts. (O'Connor, 1993: p. 161)

Concerns that are implicit in O'Connor's example are that to speak of sectarian killings actually exacerbates the problem. The preferred strategy is perhaps one of keeping silent in the hope that the problem will at best disappear, or at worst not deteriorate further. For whatever reason, the silence is perceptible elsewhere. As noted earlier, Brewer's (1998) survey of anti-Catholicism in Northern Ireland from 1600 to 1998 neglects to mention sectarian killings of Catholic civilians as a systematic policy of Loyalist paramilitaries. By including reference to several killings of Catholics, Brewer creates the impression that such killings were relatively isolated incidents and that the large number of sectarian killings conducted by Loyalists were either not related to anti-Catholicism or did not happen at all (ibid.).

The extent of denial of both the nature and extent of sectarian killing is worrying. The lessons from Northern Ireland are that even in the face of a massive escalation in the amount of killing, denial continued to be used as a mechanism for 'managing' information on such attacks. Similar levels of denial are observable elsewhere. It is perhaps an inescapable conclusion that the killing of citizens who are members of minority or marginalised groups will be regarded with less public concern and media attention than the killing of members of the dominant group. None the less, the parallels with the phenomenon of denial, including denial in the target population documented by Charny (1991) in relation to genocide would suggest that denial may well facilitate the unimpeded escalation of hate crimes and sectarian violence and create and maintain conditions for their proliferation. The very form of targeting used in hate violence and sectarian killing – namely the targeting of populations because of their identity – is reminiscent of that used in genocide. Perhaps increased public awareness and challenges to denial about these forms of violence may have some prophylactic effect on their proliferation.

CONCLUSION

Although sectarian killing is often characterised as 'mindless' and primal, it almost always reflects an ideological belief structure. The violent attack itself is construed as in some way serving the cause of asserting, reinstating or proving that superiority and subjugating the (inferior and dangerous) target group by the terror resulting from the act of violence. Sectarian killing, like racism, sexism, homophobia and religious hatred, is supremacist.

The details and rationale of exactly how a given population is construed to constitute a threat, and the nature of the supposed threat, varies contextually according to geography and history. What appears to be constant is the way in which violence against a particular population is explained in terms of 'defence' or 'reaction' against threat, rather than in terms of how it is perceived by a wider set of observers, as terror or 'sectarian killing' targeted at unsuspecting and defenceless members of the 'target population'.

In Northern Ireland, killing has been highly routinised with commonly recognised protocols governing its operations. Paramilitary organisations 'claim responsibility' for killings or other operations using officially recognised codewords. Not all killing, for example, is regarded as equally problematic or illicit. Setting aside the major fault-line in the society (whereby the killing of a member of the 'other side' will generally be regarded differently – as less problematic and more justifiable – than the killing of a member of 'one's own side') there are other 'rules of combat' which influence the manner in which a particular form of killing is regarded. The various paramilitary organisations have over the years explicitly stated what they consider to be 'legitimate targets', which include those bearing arms or carrying information to the enemy, those performing services for the enemy, and those representing or promoting the political cause of the enemy.

Implicit in all of these rules is the principle that it is the *behaviour* and not the *identity* of the person that qualifies him or her as a target.

One has choice about one's behaviour, what organisation one is affiliated to, or what role one occupies in one's own community. One does not have a corresponding choice about one's identity; about being Nationalist/Catholic, Unionist/Protestant, black/white: these are identities that are ascribed by the larger society. It is the distinction on which the difference between war and genocide is built. In war, one targets the combatants on the other side, in genocide one targets the entire population.

For this reason, sectarian killing in Northern Ireland is a matter of grave concern. Deaths of civilians are rarely perceived by combatants as being equally as problematic as the deaths of their comrades or members of their own community. Accidental civilian casualties, described as 'collateral damage' or 'accidents', are increasingly the most vulnerable population in times of war and political conflict. However, with sectarian killing and hate crime it is this most vulnerable section of the population that is explicitly targeted. Their very vulnerability renders this strategy comparatively risk-free in terms of the danger to their assailant of reprisal. The effect of such targeting is not only the death of or injury to the actual victim, but also the intimidation and terrorising of the population from which the victim is drawn.

This in turn has served to increase the mutual demonisation of and social and political distance between the two communities in Northern Ireland. The increased prevalence of sectarian attack since the ceasefires and the increased numbers of sectarian killings prior to the ceasefires represent a shift in the form of the Northern Ireland conflict itself – away from a contest about sovereignty and national identity and towards an internal ethnic conflict between two opposing groups.

4   The Young as Victims

In his keynote address to a conference in Belfast in June 2000, Olara Otunnu, Special Representative of the Secretary-General of the United Nations with Responsibility for Children and Armed Conflict, said:

> Children like to reach out to each other instinctively and play with each other and be children. The Troubles have not made is possible for this to happen because of:
>
> - The way in which some of the children here in Northern Ireland have lost their loved ones in the violence;
> - The extended exposure to violence and the threat of violence and the use of some young persons in the process of the violence;
> - The way in which young people have been subjected to the prejudice of adults;
> - The polarisation within the community;
> - Indoctrination about the other side, the other group, and the hatred that comes with that;
> - And of course when you have Troubles like you've had here in Northern Ireland is very difficult to pay adequate attention to what really matters for young people, economic and social development that assures of a brighter future. (CCIC, 2000)

This chapter addresses the effects of the Northern Ireland conflict since 1969 – the so-called 'Troubles' – on children and young people in Northern Ireland. The particular hazard faced by children and young people in Northern Ireland as a result of the Troubles is described in terms of the impact upon them.

As is clear from work elsewhere (Fay et al., 1999a) and from earlier chapters, it is apparent that the risk of being a victim of Troubles-related violence is not evenly distributed across different geographical areas or sections of the population. Since 1969, over 3700 people in total have been killed in Northern Ireland due to the political conflict.* The official estimate is that a further 40,000 people have also been injured. However, this figure is likely to be low since not all injuries were officially reported. Over 90 per cent of all those killed were male. Of all deaths, 60 per cent are attributed to the activities of Republican paramilitaries, 28 per cent to Loyalist paramilitaries, 2 per cent to the police and 10 per cent to the British Army. Approximately 42 per cent of those killed came from the Catholic/Nationalist community and 29 per cent of those killed came from the Protestant/Unionist community, with a further 17 per cent from outside Northern Ireland (many of them British soldiers serving in Northern Ireland), with 12 per cent for whom the religious affiliation is unknown.

Young people account for a large proportion of those killed, with a quarter being aged 21 or under. The 19–20 age group contains the highest number of deaths for any age group in Northern Ireland. Of all age groupings, the 18–23 age range contains the highest number of deaths, at 898. This age group alone accounts for 25 per cent of all deaths in the Troubles. People aged 29 years or under account for over half the deaths in the Troubles to date. Whilst the death rate for the 0–14 age group is below the average death rate for the overall population, both the 15–19 and the 20–24 age groups show a death rate that is substantially higher than that for the total population.

RESPONSIBILITY

In both the under-25 and the under-18 age group, Republican paramilitaries are responsible for the largest share of the deaths, followed by Loyalist paramilitaries, with the security forces accounting for the third largest share.

Republican paramilitaries are responsible for the largest percentage of deaths of any group in both the under-25 age group (55 per cent) and the under-18 age group (34.6 per cent). Republican paramilitaries are responsible for 58.8 per cent of all deaths, compared to 55 per cent of those under the age of 25 and 34.6 per cent of those

---

* Applying the death rate (2.2 per thousand) to the population of the UK as a whole, the equivalent number of deaths would be 129,734. Applied to the US, the equivalent number of deaths (in addition to the number of deaths due to criminal killings) would be 588,720; in Israel (excluding the West Bank and the Gaza Strip), 12,416; in South Africa, 89,283. These figures are calculated on a population estimate of 1.675 million in Northern Ireland and estimates of population for the US and the UK at July 1998 from the CIA World Fact Book and the 1997 Census of South Africa.

under the age of 18. It follows that a substantial number of deaths of Catholic children and young people have been caused by Republican paramilitaries (for more information see Fay et al., 1999a). Loyalist paramilitaries are responsible for 27.9 per cent of all deaths, compared to 21.3 per cent of deaths of the under-25s and 28.8 per cent of deaths of the under-18s. Security forces are responsible for 11.25 per cent of all deaths; 17.5 per cent of deaths of the under-25s and 26.1 per cent of deaths of the under-18s. Although Republican paramilitaries overall hold the most responsibility for deaths at all ages, there is a marked increase in the share of total deaths of young people due to the security forces, and this is particularly striking in deaths of those under the age of 18.

In the case of the under-18s, the IRA again are responsible for the largest number of deaths, followed by the British Army, but the variation in the scale of difference in the two age groups is not quite as marked. In the under-25 age group, the IRA were responsible for by far the largest number of killings. The difference between the IRA and the next largest – the British Army – is quite marked (610 to 182) – whilst the difference in the under-18 age group is not as great (73 to 58).

RELIGION

Table 4.1 shows the numbers of under-25s and under-18s killed, according to the religious community with which they were identified.

Table 4.1   Religious Affiliation of Under-25s and Under-18s Killed, 1969–98

	Under-25s		Under-18s	
	No.	%[1]	No.	%
Catholic	615	48.1	190	73.9
Protestant	231	18.1	50	19.5
Non-Northern Ireland[2]	362	28.3	12	4.7
Unknown	68	5.3	5	1.9
Total	1276	100.0	257	100.0

[1]   Rounded.
[2]   Refers to those who are not residents of Northern Ireland.

Catholics make up the largest group. However, a marked difference between the age categories emerges. Whilst Catholics account for just over 48 per cent of the under-25s killed, they account for almost 74 per cent of the under-18s killed. In the total death figures for all ages, Catholic deaths also outnumber Protestant deaths both in relative and absolute terms. However, the scale of the difference between Catholic and Protestant deaths is much less in the total death figures for all ages than it is for the under-18 age group. Almost three-quarters of children (as defined by the United Nations Convention) killed in the Troubles have been from the Catholic community.

The cause of death in younger age groups follows the pattern of the overall population of deaths: shooting in the majority of cases of deaths of the under-18s (53 per cent, 137 deaths), followed by explosion (34 per cent, 87 deaths). The use of firearms and explosives have caused the overwhelming majority of fatalities amongst children and young people However, the third most frequent cause of death – although much less frequent – is death by rubber or plastic bullets (3 per cent, 8 deaths). In all, 13 people under the age of 25 have been killed by rubber or plastic bullets.

PLASTIC BULLETS

Militarised policing in Northern Ireland developed various strategies for intervention in street violence and rioting. Successive security strategies and developing military technology have seen the deployment of CS gas, water cannon and rubber and plastic bullets in the face of civil unrest. Rubber bullets were first to be used, but were replaced by plastic bullets following complaints about the severity of injury caused by the rubber bullet. However, severe injury continued to result.

Plastic or rubber bullets, also referred to as baton rounds, are used in riot situations against unarmed combatants. They have frequently been deployed in situations involving young people and children, who may be throwing stones or petrol bombs. However, there have been a number of cases where bystanders have been shot, where poor visibility, panic or other factors have led to shots being fired erroneously or where baton rounds have been fired at lethally short range.

By 1991, the use of plastic bullets in Northern Ireland had led to the deaths of an estimated 17 people, 10 of whom were aged 18 or under (see Table 4.2). RUC officers fired four of the fatal bullets and members of the British Army fired the remainder. Unknown numbers have been injured, some seriously and permanently, by plastic and rubber bullets. Arguably children are more vulnerable because of the size of the bullet relative to the size of a child's body. Because of the danger to children there has been a campaign to ban the use of plastic bullets in crowd control and riot situations.

Table 4.2   Ages of Persons Killed by Plastic Bullets, August 1969–May 1999

Age	Male	Female	Total
10	1	0	1
11	2	0	1
12	2	0	2
13	1	0	1
14	0	1	1
15	2	0	2
16	1	0	1
18	1	0	1
21	2	0	2
22	1	0	1
33	0	1	1
40	1	0	1
41	1	0	1
45	1	0	1
Total	15	2	17

Source: Committee on Administration of Justice, cited in *Sunday Tribune*, 13 November 1999.

THE SIGNIFICANCE OF GENDER

Marked segregation of gender roles, especially in relation to experiences of Troubles-related violence, is a feature of many of the communities worst affected by the Troubles. Males tend to have more direct experience of violence, such as being directly involved in physical attacks or sectarian verbal abuse, whereas females are more likely to be witnesses to such events (Fay et al., 1999b).

As stated elsewhere (Fay et al., 1999b), the overwhelming majority of those killed in the Troubles have been male. In both genders, the Troubles-related death rate is related to age. The number of deaths for both genders peaks at the ages of 19 and 20, with declining death rates for all age groups thereafter. Of those killed, 93.3 per cent of those aged 18 and under were male. Overall, 91.1 per cent of those in all ages groups killed in the Troubles have been male. Of all male under-24s killed, 13.48 per cent comprise 20-year-olds, whilst 19-year-old females comprise 15 per cent of all female under-24s killed. Death as a result of the Troubles is highly differentiated by gender, and this is significant particularly in relation to the culture of violence.

Perhaps as a result of these material gender differences, male experience and expectation take a particular form. In families where a member had been killed or injured, marked differences between the fears for the male and female children in the family have been found (Smyth et al., 1994). Typical family fears for young men were that they would be targets of violence, that they would seek revenge for a death or injury in the family, that they would become involved in paramilitary violence, and that ultimately the family would experience another loss. This pattern is particularly apparent in areas where levels of Troubles-related violence are high (Smyth, 1996).

Interview data suggested that young males react to news about attacks on their community in ways that illustrate their relationship with violence. They described how they tried to 'forget about' deaths that had happened in their community. The combination of the fact that young males are the prime target and simultaneously the perpetrators of violence yet are socialised into a kind of stoicism is perhaps related to the reproduction of violence itself. Male culture, particularly in communities worst affected by the Troubles, is not generally permissive of male emotional expression, with the possible exception of anger. Anger in males is often channelled in particular (violent) ways. In interview, several informants described how several males in the family joined paramilitary organisations after the death of the father and a cousin. This decision to join paramilitary organisations was attributed by informants to anger at the deaths of close relatives. Furthermore, in certain communities males are cast in the role of defending their community and their ability to deal with threat or attack is perhaps a residual site of male achievement.

Whilst male roles in the family and gender culture in the community may predispose some young males to become involved in retaliation and further violence, this is not inevitable. One informant explained his own resistance to 'joining up' in terms of his awareness of the impact of bereavement on his own family. He referred to his reluctance to cause the pain of bereavement to another family, since he knew from first-hand experience how painful and difficult it was, particularly for the children. He referred to this awareness in order to explain his resistance to the use of violence in retaliation. He was a child when his father was killed and, in his view, children (such as he was at that time) are innocent and undeserving of the pain of bereavement, irrespective of the identity or actions of their parents. Therefore he was unwilling to inflict that pain on other children by depriving them of a parent.

For other young males, retaliation and violent activity hold an irresistible pull. Families can be aware of this and attempt to monitor the movements of young males in order to prevent their 'getting involved'. In some cases families have gone as far as moving home (where they can afford to do so) in order to remove young males from the context where there are opportunities of seeking revenge or 'getting involved'.

POLITICAL AFFILIATION

Popular consciousness about children and the Troubles attributes adjectives such as 'innocent' to children, suggesting that in all cases children are passive victims of the Troubles. Whilst Northern Ireland has not seen the same level of military involvement of children that has been apparent in other conflicts – Sierra Leone, for example – none the less, some children and young people in Northern Ireland have been actively involved as combatants. Political affiliation was determined by the 'claiming' of those who died by particular para-military organisations or by the security forces. Obituaries often described the deceased in terms of his or her rank within the organi-sation, and rolls of honour from various organisations were used to cross-check the attribution of individuals to particular organisations.

Most children and young people killed in the Troubles were civilians, especially in the under-18 age group. The highest number of children who died as combatants, died within the ranks of Republican paramilitaries, the IRA (21) and their junior wing, Na Fianna (14). The Official IRA had 3 combatants aged under 18 killed and 2 in the Fianna branch of their organisation. Both the other categories of combatants – Loyalist paramilitaries (UDA with 4 deaths and UVF with 3) and the security forces (British Army with 5 deaths, 3 of whom died in England) – have also recruited and armed persons legally defined as children. Deaths of combatants aged under 18 peaked in 1972, with 18 combatants under the age of 18 dying that year. Deaths among combatants aged under 18 subsequently declined, partly as a result of the British Army policy shift that meant that they no longer sent soldiers under the age of 18 to serve in Northern Ireland, although they continue to be recruited into the army.

Recruitment of those who are legally children under the terms of the United Nations Convention on the Rights of the Child – namely those under the age of 18 – into paramilitary organisations has been an ongoing feature of Northern Ireland's Troubles. Whilst the term 'child soldier' tends to be associated exclusively with conflicts in the developing world, Northern Ireland, too, has seen children recruited and armed as combatants by all armed parties to the conflict. This has included the British Army which recruits from the age of 16 and which, until the early 1970s, sent soldiers under the age of 18 to serve in Northern Ireland. By 1998, 6 British soldiers aged under 18 had been killed in Northern Ireland, alongside 21 IRA volunteers, 13 Fianna, 3 Official IRA and 2 Official Fianna, 4 UDA and 3 UVF volunteers. Just over 96 per cent (50) of all these (52) were male, compared with 76 per cent males of total civilian children killed.

Olara Otunnu, whilst visiting Northern Ireland in June 2000, commented:

> the paramilitaries who have been recruiting and using children to participate in violence and be part of that process must stop doing this because when violence becomes normalised in the life of children, and becomes a way of life it is very difficult to wean young people from that. (CCIC, 2000)

Whilst Northern Ireland adolescents undoubtedly undergo similar maturational processes to adolescents elsewhere, certain contextual factors differentiate some of Northern Ireland's experience from that of other Western societies. The meaning attached to certain forms of violence has consequences for the degree of community sanction for it. Rioting or stone-throwing conducted by children and young people against the police in Northern Ireland has often been condoned and supported by adults. Therefore rioting or attacks on the security forces, for example, can acquire 'non-delinquent' meaning at a local or community level, thus public attitudes to violence and the socialisation of young people in relation to the legitimacy of violence in Northern Ireland may not correspond with attitudes and practices in other Western societies. In one community examined, an explicit debate was ongoing between the young people in the community who argued that law and order had broken down and the only way to protect the community and achieve its goals was through street violence. The older cohort in the community, many of whom were parents of these young people, had advocated peaceful protest which had not achieved the desired outcome, and felt disempowered in the face of the seeming logic of the young people's argument for violence.

The transition from street protests involving rioting and stone-throwing to more organised and focused activity is undertaken by some young people, usually males. So-called recreational rioting and sectarian street fights with peers from 'the other side' can provide early socialisation into the tolerance of the risk, danger and excitement that violence entails. Feldman (1991) describes how the militarisation of certain local communities in Northern Ireland together with relatively easy access to firearms has created the conditions for what he refers to as the transition 'from hardman to gunman'. Prior to militarisation of these communities, 'hardman' status was achieved through fist-fighting and other feats. Feldman discusses how the introduction of weapons has shifted the status from 'hardman to gunman', a more complicated and dangerous challenge than that which faced males in these communities prior to militarisation.

A form of status is to be achieved within the community by engaging in paramilitary violence. Young men interviewed in a Protestant area professed the ambition of forming their own para-military organisation. The paradox in this context is that only by completely devaluing his life by being prepared to lose it, can a young man be seen to achieve a sense of his own value. By achieving notoriety in such manner his activity must be predicated on the will-ingness to dispense with his own life and the life of others.

Within militarised communities where peace-time policing arrangements do not exist, normative adolescent rebellion against authority can quickly escalate into dangerous and sometimes lethal confrontation with an armed group. Paramilitary organisations engaged in 'policing' such communities have been asked by some residents to curb vandalism and petty crime. Without the resources of a peace-time police force at their disposal, they can neither put offenders on probation nor incarcerate them. The penalties that are easily at their disposal are almost invariably violent. In the course of conducting research in this field, we encountered no young people who supported the administration of violent punishments to young people in such communities. Yet with the growth in paramilitary hegemony in certain communities, a small number of young people, largely males, set about challenging, either explicitly or implicitly, the authority of the paramilitary organisation. In these cases the young males can quickly become targets for punishment beatings and shootings. In interview, one young man explained his defiance of the paramilitary organisation that had beaten him several times by asserting, 'Nobody is going to tell me what to do.' When asked about the danger of his position, he responded, 'You [I] have to die sometime!' Adolescent defiance, which in other contexts will lead to brushes with authority, in the context of militarisation and blocking of most routes to the achievement of status for young males, can lead to violent injury and, on occasion, death.

PUNISHMENT BEATINGS AND SHOOTINGS

Official figures would suggest that Northern Ireland is a more law-abiding society in general than, for example, the rest of the United Kingdom. However, the reluctance, particularly though not exclusively in Catholic areas, to report crime to the police or to call on the police to intervene would indicate that the true extent of the law and order problem may be underestimated in official Northern Ireland figures. None the less, *The Northern Ireland Communities Crime Survey* (O'Mahony, 1997) and other international surveys (Mayhew and Van Dijk, 1997) show that victimisation rates (which include crimes not reported to the police) are considerably lower in Northern Ireland than in any other Western country. Local communities are divided on the issue of policing of communities, with some advocating paramilitary policing in the absence of an acceptable state police force and others horrified at the brutality of the punishments meted out and the summary nature of the attribution of guilt. These kinds of dilemmas and the practice of summary punishment at the hands of local people can be seen in other societies that have experienced conflict. Lynchings and beatings as punishments for petty crime are administered in local communities in, for example, Guatemala and South Africa.

In Northern Ireland, this kind of punishment is administered as a disincentive to petty crime and what is referred to as 'anti-social behaviour', which can include vandalism, burglary, theft and other misdemeanours. They are carried out by members of paramilitary organisations and usually take the form of attacks with sticks, iron bars or firearms, ranging in severity, and including extremely brutal beatings – in one case the impaling of the victim's arms and legs. Severe mutilation, permanent disability or death can result.

Punishment beatings in some areas operate on a tariff system with an incremental scale of penalties, where repeated offences can lead to the victim being ordered to leave the country. At least one voluntary organisation facilitates the flight of young people in order to help them avoid the ultimate sanction, the death penalty. The victims of such beatings are almost invariably male, working class and in their teens or early twenties.

According to Northern Ireland Office statistics, in the period 1973–97, a total of 2096 people were victims of 'punishment shootings', 214 of whom were under the age of 20. A further 1283 people were casualties of 'punishment beatings' in the period 1982–97, of whom 287 were under the age of 20. The latter period (1988–2000), which includes the period of ceasefires from both Republican and Loyalist paramilitaries, shows a continuity of such attacks. Data for individual years indicates that after the ceasefires there was no dramatic reduction in attacks, but the share of assaults increased relative to shootings (see Table 4.3).

Table 4.3   Number of Casualties of Paramilitary-Style Attacks

	Loyalist		Republican		Total	
	All ages	Under 20	All ages	Under 20	All ages	Total under 20
Assaults						
1982–97	528	104	755	183	1283	287
1988–2000	715	167	756	229	1471	396
Shootings						
1973–97	868	91	1,228	123	2096	214
1988–2000	615	114	479	146	1094	260

Sources: RUC and Central Statistical Office, personal correspondence with M. Smyth, January 2001.

Concerted campaigns against punishment beatings and shootings have led to increased public awareness of and outcry against the use of punishment attacks. In March 1999, the IRA, in a statement to the *Andersonstown News*, said:

> We want people to support the restorative justice approach by bringing their problems to the dedicated and highly trained workers operating in the programmes rather than to the IRA. We believe they now offer the best solution to resolving the severe problems of anti-social behaviour in our districts. (Moloney, 1999)

Perhaps this statement augurs a departure from the methods of the past and the beginning of new non-violent initiatives as part of the process of peace-building.

THE IMPORTANCE OF PLACE

This account of life in militarised communities will be unfamiliar to many within Northern Ireland. This is because vast differences exist between geographical locations in their experience of the Troubles and the attendant effects that the Troubles have had, such as militarisation. In Chapter 2 we discussed the importance of location as a determinant of experience of the Troubles. A large section of the population, and many of those who have responsibility for the education and care of young people in Northern Ireland, live in areas where the Troubles have had relatively little effect. This is manifest if we look at how Troubles-related deaths within Northern Ireland are concentrated in a relatively small geographical area. The six Northern Ireland postal areas BT11, BT12, BT13, BT14, BT15 (North and West Belfast) and BT48 (Derry Londonderry city) account for 33.5 per cent of all deaths under the age of 25 (58 per cent of deaths under 18). Young people – particularly males between the ages of 12 and 20 – comprise the majority of fatalities of the Troubles. Qualitative data confirms that young people in these areas are particularly at risk of becoming victims (or perpetrators) of violent acts.

Another category of children with intense experience of the Troubles are the children of the security forces. The taboo of talking to civilians has meant that it is difficult to collect data on this group and consequently little is known about them. One young woman interviewed described her childhood experience of growing up in a family associated with the security forces. She learned from the age of five not to trust others outside the family, not to give anyone her name, address or phone number. Her family moved house every few months, and as a child she kissed her father goodnight each night for years knowing that she might never see him alive again. She learned from an early age how to dial two nines on the phone and wait for instructions to dial a third nine (the emergency services) if a stranger approached the front door. Whilst such children do not usually live with the economic deprivation that children in the worst affected communities also face, they can experience extremes of social isolation and alienation from the wider community.

As with adults, the highly geographically differentiated distribution of the Troubles has implications for Northern Ireland's children. Some children living in areas with the highest death rates are likely to have a great deal of experience of the violence of the Troubles, whilst other children living in relatively peaceful areas have very little experience.

This marked geographical differentiation renders the concept of the 'average Northern Irish child's' experience somewhat misleading. Since children's experience is widely diverse, the majority of children have little experience of the Troubles, yet a relatively small number of children have very intense, concentrated and long-term experiences of Troubles-related events. The account of one young woman of 15 starkly illustrated this. When she was 11, her aunt was shot dead walking across the road beside her. Her aunt's dead body fell on top of her, and in the ensuing panic, the 11-year-old girl was forgotten about. About a year later, a gunman entered her home and shot her uncle dead. She had been standing in the kitchen with her mother and younger brothers. Two years after this incident, her brother was shot dead.

This young woman's history illustrates how some children and young people have multiple experiences of Troubles-related loss. This number of children who fall into this category is small in comparison to the overall population of children, and they almost invariably live in militarised and marginalised communities. Life in such communities almost guarantees that children are also affected by the other problems associated with marginalisation. This marginalisation in turn has its own consequences: they are at risk not only from the worst effects of the Troubles, but also of being ignored.

The children and young people who are likely to be the most negatively affected by the Troubles and are likely to have the highest level of need are perhaps least likely to access what services there are. In terms of social support or mental health services, the overall level of provision in Northern Ireland as a whole for this age group fails to meet the ordinary everyday needs of the age group. The prospects are therefore poor for those who have specific needs that might require (new) specialist services or the retraining of staff to enable them to deal comfortably with Troubles-related issues faced by children.

DEPRIVATION AND VIOLENCE

It is clear that it is the areas with the highest level of Troubles-related violence that experience the highest levels of deprivation and family poverty (Fay et al., 1999a). Children in these areas live not only with poverty, but also with the effects of militarisation and the interplay between violence and deprivation.

In order to illustrate this, death rates for particular locations in Northern Ireland were compared with their deprivation scores. Work conducted in the early 1990s in the Micro Statistics Centre at the University of Manchester produced indicators of spatial deprivation that can be used for this purpose (Robson et al., 1994). Table 4.4 shows the six district council areas with the highest rates of fatal incidents per 1000 population taking place within their district council area. The corresponding ranks for the rates of resident deaths for each council area and each area's spatial deprivation score according to the Robson index are also shown. The fatal incident rate is based on the number of fatal Troubles-related incidents occurring within the district council area, whilst the resident death rate is based on the number of residents from the district council area who have been killed in the Troubles. In some areas, such as in the border regions, there is a high rate of fatal incidents but a comparatively low rate of resident deaths. This is due to the number of security force deaths that occurred in the area. Conversely, in some districts – for example, in Belfast – the rate of resident deaths and the rate of fatal incidents occurring in the district are comparable, since the majority of those killed were killed in their home district. The geographical variation in the experience of the Troubles means that some areas witnessed more deaths of non-residents, whilst in others the majority of those killed were residents.

What emerges clearly from Table 4.4 is that of the six districts that ranked highest on fatal incidents, four were among the six worst deprived. Armagh and Cookstown were the exceptions. Strabane, which ranked highest on deprivation in the region, ranked eighth on the rate of fatal incidents. Therefore the relationship between deprivation and violence is not a simple one. (It is complicated, for example, by factors such as the disproportionately large number of members of the security forces killed and the above-average income of members of the security forces.) The correlation coefficients of the two violence scores with the deprivation score across all 26 districts were 0.76 and 0.52 respectively. There was a higher level of association between the number of fatal incidents taking place in a district and deprivation than between the number of residents killed and deprivation. The difference between these two death rates is worth noting. The number of fatal incidents that take place in a district seems to provide a better measure of the intensity of the violence affecting the area. In summary, the intensity of violence and deprivation do seem to be positively associated.

Table 4.4   A Comparison of Violence (1969–98) and Deprivation (1994) in Selected Districts

District Council	Fatal incidents rank	Deaths of residents rank	Deprivation rank (out of 26)
Belfast	1	1	2
Newry and Mourne	2	9	4
Dungannon	3	3	5
Derry Londonderry	4	6	3
Armagh	5	2	13
Cookstown	6	4	8

The implications of this for children and young people are serious. Those children and young people who face the worst challenges posed by the Troubles in terms of militarisation, injury and loss are likely to be those children who have the fewest socio-economic resources available to them. Socio-economic deprivation is likely to have negative implications for the coping abilities and resilience of precisely those young people most in need of resilience and coping strategies. Some of this is already manifest in the worst-affected communities in Northern Ireland.

EDUCATION

The research conducted by CCIC took the form of interviews with children and young people about the impact of the Troubles on their education and experiences at school. The project interviewed 85 young people across Northern Ireland and found the following:

- A link between areas of violence and educational achievement

- The development of a culture of violence in the most affected areas
- A negative impact of the Troubles on adult–child relationships
- A culture of silence and denial which developed as a way of coping with the violence of the Troubles
- The inclusion of drug and alcohol abuse in young people's coping strategies
- Inadequacies in services geared towards the worst-affected communities.

The interviews were taped and transcribed for analysis, and coded by a coding regime devised using QSR NUDIST Qualitative Data Analysis software. Table 4.5 shows the range of themes related to education that emerged in the interview transcripts. The table shows the number of interviews in which each theme appeared, the number of text units coded for each theme and the text unit rank. A text unit is composed of a number of lines of text. Text unit rank shows the rank in terms of the number of text units devoted to a given theme.

The most frequent themes that emerged, both in terms of the number of interviews mentioning it and the amount of attention in interview devoted to the theme by the young people interviewed, was violent sectarianism. This was followed by reported problems with teachers, danger in travelling to school, education suffering, problems with gangs and expulsion. Clearly, from the perspective of pupils, problems related to the Troubles are identifiable within schools, and many of these young people are concerned that their education is suffering as a result. Some of the young people interviewed reported that teachers had lost control in schools serving the worst-affected areas, and most of those young people in this situation wanted teachers to reclaim control of the school.

Partly as a result of these difficulties in schools, no doubt compounded by other difficulties related to socio-economic deprivation in communities and resourcing of education, many young people in areas worst-affected by the Troubles leave school without educational qualifications. Levels of educational attainment – and consequently life chances and expectations – in communities worst-affected by the Troubles are often low, leaving young people with few incentives to invest in the wider society. Young people in such situations can feel that they have little to lose, and so are not dissuaded by impulses for self-protection from high-risk behaviours in relation to drugs, sex and violence.

Table 4.5   Education Themes that Emerged in Interviews with Young People

	No. interviews	No. text units	Text unit rank
Sectarianism/violence	10	727	2
Danger in travelling to school	8	399	7
Problems with teachers	7	842	1
Education suffers	6	455	5
Gangs	5	236	9
Catholic schools	5	42	17
Expulsion	4	617	3
Bullying	4	365	8
No discipline	4	105	10
Integrated schools	4	70	12
Teachers are no good	3	45	16
Hate schools	3	426	6
Schools need to help more	3	55	15
Teachers have no control	2	64	14
Homework	2	74	11
Training schools	2	575	4
Work harder in school	2	66	13
Detentions	1	20	19
Protestant schools	1	35	18
Truancy	1	8	20

Education and Gender

Recent attention has been focused on gender differences in educational performance, and the 'feminisation' of activities such as reading. Young men often regard the pursuit of educational goals as 'uncool', and male educational attainment generally lags behind that of females. If this trend is placed alongside high levels of male unemployment and the gender patterns of involvement in political and anti-social violence discussed above, a disturbing picture emerges. Young men and boys in communities with high levels of deprivation and violence begin to experience at an early age within the school system the marginalisation that culminates in the 'roleless-ness' that characterises male lifestyles in many such areas (see, for example, Leonard, 1992; Finlay et al., 1995). Educational failure compounds and underpins the situation.

IMPLICATIONS FOR CITIZENSHIP

Whilst the young people interviewed showed signs of awareness and openness to the 'other side', there was also evidence of suspicion, anger and at times hatred, directed at the other community – in spite of involvement in cross-community schemes and some positive parental influence. Children and young people's attitudes are formed in the context of the other things that happen to them, and maintenance of open-minded attitudes in the context of violently divided communities is clearly impossible for many of them. However, perhaps it is not only children and young people from highly segregated areas that suffer as a result of the divided nature of this society. All children suffer to some degree as a result of the influence of three decades of violence on the culture, manifest by, for example, the proliferation of residential segregation.

The hidden effects on children of living in a divided society gives rise to anxiety about possible warping and restriction of children's education and socialisation. The work of consciously constructing models for dealing in healthy, open and mutually respectful ways with the different views, aspirations and traditions, has begun in Northern Ireland, and some of that work takes place within schools. The goal of ensuring that children can grow up with positive models of inclusiveness, and skills for resolving conflict perhaps reduces the chances that children and young people will grow into adults who are ill equipped to deal successfully with the differences contained within the wider political community. In the past, the atmosphere of fear together with the feelings of powerlessness incurred by the so-called democratic deficit and ongoing violence, meant that the full capacity for citizenship could not be developed (Smyth, 1995a, 1995b). Should such development be inhibited it will have far-reaching implications not only for children, but also for the society at large and for the long-term prospects for peace.

CONCLUSION: A CULTURE OF VIOLENCE?

Children in Northern Ireland – not just children in the worst affected areas – have grown up with mixed and confusing messages about law and order and right and wrong. The political situation has led to the widespread legitimisation of violence for political reasons. This legitimisation has depended on the collective identities of the various communities as victims. Republicans see themselves as victims of the British state; Loyalists see themselves as victims of the IRA, and security forces see themselves as targets of IRA attack and threatened by various insurgents who aim to overthrow the state and the rule of law. In defence of their various positions, all have justified the use of various forms of violence.

Set alongside a popular culture that often celebrates and promotes the use of violence, the scale of the damage to and brutalisation of young people and children has yet to be assessed. In fiction, entertainment and video games targeted at a young market, violence is presented as thrilling, entertaining, sexy, powerful and exciting. It is therefore not surprising that adolescents, especially young men, often attach positive values to toughness and aggression. Young people's experiences of death and violence have made them 'streetwise' (a phenomenon also reported by Straker et al., 1993).

In order to survive the violence and brutality of the Troubles, many people, including many children and young people, have become habituated to violence. Violence is minimised, and in the past this has enabled people to survive psychologically. This was illustrated in a group interview with young people, who, when asked to discuss the kind of community they wanted to live in, hesitated at the thought of living in a community without riots, because 'there was nothing else to do'. There is an urgent challenge to provide children and young people with opportunities to learn alternative values and to learn the skills of dealing with aggression without resorting to old patterns of behaviour. Children and young people require help in reshaping behaviours that were arguably appropriate to the violence, in a context where violence is to be consigned firmly to the past.

An earlier report by Olara Otunnu to the United Nations pointed out:

> Cessation of hostilities does not mean that war is over, particularly for children who have been extensively exposed to the culture of violence. Only with a systematic programme of healing and reintegration into society can the cycle of violence be broken. The healing and rehabilitation needs of children should, therefore, constitute a central theme and not an afterthought of post-conflict peace-building programmes ... Some of the issues and needs that

should be addressed in a collaborative manner include: prioritisation of child rights within the terms of peace accords and in the mandates of peacekeeping operations, the demobilisation of child soldiers and their social reintegration, the return and reintegration of displaced and refugee children, mine clearance and mine-awareness programmes, psychological recovery, educational and vocational training, and issues of juvenile justice. Promotion of compliance with international standards and re-establishment of local norms that promote child protection and welfare also merit priority attention. (United Nations, 1998: para. 121)

'Words on paper cannot save the children in peril', says the report-which goes on to describe the conditions necessary for 'post-conflict peace-building'.

In post-conflict situations, sustained assistance for reconstruction is required in order to consolidate peace and to support indigenous rehabilitation capacity. A critical component of such assistance must focus on the needs of children, particularly the 'crisis of the young'. The Special Representative believes that the prospects for recovery in many countries depends very much on recuperating the young and restoring to them a sense of renewed hope. In this connection, the Special Representative calls on key actors responsible for designing post-conflict peace-building programmes, in particular the World Bank, the European Union, UNDP and bilateral development agencies, to make the needs of children a central concern from the outset of their planning. Moreover, post-conflict peace-building must not mean a return to the status quo ante, a return to the conditions that gave rise to the conflict in the first place. In order to prevent the recurrence of conflict and to rebuild lasting peace, we must work systematically to transcend the distorted relationships of yesteryear. (Ibid.: para. 145)

What, then, are the prospects for children and young people, particularly those who have been worst-affected by the Troubles?

Back in Northern Ireland, the Good Friday Agreement of April 1998, wherein all the political parties elected to negotiate, set out and agree the conditions of a settlement, states:

The participants [to the negotiations] particularly recognize that young people from areas affected by the troubles face particular difficulties and will support the development of special community-based initiatives based on international best practice. The provision of services that are supportive and sensitive to the needs of victims will also be a critical element and that support will need to be channeled through both statutory and community-based voluntary organizations facilitating locally based self-help and support networks. This will require the allocation of sufficient resources, including statutory funding as necessary, to meet the needs of victims and to provide for community-based support programmes. (Section 6, para. 12)

Whilst in Northern Ireland, Otunnu described his experience of working in other violently divided societies, and pointed out:

Among the things that we've learnt elsewhere in the world is the importance of having the protection, the rights, and the well-being of children being clearly stated and catered for in any peace process.

    And here the example of the Good Friday Agreement is a very good one. It's one that in fact we want to use elsewhere in the world because it's one of the very few peace processes and peace agreements in which the needs and interests of children explicitly indicated. The Agreement provides that for children who have been affected by the troubles, their needs need to be met, consistent with international standards and practice. It's a wonderful model, now we have to work and encourage all the actors and translate this principle about the protection and interest, the best interest of children into realities on the ground. (CCIC, 2000)

It remains to be seen whether Northern Ireland will honour the commitment in the Good Friday Agreement and take the advice of the United Nations Special Representative. Certainly, the targeting for aid of children and young people particularly affected by the Troubles would seem an obvious first step. Fund-led initiatives would also seem to offer some role in peace building with children for the European Community and other interested parties. These initiatives could encourage and support such schemes as the provision of training and programme development assistance for teachers and other professionals involved with children and young people, the development of school curricula to include materials on civic and

political education, violence awareness programmes aimed at prob-
lematising violence, and the provision of compensatory education
schemes for those whose education and life chances have been
damaged by the Troubles.

In his closing remarks in Belfast, Otunnu concluded:

> Yet this is the moment to begin that process, to de-legitimise the
> use of violence. Competition and disagreement within societies is
> normal. Every society has conflict. The difference is whether you
> resolve this competition, this conflict – through discussion,
> debate, sitting down, voting – or whether you resort to the use of
> violence as a way of resolving this conflict and competition within
> society. And I hope that in Northern Ireland you have embarked
> on a path of peaceful ways of resolving and debating and
> mediating that conflict and competition as may legitimately exist
> within the society. (Ibid.)

These are lessons that children in Northern Ireland must learn.
Whether the adults will be able to create and maintain the
conditions under which such lessons can be learned is a recurring
and troubling question.

Part III: Survey Results

5 Experiencing the Troubles

Early in Northern Ireland's Troubles, there was some disagreement amongst psychiatrists and psychologists about the extent of exposure to Troubles-related violence and the effect of the Troubles on the population in general. Some, notably Fraser (1971; Fraser et al., 1972) maintained that observable effects of exposure to violence had occurred, whilst others such as Lyons (1974) or later Cairns and Wilson (1989) tended to support the view that traumatic symptoms rapidly improved after a violent event and that those exposed to the violence of the Troubles coped successfully. Since that early debate, although there has been some investigation of the impact of the Troubles on attitudes and moral development, there has been remarkably little consistent interest in the specific mental health or other effects of the Troubles on the population, nor is there any generally recognised and reliable measure of the general effects of the Troubles on the population of Northern Ireland.* It was in this context that the study was established.

In the wake of ceasefires from 1994 onwards, a group of people from all sections of the population in Northern Ireland who had direct experience of being bereaved or injured in the Troubles were brought together to discuss their position and possible contribution to the new political situation. The widespread determination to see a permanent end to violence seemed to be based on the implicit recognition of the damage done by the violence of the Troubles, yet there was no reliable collated evidence of this damage, nor was there documentation of the needs that might have to be met should peace be achieved. This group formed 'The Cost of the Troubles Study', which became a limited company and a recognised charity. In partnership with academic researchers from the university sector, a study of the effects of the Troubles on the population was planned and initiated.

THE RESEARCH APPROACH

We have documented elsewhere (Smyth and Moore, 1996) concerns about the relationship of researchers to those who participate as

---

* Research has been conducted on various sub-populations such as children (Cairns, 1998), or various groups of people, such as litigants for compensation (Bell et al., 1988), or those affected by the Enniskillen bomb of November 1987 (Curran et al., 1990).

'subjects'. We wished to resist the practice of using informants or respondents simply as containers of data that must be collected. Our training in research does not necessarily equip us to consider the rights of the respondent, not does it demand that we consider the appropriation of information and the subsequent marginalisation of the respondent from the process of analysis as problematic. Yet in the context of researching the impact of violence, to proceed in this way seemed ethically problematic to us.

Like media coverage, research is usually engaged in the collection of evidence to support or contradict pre-existing ideas about the subject investigated. In neither case does the interviewee or 'subject' exert much influence, if any, on the angle of the journalist or the analysis of the researcher. Furthermore, having given consent to being interviewed, filmed or otherwise represented, usually the 'subject' exerts no further control over the manner in which the footage, soundtrack or data are deployed. This material may be used again, usually without consultation with those who generated it, when documentary media material is being compiled or in further research.

The research carried out by The Cost of the Troubles Study adopted a participatory action research approach, which entailed developing a management structure that involved a range of people with direct experience of the effects of the Troubles. The involvement of 'subjects' in managing the research addressed the ethical considerations related to the marginalisation of 'subjects' mentioned above. One of the most devastating after-effects of trauma is the sense of disempowerment that can result. Working according to a principle of partnership was an attempt to avoid further disempowering those whose lives and experience we had set out to research and document. The use of a participative approach to the research was one way of addressing our responsibility for the impact of our work on those whose experiences we sought to explore and understand.

Improving democratic access to the research process for individuals from the researched population was a strategy aimed at improving our accountability as researchers and allowing those from the researched population to protect their interests. The term 'participatory action research' has been applied to a variety of strategies which attempt to engage the researched population in various ways. The approach we adopted had been developed in previous work (such as Templegrove Action Research, 1996) and in this case entailed, for example, involving those who were bereaved or injured in the Troubles in the management of the research project. The involved lay management in monitoring the ethical aspects of research practices, and in the analysis by discussion and the reviewing of findings. The work also operated a policy of informed consent with participants, entailing a detailed process of providing transcripts to all interviewees, discussion and agreeing of transcripts, collaboration with interviewees on issues such as anonymity, and presentation of findings.

Elsewhere (Fay et al., 1999a) we have described how we decided to depart from the professional norm in our approach to the issue of professional value freedom. Researchers investigating violence and its effects inevitably face ethical concerns arising out of the claim to value freedom and objectivity. These are dealt with more fully elsewhere (Smyth and Robinson, 2001). Survey-based approaches to research conjures up images of systematic door-to-door collection of data, anonymity, and responses that can be coded numerically. However, in researching the impact of the Troubles, ethically the research team had to anticipate their strategy when an interviewer uncovered distress or unmet needs. Traditional methods would simply record distress as data whilst the interviewer remained detached. However, for ethical reasons we equipped interviewers with the information necessary to refer respondents in need with a range of supportive services. The demands placed on interviewers were also anticipated. At an earlier phase of the work, the experience of working on the database on deaths and the daily handling of the tragic and often heartbreaking details of people's lives had an emotional impact on the researchers. We were constantly reminded of the nature of the data we were handling and had to deal with our emotional responses to it. Yet we were also concerned that we would begin to see the data as 'just data', forgetting its human context, a process of becoming habituated to handling data on death. We tried to practise the discipline of remembering that these data represent the suffering and loss of human lives in the context of a society that often copes with the scale of loss by denying it. This, although necessary for the ethical reasons outlined above, increased rather than reduced the demands on research staff. This approach also challenges models of scientific or professional distance, and runs counter to the culture of silence and denial that is commonly used to cope with the tragedies of the Troubles. Whilst we as researchers have been socialised as professionals, or as members of a society into these approaches, we attempted not to 'retreat' from the data into silence, denial or professional distance. Rather, we have not tried to deny our personal responses to working with the data and the people who generated it. We used our personal responses to the data to inform our interviewer training and support, and ultimately our analysis. It also informed the way we set about conducting the survey.

We had anxieties about 'cold calling' at people's homes without warning, since we anticipated that some people who had had traumatic experiences of the Troubles would choose not to participate or to have interviewers call at their homes. We wished to avoid invading the privacy or causing undue distress to people who had been affected and who did not wish to participate. Therefore we wrote in advance, informing people of our intention to call and ask them to complete a questionnaire on their experiences of the Troubles and the effects on them.

In total, 57 of the 3000 people we wrote to contacted us. Of these, 7 wanted to make specific arrangements to meet the interviewer, as they weren't always available; 18 wrote letters, most saying politely that they did not want to participate; 3 people wrote saying that they were disabled or infirm and felt it 'inappropriate' to participate. One written reply put forward the view that the Troubles were caused by 'our departure from the Lord and the Word' and that that was all she wanted to say on the subject. Another person wrote, stating 'the following testimony is the *only* contact I intend to have with the study team per se', and went on: 'As with the majority of such studies as yours, your remit begins in the middle and asks all the wrong questions.' This correspondent finished: 'The theme of the "troubles" is a string of death, injury, and tears. The cost of the "troubles" is the cost of Eden's apple bite: knowledge, sorrow, and a taste of freedom!' One letter simply stated, 'I do not wish to participate in your survey. The troubles have not affected me greatly over the years, as it has done to others. Therefore it would be of more beneficial [*sic*] to your work if you found someone else to help you. I do not wish to be contacted further, and I thank you for writing to me in the first place.'

Since we anticipated that we would uncover distress and unmet needs in interviewees when doing the survey, we compiled a list of agencies and their contact details that offered support or help in this field. Using this information, a leaflet containing relevant information was drawn up for interviewers to distribute as appropriate. The leaflet also contained basic advice and information about common responses to the Troubles, and this part of the leaflet was written in collaboration with two women who had been bereaved and injured in the Troubles. We also alerted a number of agencies to the work we were doing and warned them that respondents might be directly referred to them as a result.

This work was carried out at a delicate time in the Northern Ireland peace process. As researchers, we were conscious of the responsibility to contribute in positive ways to political progress and peace. Since the information we collected was laden with political meanings, and the issues we were researching were sources of grievance and therefore open to political use, it was easy to see that our work was not 'objective' or 'neutral'. The data we collect has been used by one or other parties to the Northern Ireland conflict to 'prove' their cause. Researching and publishing such data in the midst of a continuing conflict brings with it responsibilities. Once published, the authors lose control over how the work is used or interpreted. Our work might be used in ways that will contribute to the entrenchment of positions, and thence to more bloodshed and loss of life. There is no possible evasion of this responsibility. The work is conducted and published in the belief that more and better evidence of the awful price paid by this community will support, inspire and motivate some people to pursue new ways in which we can peacefully and successfully address our situation. Although the bare statistics cannot properly represent the pain and suffering of individuals, families and communities, we also hope that the evidence we collect will help persuade those in authority to devote resources where they are most needed in order to redress the damage that has been done by almost thirty years of the Troubles. Some of our work may also be useful in shedding light on the legacy of the Troubles, particularly within some of the areas and sub-populations worst affected, and thereby illuminate the routes towards new and effective ways of repairing the damage of the past.

The Remit of the Project

The aim of the work was to document the effects of the Troubles on the population of Northern Ireland as a whole, and to elucidate any patterns or trends in the way the effects of the Troubles were distributed within the population. The aims of the survey, which was conducted as part of the project, were to establish the prevalence of emotional and physical sequelae arising out of the Troubles in Northern Ireland, and to identify the needs (medical, emotional, social, financial) of those affected. The survey involved administering a questionnaire to a representative sample of the population of Northern Ireland. No existing questionnaire was adequate for this purpose and it was necessary to develop an instrument for this purpose. A tripartite research strategy was employed in order to achieve this:

- Phase one of the project identified the full range of self-help groups established by people adversely affected by the violence of the Troubles at that time. A directory of groups and services available to those experiencing physical or emotional after-effects related to the Troubles was drawn up and made available to all interviewers who could then pass it to respondents where appropriate. Phase one also produced a database of deaths in the Troubles from 1969 to date. This database was used to calculate death rates in all of the electoral wards in Northern Ireland. Originally the database of deaths had been compiled primarily to provide a sample frame for the survey. However, the database of deaths was of interest in its own right, and an analysis of this database has been published separately (Fay et al., 1999a).
- Phase two involved conducting interviews with 85 people to generate in-depth accounts for qualitative analysis. These data, excerpts from which were also published separately (Smyth and Fay, 2000), also informed the design of a questionnaire. (For more information on the issues encountered and methods used in designing and operationalising the survey, see Appendix 2.) This was used in the field survey of a representative sample of 3000 people drawn from the general population.
- Phase three consisted of the conduct and analysis of the survey.

Why a Survey?

Although it is clear that the rich data on the experiences and effects of the Troubles in the project were contained in the in-depth interviews, a survey of a sample of the general population was also considered necessary. This was because it was anticipated that policy-makers might be more easily persuaded by the findings of a survey that 'tested' the wider validity and reliability of the qualitative data. Therefore, whilst the qualitative data were used to inform the design of a questionnaire, and were also presented in a separate book (Smyth and Fay, 2000), video (The Cost of the Troubles Study, 2000) and in an exhibition (The Cost of the Troubles Study, 1999), the quantitative data would provide a more reliable picture of how certain experiences and effects were distributed in the general population.

In the survey of Northern Ireland, designed to elicit data on experience and effects of the Troubles, a total of 1346 persons were interviewed. Alongside the specific questions about experience and impact of the Troubles on their lives, people were also asked general questions about themselves and their household. The sample was drawn from three very different sets of wards, which were classified according to their Troubles-related death rates. Differences between these three sets of wards are analysed later in the chapter. First, we describe the kind of people interviewed and their experiences of the Troubles.

THE SAMPLE

Although household size varied from 1 person to 28, 1005 respondents (74.3 per cent) were living in 1- to 4-person households. The modal group, 334 (24.7 per cent), lived in 2-person households. A further 218 (16.1 per cent) lived alone and 36 (2.7 per cent) lived in households with 8 or more people.

Respondents and their households represented a population of 4513. The age structure of the population was similar for both males and females. Approximately-one fifth (21.8 per cent) of the sample household population were below the age of 15, with 21.1 per cent of males and 22.4 per cent of females falling into that category. In terms of working age, 71.2 per cent of males and 68.5 per cent of females were between 15 and 65 years of age.

In the mid-year estimate for the Northern Ireland population in 1996, women made up 53 per cent of the population aged over 24 in Northern Ireland. Given that only adults were interviewed, the sample gender balance reflected that in the overall population with 624 respondents (46.4 per cent) being male and 722 (53.6 per cent) female. Two-thirds of respondents were between the ages of 25 and 59, with the largest single number in the 40–59 age group (421, or 32.3 per cent of respondents). 201 (15.5 per cent) respondents were below the age of 20 and 172 (13.2 per cent) aged 65 and above. The sample was concentrated more in the younger age groups than was the Northern Ireland population as a whole. Thus almost 45 per cent of the sample was aged less than 25 years compared to just over 39 per cent of the general population. Similarly, 13.3 per cent of the sample household population were aged 60 or over compared to 17 per cent of the Northern Ireland population. Given that the sampling procedure emphasised a cluster of wards with high death rates, some of which also had high concentrations of younger people in their populations, such differences were to be anticipated.

The majority of respondents, 684 (51.4 per cent), were married and 406 (30.5 per cent) were single. Single parents constituted only 2.2 per cent of all respondents.

Approximately two-thirds of the respondent population were Catholic and one-third Protestant, with 34 respondents (2.5 per cent) failing to answer the question relating to religion.

The majority of households in the sample – 819 (62.5 per cent) out of 1310 – had no household members at school. A further 345 (26.4 per cent) of households had 1 or 2 members, and 89 (6.8 per cent) had 3 members still at school. There were slightly more households 962 (73.7 per cent) with no males at school compared to the equivalent number of households – 930 (70.9 per cent) – with no females at school respectively. There are also more households – 94 (7.2 per cent) – with 2 females at school than 2 males – 77 (5.9 per cent). Similar patterns emerge for households with three members at school, with 30 (2.3 per cent) having 3 females and 17 (1.3 per cent) having 3 males at school. These figures may reflect the difference between males and females in the age structure of the sample household population, where there were 700 males below the age of 20 compared to 785 female.

The majority of households (1170, or 89.8 per cent) did not have anyone in higher education. However, households with 1 female in higher education (77) outnumbered households with 1 male in higher education (59), indicating that, in the sample, there were more females than males in higher education.

The majority of respondents (51.6 per cent) had no formal qualifications. Out of those with some qualifications (48.4 per cent), the most common qualification was O levels or GCSEs (held by 32.5 per cent), compared with 21.3 per cent who had CSE/NVQs and 20.7 per cent who had A levels or B.Techs. Of all respondents, 6 per cent had a higher education degree of some kind.

Over a third (516, or 39 per cent) of households had no members in either full- or part-time employment. However, 313 (23.6 per cent) households had 1 member and 346 (26.1 per cent) households had 2 members in either full- or part-time employment. Households that had 3 or 4 people in employment accounted for 127 (9.5 per cent) in the sample, and 22 (1.7 per cent) of sampled households had 5–7 people in either full- or part-time employment.

When employment was analysed by gender, a greater proportion of households (765 or 57.7 per cent) had no females in employment compared to the equivalent figure for males (654, or 49.1 per cent). Women working in the home, in both larger and single-sex households could explain this. Over a third of households (460 or 34.7 per cent) had only 1 female in employment. This compares with the male statistic of 534 (40.1 per cent of households).

Over a third (37.5 per cent) of households did not have anyone in the household receiving benefit. In 435 (33.3 per cent) of households one person was receiving benefit, and in 293 (22.4 per cent) households two people were receiving benefit. One household, suggested earlier to be an institution of some kind, had 28 males all on benefit.

A significant proportion (14.1 per cent) of respondents were receiving the Jobseeker's Allowance, with a further 27.1 per cent receiving income support, some 27.6 per cent on housing benefit and 39.7 per cent on child benefit. The benefits received by the respondents reflected to a certain extent the age structure and socio-economic status of the respondent population. In some cases, percentages also reflected share of economically active respondents. For example, 12.8 per cent of respondents were registered unemployed and 14.1 per cent were receiving the Jobseeker's Allowance.

The majority of respondents (738, or 54.6 per cent) owned their home and a significant proportion of respondents (611, or 45.2 per cent) rented their accommodation. Only 3 respondents lived in co-ownership housing. Housing tenure in the sample was related to the type of accommodation and to whether it was a public or private housing development. Almost half (654 out of 1347, or 48.6 per cent) the households lived in a whole terraced house or bungalow, whilst households living in a whole house or bungalow – irrespective of whether it was semi-detached, detached or terraced – constituted 95.1 per cent of the sample population. Only 29 (2.2 per cent) households lived in a flat in a block of flats.

Approximately half (51.3 per cent) the households in the sample lived in current or former Northern Ireland Housing Executive or other public housing. Of these, approximately one-fifth lived in a rural area; the remainder were located in a town or city. Approximately one-fifth (266 out of 1320 households, or 20.2 per cent) lived in a private development and a similar proportion said they were living in a 'rural or isolated setting'. Only 16 respondents (1.2 per cent) lived in sheltered housing located either in a town or city. These patterns are a product of a combination of factors such as geography and the social and economic environment, all of which determine the type of housing provision available in the various areas in which the respondents' population was located.

In terms of perceived housing segregation, a majority of 787 out of 1344 respondents (58.6 per cent) saw the area in which they lived as segregated. When cross-tabulated with religion, perceived housing segregation tended to be higher amongst Catholics than Protestants. Of those who perceive their area as segregated, the majority (81.8 per cent) were Catholic.

In relation to income, re-analysis showed that the largest single group of respondents, (30.4 per cent) earned between £100 and £250 per week, followed by 27.5 per cent who earned less than £100. When taken together, more than half the respondents to the question on income, 440 out of 760, earned less than £250 per week. A further 8.9 per cent of respondents earned between £12,000 and £16,000 and only 10 (or 1.1 per cent) of respondents earned more than £30,000. When compared with the distribution of household income in Northern Ireland, these figures suggest that household income in the sample was below the Northern Ireland average. In 1996, average household income exceeded £300 per week – a quarter of the sample had a weekly income of less than a third of this figure.

The level of income is related to a number of features of the sample, such as the proportion of the population who receive benefits, the age and gender of respondents, employment opportunities and the employability of the respondent population. One of the most important factors, particularly in relation to the two questions enquiring about income, is how respondents gave data on income. The key was whether they gave weekly or yearly figures for income.

In terms of weekly incomes, 32 per cent of households had an income between £100 and £249, while 58.1 per cent of respondents had household incomes of less than £500. This may be attributed to a combination of factors such as the number of people receiving benefit and household size. Earlier it was noted that 24.7 per cent of respondents were living in 2-person households and 16.1 per cent were living alone. Clearly, smaller households will tend towards lower household incomes. It is important to note that the response rate for this question was poor, with only 597 cases (44 per cent of the sample) answering these questions.

KEY VARIABLES

Previous analysis of political violence in Northern Ireland undertaken by The Cost of the Troubles Study highlighted the significance of certain key variables – location, gender and religion, and also age and socio-economic status. It has been demonstrated that these are crucially associated with an individual's experience of the Troubles. In addition, the majority of direct casualties of violence have been male, suggesting that the Troubles have been a predominantly male phenomenon.

The Importance of Location

The significance of location as a factor in the patterning of violence is now explored, mainly through analysis by cross-tabulation, given the categorical nature of the variables concerned. For each of the cross-tabulations, Chi Square tests were performed to ensure that the differences reported here were systematic rather than random. Given the large number of cross-tabulations, a significance level of 0.005 was used as the benchmark, in preference to the 0.05 significance level. With the 0.05 level, 1 in 20 cross-tabulations may show random rather than systematic differences. In this exercise, since over 80 cross-tabulations were performed, a potential four dubious relationships may have appeared within the set had the 0.05 level been employed. However, raising the level to 0.005 may exclude certain significant relationships but in the interests of excluding the spurious relationships, this was regarded as more acceptable and rigorous.

Earlier (see Chapter 2) we analysed the uneven spatial distribution of political violence in Northern Ireland. From this analysis, it is clear that certain areas have suffered disproportionately. This uneven geographical distribution of the conflict was the primary reason for the choice of sampling procedure used. In order to analyse the role of location in the Troubles, a new variable was created with just three values and all data was coded in one of three categories: wards with the *highest intensity* of violence; wards with *medium intensity* of violence and wards with *low intensity* of violence. Ideally, analysis by individual ward would have revealed further detail in the distribution of Troubles' effects. However, due to the low returns in some wards, the analysis only worked at the level of these ward groups.

These groups of wards, however, are distinguished by more than just their level of violence. Table 5.1 records reported weekly household income for each of the three groups of wards.

Table 5.1   Weekly Household Income by Ward

Income	% in Highest intensity	% in Middle intensity	% in Least intensity
Less than £100	24.5	12.6	5.3
£100–249	45.6	38.2	18.5
£250–499	15.0	13.5	12.8
£500–999	4.8	4.3	3.7
(Number)	(147)	(207)	(243)

The group with the highest intensity of violence contained more households with extremely low incomes than the other two groups. Almost a quarter of households in this group reported an income of less than £100 per week. A further 70 per cent had incomes of less than £250 per week. Overall, for the lower income categories, household income varies inversely with degree of violence. Thus, the wards with least violence had the lowest proportion of households in the bottom income categories. While not shown in the table, wards with the lowest levels of violence also had the highest proportion in the upper income categories.

Elsewhere (Fay et al., 1997) we found that there was not a high correlation between spatial indices of deprivation and ward death rates throughout Northern Ireland. It was hypothesised that the relationship was obscured by the inclusion of deaths of members of the security forces who did not tend to live in areas of acute deprivation. Here, however, by selecting the group of wards with highest death rates for residents, we also included some of the region's most deprived wards.

Table 5.2 offers a socio-economic profile of households and respondents in each of these ward groups.

The wards with the highest intensity of violence stand out as characterised by low levels of employment and high benefits dependency. These wards also contain the highest rates of respondents with no educational qualifications, who are also concentrated in public sector rented accommodation, which is also, for the most part, religiously segregated.

Table 5.2   Socio-economic Characteristics of Households and Respondents by Ward

	% in Highest intensity	% in Middle intensity	% in Least intensity
No household members receiving benefits	16.2	46.7	51.7
No household members in employment	57.0	29.2	29.8
Respondents with no qualifications	62.1	46.6	45.5
Respondents residing in public or previously public sector housing	86.1	32.7	32.6
Respondents residing in rented housing	74.7	30.6	28.0
Respondents living in a religiously segregated area	91.9	50.1	29.9
(Number)	(471)	(474)	(407)

The labour market profile of respondents in these wards reinforces this picture (Table 5.3).

Table 5.3   Labour Market Profile of Respondents by Ward

		Highest intensity	Middle intensity	Least intensity
In full-time employment	no.	99	193	170
	%	35.5	58.0	66.9
In part-time employment	no.	28	51	42
	%	10.0	15.3	16.5
In training	no.	10	2	1
	%	3.6	0.6	0.4
Unemployed	no.	109	44	22
	%	39.1	13.2	8.7
Permanently sick or disabled	no.	33	43	19
	%	11.8	12.9	7.5
Total	no.	279	333	254
	%	100.0	100.0	100.0

In the wards that had experienced the greatest degree of violence, lower percentages of respondents were in work. The percentage unemployed in these wards was three times that in middle intensity wards and more than four times that in low intensity wards.

While this is predictable at one level, it also complicates the analysis. Identifying effects specifically caused by the Troubles requires separating out other possible causal factors like deprivation. In practice, this is rarely easy to accomplish. Of course, it has been argued that deprivation and political violence are intimately related – that grievance at inequality and discrimination fuels violence. However, such arguments could be equally applied to peripheral housing estates in Britain where poverty and squalor can be linked to local crime, which can be seen as a product of socio-economic marginalisation rather than as a separate factor. Thus some of the difficulties in identifying the impact of the Troubles begin to emerge in this analysis.

Experience of Violence

Given how these wards were sampled, it is unsurprising that the 'highest intensity' wards should record the highest scores in reported experience of violence. Nevertheless, almost 55 per cent of respondents in highest intensity wards reported a lot or quite a lot of experience of the Troubles (Table 5.4). A further quarter of respondents in these wards reported some experience of the Troubles. Such findings suggest that for almost 30 years in certain places in Northern Ireland, the Troubles have almost been a way of life.

Table 5.4   Experience of the Troubles by Ward

	% in Highest intensity	% in Middle intensity[1]	% in Least intensity[1]
A lot	25.9	11.9	5.5
Quite a lot	28.9	16.6	12.0
Some	24.2	29.6	26.3
A little	10.2	17.9	16.8
Very little	9.9	20.3	35.3
None	0.9	3.6	4.3
Total %	100.0	100.0	100.0
(Number)	(463)	(469)	(400)

[1] Rounded.

Interestingly, when respondents were asked to specify the nature of their experience, a smaller proportion in the highest intensity wards referred to peripheral experiences such as reading news reports about the Troubles. This might suggest that the Troubles were more a lived reality for these respondents than a series of media events. The kinds of experience reported more frequently in these wards were 'being stopped and searched by the security forces', 'being wary in the presence of people from the other community', 'having to take extra security precautions to secure my home or workplace' or 'having to change normal routes, routines or habits because of safety'. For other questions, for example, 'being stopped at a checkpoint', respondents in high intensity wards reported this experience at about the same level of frequency as for the other two groups of wards. In responses to the group of health questions in the questionnaire, those in wards with the most intense violence consistently reported more health problems than in other wards. Although this may reflect health problems associated with deprivation, a third of respondents indicated that Troubles-related incidents had an effect on their general health and a fifth reported similarly for Troubles-related bereavement. Thus some evidence emerged that the Troubles have impacted negatively on health, particularly in wards with the highest levels of violence.

Table 5.5   Experience of Having to Conceal Things in Order to Feel Safe, by Ward

		Highest intensity	Middle intensity	Least intensity[1]
Very often	no.	71	30	14
	%	15.2	6.4	3.4
Occasionally	no.	188	59	35
	%	40.2	12.6	8.6
Seldom	no.	90	75	75
	%	19.2	16.0	18.4
Never	no.	119	305	283
	%	25.4	65.0	69.5
Total	no.	468	469	407
	%	100.0	100.0	100.0

[1] Percentage figures rounded.

For other types of experience of the Troubles, the highest intensity wards showed marked differences from the other two groups of wards. Tables 5.5, 5.6 and 5.7 relate to direct experience of the Troubles.

Table 5.6   Experience of Having a Neighbour Killed, by Ward

		Highest intensity[1]	Middle intensity	Least intensity
Several times	no.	31	13	4
	%	6.6	2.8	1.0
More than once	no.	76	48	51
	%	16.2	10.3	12.5
Once	no.	134	69	29
	%	28.6	14.7	7.1
Never	no.	227	338	323
	%	48.5	72.2	79.4
Total	no.	468	468	407
	%	100.0	100.0	100.0

[1] Percentage figures rounded.

Table 5.7   Extent to which Experience of the Troubles has Affected Individuals' Lives, by Ward

		Highest intensity[1]	Middle intensity[1]	Least intensity
Complete change	no.	81	12	6
	%	17.4	2.6	1.5
Radical change	no.	51	42	26
	%	10.9	9.0	6.5
Some change	no.	198	199	124
	%	42.5	42.4	31.0
Small impact	no.	113	171	190
	%	24.2	36.5	47.5
Not at all	no.	23	45	54
	%	4.9	9.6	13.5
Total	no.	466	469	400
	%	100.0	100.0	100.0

[1] Percentage figures rounded.

Overall, the high intensity wards reported in the 'very often' category more than twice as much as in middle intensity wards and more than four times as often as those from low intensity wards. This pattern is repeated across almost all the variables for direct experience of the Troubles. Indeed, those in the highest intensity wards scored ten times higher than least intensity wards in positive responses to the question about 'feeling very often blamed for the Troubles'. Furthermore, in the highest intensity wards, 28 per cent reported having their home attacked very often or occasionally – 10 per cent reported that they had had their home destroyed. Similarly, in the high intensity wards, almost 40 per cent of respondents reported being caught up in riots several times, whilst almost three-quarters had been in a riot at least once.

Those in the highest intensity wards reported having other kinds of intense experiences of the Troubles more frequently. Over half of respondents in high intensity wards reported having a neighbour killed, compared to one in five in the least intensity wards. Just less than half reported having a friend killed. More than a third reported having a member of the immediate family injured. A fifth had a member of their immediate family killed.

It seems likely that the increased rates of reporting of Troubles-related experience in highest intensity areas is related to the finding that individuals living in these wards felt that their lives had been more altered by the Troubles than those living elsewhere.

Just over 28 per cent of residents in highest intensity wards reported either a 'radical change' or a 'complete change' compared to 11.6 per cent in wards of next intensity. The proportion reporting some form of change was almost twice as high as in the least intensity wards.

Those in wards least affected by the Troubles tended to blame Republican and Loyalist paramilitary organisations more in their attribution of responsibility for the Troubles, with combined scores between 75 and 80 per cent for 'responsible' or 'most responsible'. Wards with highest intensity tended to blame Loyalist, though not Republican, paramilitaries. Most of all, however, they tended to blame the RUC, the British Army, Loyalist politicians and British politicians with scores in excess of 75 per cent for each.

The survey also examined the kind of help used by respondents in each of the three locations. Table 5.8 shows the kind of help that respondents reported using.

Table 5.8   Sources of Help Sought/Obtained, by Ward

Have you ever sought/obtained help from the following?	High intensity No. (%)		Medium intensity No. (%)		Low intensity No. (%)	
	Yes	No	Yes	No	Yes	No
Psychiatrist	45	394	11	453	7	391
	(10.3)	(89.7)	(2.4)	(97.6)	(1.8)	(98.2)
Clinical psychologist	14	422	2	464	2	396
	(3.2)	(96.8)	(0.4)	(99.6)	(0.5)	(99.5)
GP/local doctor	171	272	57	410	40	360
	(38.6)	(61.4)	(12.2)	(87.8)	(10.0)	(90.0)
Community nurse	67	370	2	463	8	389
	(15.3)	(84.7)	(0.4)	(99.6)	(2.0)	(98.0)
Alternative health practitioner	10	427	0	465	0	398
	(2.3)	(97.7)	(0.0)	(100.0)	(0.0)	(100.0)
Chemist	137	302	23	442	14	385
	(31.2)	(68.8)	(4.9)	(95.1)	(3.5)	(96.5)
Social worker	46	391	3	462	2	396
	(10.5)	(89.5)	(0.6)	(99.4)	(0.5)	(95.5)
Child guidance counsellor	10	424	0	465	0	398
	(2.3)	(97.7)	(0.0)	(100.0)	(0.0)	(100.0)
School welfare/educational psychologist	16	419	1	463	0	398
	(3.7)	(96.3)	(0.2)	(99.8)	(0.0)	(100.0)
Teacher	37	398	2	463	2	396
	(8.5)	(91.5)	(0.4)	(99.6)	(0.5)	(99.5)
Counsellor	23	412	7	458	6	392
	(5.3)	(94.7)	(1.5)	(98.5)	(1.5)	(98.5)
Self-help group	40	396	3	462	4	394
	(9.2)	(90.8)	(0.6)	(99.4)	(1.0)	(99.0)
Marriage counsellor	3	433	2	463	0	398
	(0.7)	(99.3)	(0.4)	(99.6)	(0.0)	(100.0)
Social security agency	104	333	3	462	1	397
	(23.8)	(76.2)	(0.6)	(99.4)	(0.3)	(99.7)
Citizens' Advice Bureau	64	372	7	458	3	395
	(14.7)	(85.3)	(1.5)	(98.5)	(0.8)	(99.2)
Samaritans	2	434	3	462	1	397
	(0.5)	(99.5)	(0.6)	(99.4)	(0.3)	(99.7)
Minister or priest	70	367	26	439	20	379
	(16.0)	(84.0)	(5.6)	(94.4)	(5.0)	(95.0)
Faith healer	3	432	4	459	1	394
	(0.7)	(99.3)	(0.9)	(99.1)	(0.3)	(99.7)
Lawyer or solicitor	90	346	30	434	15	380
	(20.6)	(79.4)	(6.5)	(93.5)	(3.8)	(96.2)
Work colleagues/ personnel department	13	423	2	461	1	394
	(3.0)	(97.0)	(0.4)	(99.6)	(0.3)	(99.7)
Accountant	3	433	1	461	0	395
	(0.7)	(99.3)	(0.2)	(99.8)	(0.0)	(100.0)
Local politician	117	318	15	446	14	381
	(26.9)	(73.1)	(3.3)	(96.7)	(3.5)	(96.5)
Community worker	115	322	6	455	9	386
	(26.3)	(73.7)	(1.3)	(98.7)	(2.3)	(97.7)
Other voluntary organisation	92	344	3	460	5	389
	(21.1)	(78.9)	(0.6)	(99.4)	(1.3)	(98.7)

In this breakdown of where respondents reported receiving help, significant differences between the different groups of wards emerge. Those in high intensity locations obtained help more frequently from all but two sources – the Samaritans and a faith healer. However, the numbers involved are so small that they do not affect the overall significant pattern – much larger numbers from high intensity areas seeking help.

There is variation between the three locations in the pattern of where help was most frequently obtained. Areas of highest intensity sought help from GP or local doctor, chemist, local politician, community worker, social security agency, other voluntary organisation and lawyer or solicitor, in that order. Respondents in areas of medium violence also sought help from their GP or local doctor most frequently, but second most frequent was their lawyer or solicitor, followed by their minister or priest, chemist, local politician, psychiatrist, and counsellor. (Not all of those seeing psychiatrists would have been seeking help: some were seeking forensic psychiatric reports in the pursuit of financial compensation claims.) In areas of low violence, the pattern differed again. There, respondents sought help most frequently from their GP or local doctor, then from their minister or priest, then lawyer or solicitor, local politician, chemist, community worker, and community nurse.

It would seem that a higher percentage of those in areas of high intensity violence seek and obtain help of some kind, and when they obtain help, they are less likely to use their minister or priest, solicitor, psychiatrist, counsellor or community nurse than those in medium or low intensity areas. Conversely they were more likely than any of the other locations to use the social security agency and other voluntary organisations. The higher levels of deprivation in these areas may explain this.

Significant differences also emerged between the three areas in terms of where respondents received their best help (Table 5.9).

Table 5.9 shows that in all three locations, respondents reported receiving their best help from their spouse, followed by either parents or other close family. This was followed by close friends, neighbours, local doctor or children. Local doctors were the most likely non-family helper to be regarded as a source of good help. However, the overall results show that overwhelmingly family, friends and neighbours have provided the most valued help with the effects of the Troubles.

Table 5.9   Sources of Best Help, by Ward

Source of best help		Highest intensity	Middle intensity	Least intensity	Total
Spouse	no.	90	32	29	151
	% within source	59.60	21.19	19.21	100.00
	% within ward	24.13	16.16	9.35	17.14
Children	no.	17	5	9	31
	% within source	54.84	16.13	29.03	100.00
	% within ward	4.56	2.53	2.90	3.52
Parents	no.	76	18	28	122
	% within source	62.30	14.75	22.95	100.00
	% within ward	20.38	9.09	9.03	13.85
Other close family	no.	65	21	17	103
	% within source	63.11	20.39	16.50	100.00
	% within ward	17.43	10.61	5.48	11.69
Close friends	no.	22	8	11	41
	% within source	53.66	19.51	26.83	100.00
	% within ward	5.90	4.04	3.55	4.65
Neighbours	no.	1	7		8
	% within source	12.50	87.50		100.00
	% within ward	0.27	3.54		0.91
Work colleagues	no.		2	1	3
	% within source		66.67	33.33	100.00
	% within ward		1.01	0.32	0.34
Those in similar position	no.	6	3	9	18
	% within source	33.33	16.67	50.00	100.00
	% within ward	1.61	1.52	2.90	2.04
GP/local doctor	no.	12	7	1	20
	% within source	60.00	35.00	5.00	100.00
	% within ward	3.22	3.54	0.32	2.27
Psychiatrist	no.	3	2	1	6
	% within source	50.00	33.33	16.67	100.00
	% within ward	0.80	1.01	0.32	0.68
Alternative health practitioner	no.	1			1
	% within source	100.00			100.00
	% within ward	0.27			0.11
Chemist	no.		1		1
	% within source		100.0		100.0
	% within ward		0.51		0.11
Social worker	no.	1			1
	% within source	100.00			100.00
	% within ward	0.27			0.11
School welfare/ educational psychologist	no.	1			1
	% within source	100.00			100.00
	% within ward	0.27			0.11
Teacher	no.			1	1
	% within source			100.00	100.00
	% within ward			0.32	0.11
Counsellor	no.		3	1	4
	% within source		75.00	25.00	100.00
	% within ward		1.52	0.32	0.45

Table 5.9   *continued*

Self-help group	no.	1			1
	% within source	100.00			100.00
	% within ward	0.27			0.11
Citizens' Advice	no.	1			1
Bureau	% within source	100.00			100.00
	% within ward	0.27			0.11
Minister/priest	no.	7	3	2	12
	% within source	58.33	25.00	16.67	100.00
	% within ward	1.88	1.52	0.65	1.36
Lawyer/solicitor	no.	3	3		6
	% within source	50.00	50.00		100.00
	% within ward	0.80	1.52		0.68
Personnel	no.	1			1
Department at work	% within source	100.00			100.00
	% within ward	0.27			0.11
Received appropriate	no.	65	83	200	348
help from no one	% within source	18.68	23.85	57.47	100.00
	% within ward	17.43	41.92	64.52	39.50
Total	no.	373	198	310	881
	% within source	42.34	22.47	35.19	100.00
	% within ward	100.00	100.00	100.00	100.00

Table 5.10 describes how respondents evaluated the help they had received. It does not reflect responses from the substantial number of respondents to whom this question did not apply, since they did not seek help.

Table 5.10   Level of Satisfaction with Help Received, by Ward

Was help satisfactory?		High intensity		Medium intensity		Low intensity	
		Yes	No	Yes	No	Yes	No
Sympathetic and	no.	191	30	66	16	41	11
helpful	% within ward	45.4	7.1	14.4	3.5	10.6	2.8
Adequate only	no.	36	57	25	44	17	32
	% within ward	8.8	14.0	5.5	9.7	4.4	8.3
Insensitive	no.	8	80	5	63	1	49
	% within ward	2.0	19.9	1.1	13.8	0.3	11.9
Harmful	no.	5	83	1	67	1	46
	% within ward	1.2	20.6	0.2	14.7	0.3	11.9
Judgemental	no.	8	81	7	61	3	44
	% within ward	2.0	20.1	1.5	13.4	0.8	11.4
Critical of me	no.	6	82	5	62	3	44
	% within ward	1.5	20.4	1.1	13.7	0.8	11.4
Couldn't find	no.	6	79	2	59	5	39
help	% within ward	1.5	19.6	0.4	13	1.3	10.1
Didn't need	no.	54	77	70	63	103	38
help	% within ward	13.0	18.6	15.4	13.8	26.4	9.7

In all cases, with the exception of the last category, 'Didn't need help', response levels are highest in the high intensity location, reflecting the greater use of help. Generally, help was evaluated positively, with a small but consistent minority of respondents in all three locations reporting dissatisfaction with the help they received.

The sharp differences amongst these groups of wards in reporting particular effects of the Troubles can be summarised as follows:

- Over 33 per cent of respondents in wards of highest intensity reported painful memories compared to 20 per cent in the middle intensity group
- Over 25 per cent in wards of highest intensity reported dreams and nightmares compared to around 12 per cent in the middle intensity group
- Around 33 per cent of respondents in wards of highest intensity reported involuntary recall compared to around 12 per cent in the middle intensity group
- In wards of highest intensity, 30 per cent felt some form of guilt at surviving compared to 11 per cent in the middle intensity group
- Almost 25 per cent of respondents in wards of highest intensity had taken some form of medication for such effects compared to just under 12 per cent in middle intensity wards
- 22 per cent of respondents in wards of highest intensity reported an increase in alcohol consumption related to the Troubles compared to just over 4 per cent in middle intensity wards
- Those in high intensity wards had more severe experiences and reported more severe effects of the Troubles than those in the other two wards
- Those in high intensity wards sought help more frequently than those in other wards
- In all cases, help was sought primarily from friends and immediate family although some differences emerged in help sought outside the family between the three locations
- Over 40 per cent of those who sought help in high intensity wards were unable to find satisfactory help, compared to 29 per cent in medium intensity and 29 per cent in low intensity wards

- Over 83 per cent in high intensity wards believed that nothing could help them, compared to just over 4 per cent in medium intensity and just over 12 per cent in low intensity wards
- Over 23 per cent had taken medication in high intensity wards compared to almost 12 per cent in medium wards and just over 9 per cent in low intensity wards
- Of those who used medication, over 52 per cent of those in high intensity wards were on medication permanently, compared to 9 per cent in medium intensity and 35 per cent for low intensity wards
- Those using medication in high intensity wards were likely to be using it for sleep disturbance, sedation or anti-depressive purposes, whereas those in low intensity wards used them for pain control rather than for anti-depressive purposes.

Indeed for every 'effects' variable, differences of this order are observable. Differential experience and effects of the Troubles would seem to be conditioned by location. These responses suggest that there have been three key dimensions to life in the areas most affected by the Troubles:

1. There is the much greater exposure to violence both from para-military organisations and the security forces – a set of experiences almost unmatched in the rest of Northern Ireland (this group of wards regularly reported experience of Troubles' related activity at twice the rate for middle wards and four times the rate for least intensity wards)
2. There are insecurities and fears in being outside one's own area and an acute wariness of outsiders, reflected, for example, in efforts to conceal where one lives
3. There is a strong pattern of segregation – over 25 per cent of those from highest intensity wards who were employed, worked only with members of their own community.

Whilst these finding might seem to be an artefact of the sampling procedure, they are, however, exactly what the sampling procedure was designed to illustrate – the stark and pervasive differences in people's lives resulting from continued proximity to violence.

Segregation

Having examined the significance of location in experiencing the Troubles by reference to three sub-samples of ward with high, medium and low intensity death rates, segregation as a further dimension of the issue of location will be examined. A considerable volume of literature points to the degree of religious segregation within the Northern Ireland community. Segregation has been exacerbated by the Troubles, since individuals and families fled from mixed areas to converge on places where they felt safe. In spite of this quest for safety, those living in 'enclaves' have not been insulated from the Troubles, as is evidenced by a comparison of the responses of those living in segregated areas with those in non-segregated areas. Caution about attributing significance to these findings is necessary since religious segregation is a widespread phenomenon in Northern Ireland. Nevertheless, over 500 respondents in the survey claimed that they did not live in segregated areas.

Those living in segregated areas said they had much more experience of the Trouble than those living in non-segregated areas. The percentage of respondents living in segregated areas who reported experiencing the Troubles 'a lot' was almost four times higher than for those who did not live in segregated areas. For 'quite a lot' the percentage was more than twice as great. Conversely, reports of experience of the Troubles in the 'very little' or 'none' category accounted for almost 40 per cent of those living in non-segregated areas compared to under 15 per cent in segregated areas.

Similar differences appear between segregated and non-segregated areas in the reported impact of the Troubles on people's lives. Over a fifth of those living in segregated areas reported a 'complete' or 'radical' change compared to a twelfth in non-segregated areas. In non-segregated areas, the majority of respondents (over a half) reported either a 'small impact' of the Troubles or that the Troubles had impacted 'not at all' compared to over a third making the same responses in segregated areas.

The very sharp differences amongst the three locations in terms of experiences and effects may be the central dimension of this sample. Other differences emerge according to gender, religion and age. In order to look at these factors, differences are examined in the context of each of the three locations – high, medium and low intensity experience of the Troubles.

Gender

Respondents were asked to report on the frequency of their experience of the Troubles (Table 5.11).

Table 5.11   Experience of the Troubles by Gender

		Male	Female[1]	Total[1]
A lot	no.	105	93	198
	%	17.2	13.1	15.0
Quite a lot	no.	124	136	260
	%	20.3	19.2	19.7
Some	no.	182	173	355
	%	29.7	24.4	26.9
A little	no.	82	114	196
	%	13.4	16.1	14.8
Very little	no.	106	169	275
	%	17.3	23.8	20.8
None	no.	13	25	38
	%	2.1	3.5	2.9
Total	no.	612	710	1322
	%	100.0	100.0	100.0

[1] Percentage figures rounded.

Although the analysis of deaths suggested that males have been the primary victims, the survey data adds other dimensions to that picture. Certainly, a higher proportion of men claimed to have experience of the Troubles, but the relative gender differences are much less stark when looking at the experiences of the living, as opposed to the statistics for those killed. Of male respondents, 37.5 per cent claimed to have experienced the Troubles 'a lot' or 'quite a lot' compared to 22.3 per cent of female respondents. Conversely, just under a fifth of men and just over a quarter of women claimed to have had very little or no experience of the Troubles. Such gender differences were reported within all three locations even though women's experiences were substantially higher in the high intensity ward group. For example, in high intensity wards, 29.6 per cent of men and 22.8 per cent of women claimed 'a lot' of experience of the Troubles compared to 8.2 per cent and 3.6 per cent in the least intensity group. It would appear that male/female differences were less pronounced in the high intensity wards although the number reporting 'a lot' in the least intensity wards was very small (22 in total, representing only 5 per cent of all respondents in this group of wards).

The term 'experience' is subject to wide interpretation. The survey examined a wide range of experiences of the Troubles, from the relatively common experience of seeing nightly news bulletins to more extreme experiences. When questioned about the nature of that experience, certain differences in the male/female experience emerged. Only the category 'very often' is examined in this analysis, since it suggests a level of intrusiveness of the Troubles in individual lifestyles. Very high proportions of both males and females had 'very often' encountered the Troubles in news reports. When it came to areas of individual active involvement – such as being in a bomb scare or straying into an area where the person felt unsafe, or being stopped and searched by the security forces, or feeling that they had to change normal routines – men experienced these roughly 50 per cent more than women. However, it should be pointed out that for each of these experiences only a minority of the sample reported having the experience often or very often. However, more than a third of all males had been stopped and searched by the security forces. Similar gender differences appeared across that range of responses in the high, medium and low intensity areas.

More intense experiences of the Troubles were also analysed. There seems to be a set of experiences – listening to their own tradition being abused, feeling blamed for the Troubles, ending relationships because of the Troubles, having schooling disrupted, experience of paramilitary punishments (though not directly) – that both genders have had in common. For some of these variables the proportion of women claiming to have experienced them was often actually higher than for men. In other situations where the tension or conflict is interactive or direct violence is involved – experience of sectarian verbal abuse and, most of all, getting into physical fights – males have much more experience.

Gender differences in the most direct experiences of the Troubles were found, although the differences were smaller. For example, 26.7 per cent of men reported witnessing a shooting compared to 18.8 per cent of women. Very similar percentages reported that a member of the immediate family had been injured or killed.

These responses suggest that, whilst the analysis of deaths due to the Troubles produces a picture that predominantly involves men (91.1 per cent of those killed in the Troubles were male), women have also experienced serious and intense aspects of the Troubles. The nature of female experience has tended to differ from that of males. None the less, women were also substantially affected, although differences between women according to their location were also quite marked. Women in highest intensity wards had greater experiences of the Troubles than women in other wards, although women's experience remained less than men's experience in high intensity wards, as elsewhere. The survey clarified the position in relation to women's experience of the Troubles. The survey demonstrated that women's experience of the Troubles was much greater than is implied by the size of the female share of all political deaths – about 9 per cent.

Table 5.12 shows only marginal differences by gender in the degree to which the Troubles affected respondents' lives. Indeed, in highest intensity wards 18.2 per cent of women reported a complete change in their lives compared to 16.4 per cent of men. Therefore, although women generally and in all three locations report less experience of the Troubles, the reported impact on their lives is roughly equal to the impact reported by men.

Table 5.12   Effect on Individuals' Lives, by Gender

		Male	Female[1]
Complete change	no.	45	54
	%	7.3	7.6
Radical change	no.	69	50
	%	11.2	7.1
Some change	no.	241	278
	%	39.1	39.2
Small impact	no.	195	272
	%	31.7	38.4
Not at all	no.	66	55
	%	10.7	7.8
Total	no.	616	709
	%	100.0	100.0

[1] Percentage figures rounded.

Religion

Analysis of the Troubles indicates that in both absolute and relative terms Catholics have been more affected by violence. They make up the majority of all fatalities and the death rates for the region's Catholic population have been consistently higher than for the Protestant population. This meant that in the survey the wards sampled because of their high death rates comprised a majority of

Catholics. This in turn influenced responses, and analysis of the experience of the Troubles by religion has to make allowance for the higher number of Catholics in the sample.

Although the respondent population comprised two-thirds Catholic and one-third Protestant, there is a relationship between religion and the experience of the Troubles. The percentage of Catholics reporting a lot of experience of the Troubles was more than three times higher than for Protestants: 18.9 per cent and 22.8 per cent of Catholics had a lot and quite a lot of experience, respectively. This can be compared to that of Protestants with 5.2 per cent and 13.8 per cent. On the other hand, 38.9 per cent of Protestants had very little experience of the Troubles compared to 15 per cent of Catholics for the same category, whilst the majority of Catholics had some experience of the Troubles.

Although there were relatively large numbers of Catholics within the sample, the percentages claiming exposure to the Troubles were higher still, suggesting, in line with findings elsewhere, that Catholic experience of conflict has been disproportionately high. Even in the high intensity wards, this difference was sustained. There, over 25 per cent of Catholics reported 'a lot' of experience of the Troubles with the comparable figure for Protestants remaining at 5 per cent. In fact, only 21 respondents in these wards were recorded as Protestant. Protestants made up 37 per cent of middle intensity wards and 51 per cent of low intensity wards. Again, the religious composition in each location can be related to the general finding of greater Catholic experience of the Troubles.

These findings are reinforced by the data in Table 5.13 which compares the effect of the Troubles on people's lives, according to religion.

According to Table 5.13, out of those experiencing a complete change in their lives due to the Troubles, 90.9 per cent are Catholic compared to only 8.1 per cent Protestant. Indeed, overall, one in ten Catholic respondents reported that the Troubles had effected a complete change in their lives. In contrast, a majority (52.5 per cent) of those in the 'not at all' category were Protestant, compared to 44.1 per cent Catholic. In general, Catholics experienced the more extreme effects of the Troubles with percentages skewed towards the upper end of the scale i.e. complete or radical change. In contrast, the effect of the Troubles has generally led Protestants to report to 'some change' or a 'small impact' on their lives. Again similar differences between the two religions were found even in high intensity wards.

Table 5.13   Effect of the Troubles on Individuals' Lives, by Religion

		Catholic	Protestant[1]	Other	Total
Complete change	no.	90	8	1	99
	%	10.1	2.1	4.5	7.6
Radical change	no.	96	14	2	112
	%	10.7	3.6	9.1	8.6
Some change	no.	368	128	8	504
	%	41.2	33.2	36.4	38.7
Small impact	no.	288	174	7	469
	%	32.2	45.1	31.8	36.0
Not at all	no.	52	62	4	118
	%	5.8	16.1	18.2	9.1
Total	no.	894	386	22	1302
	%	100	100.00	100.00	100.00

[1] Percentage figures rounded.

The contrast between the opposite ends in Table 5.13 – Catholics in the majority in the most affected categories, Protestants in the majority in the rest – reflects the general trend that the Catholics interviewed reported experiencing more extreme effects of the Troubles compared to Protestants: 10.1 per cent of Catholics and 2.1 per cent of Protestants in the 'complete change' category and 5.8 per cent of Catholics and 16.1 per cent of Protestants in the 'not at all' category. Again, it is important to remember that two-thirds of the sample population were Catholic.

Nevertheless, other sharp and significant differences are observable between religions. Catholics accounted for over 80 per cent of those suffering frequent and occasional painful memories of the Troubles. Just over 28 per cent of Catholics answered in these categories compared to just over 14 per cent of Protestants. Across a range of similar questions, including dreams of the Troubles, intrusive thoughts about Troubles-related events, losing interest in normal activities and feelings of insecurity and jumpiness, similarly significant differences were found between Catholics and Protestants. Respondents were asked if such effects had interfered with their lives. Almost 20 per cent of Catholics reported severe or moderate interference compared to 9 per cent of Protestants.

In short, the evidence of greater Catholic experience of the Troubles is supplemented by evidence of more severe and long-term effects and this was consistent across the three locations.

Disability

Analysis of Troubles-related experiences would not be complete without some reference to those suffering disability. Unfortunately, the questionnaire did not contain a question that directly related to that condition. Within the sample 39 people reported that they had been injured in a bomb explosion at least once and 33 had been injured in shootings. A small number responding in each category had suffered both bombing and shooting injuries. In total, there were 62 individuals with such injuries – about 4.5 per cent of the sample. This is dramatically higher than the ratio of 40,000 injured in the Troubles from a population of 1.5 million. A further higher number of respondents reported health deterioration as the result of Troubles-related trauma or bereavement – 287 cases, or just over 20 per cent of the total sample. Just fewer than 6 per cent of the sample (79 cases, of whom 56 reported health deterioration) reported being given pain-killing medication for conditions that resulted from the Troubles.

CONCLUSION

Of the five variables identified as being potentially significant in experiences and effects of the Troubles, location and religion stand out. Indeed, because of the high degree of spatial polarisation in Northern Ireland, which is exacerbated in those areas where violence has been most pervasive, location and religion are connected. At the outset we pointed out that the sampling procedure was weighted to 'over-represent' those areas where death rates were highest. Unsurprisingly, the most intensive and pervasive experiences of the Troubles occurred here. The survey provides evidence to support the hunch that the most intense experiences of the Troubles occurred in areas where the death rate is highest. In the remaining chapters, we will explore further the characteristics of the pattern of violence in Northern Ireland and its effects.

6 Severe Experience and Extreme Impact of the Troubles

A crucial question for this book concerns the impact the Troubles have had on people's lives. As Northern Ireland moves further along a peace process that will hopefully lead to peace, the moral responsibilities of the society to those who have been bereaved or injured in the Troubles emerge. At a certain stage in the peace process, debates began about how best to support or 'compensate' those who had been bereaved or injured, and a more ferocious debate about who properly constituted 'victims'. However, equally important questions are about the characteristics of those who suffered most and what impact it has had on their lives, and the use of systematic evidence to assess the situation.

It is reasonable to ask first about the relationship between experience of the Troubles and the impact on people's lives. The natural assumption is that the higher the degree of experience, the greater will be the impact. However, this is not a safe assumption. People respond to trauma in different ways. Other social and community factors mediate the impact of encounters with the various phenomena of the Troubles. To explore this issue, the responses to the questions in The Cost of the Troubles Study survey (see Appendix 3 for questionnaire) about experiences of the Troubles were cross-tabulated with those about the impact on people's lives (Table 6.1).

Other than the rows and columns containing actual numbers, the figures in the table are percentages of the entire sample. Thus, 3.7 per cent of the whole sample responded by declaring both that they had 'a lot' of experience of the Troubles and it 'completely changed' their lives. Interestingly, of those experiencing the Troubles 'a lot', 'quite a lot' or 'some', the common response on impact was 'some change'. Of the 198 respondents who experienced the Troubles 'a lot', just less than half indicated 'some change' in their lives compared to just over a fifth who declared a complete change. Half of those each reporting 'quite a lot' and 'some' experience indicated 'some change' in their lives compared to less than a sixth and less than a fiftieth expressing complete change respectively. It would thus appear that the relationship between experience and impact on one's life is not linear.

Table 6.1   Individuals' Experience Level of the Troubles and Impact on Their Lives

Impact	A lot (%)	Quite a lot (%)	Some (%)	A little (%)	Very little (%)	None (%)	Total (%)[1]	(Number)
			Experience level					
Complete change	3.7	3.1	0.5	0.1	0.1	0.1	7.5	(99)
Radical change	2.8	2.7	2.2	0.5	0.6		8.8	(116)
Some change	6.6	10.0	13.2	5.1	4.0	0.1	39.1	(514)
Small impact	1.5	3.3	9.7	7.8	11.7	1.4	35.3	(465)
Not at all	0.4	0.4	1.3	1.4	4.6	1.2	9.3	(122)
Total %	15.0	19.5	26.9	14.9	21.0	2.8	100.0	(1316)
(Number)	(198)	(256)	(353)	(196)	(277)	(36)	(1316)	

[1] Rounded.

Figure 6.1 points to the complexity of the relationship. The categories that reflect the most extensive experience of the Troubles have their maximum points at 'some change'. The remaining three low-experience clusters have their maximum points at 'small impact'. Thus there was a tendency for all categories of experience to report 'change' in their lives. This, however, was concentrated in just two of the impact categories. It may well be that self-reporting systems as employed in this survey will not elucidate responses at the extreme end of the scale.

However, it would be unwise to conclude that the totality of the relationship between experiencing the Troubles and their impact on people could be encapsulated by a single cross-tabulation. To explore the issue further, three exercises were undertaken:

1. To develop an indicator for the existence of post-traumatic stress and to explore the characteristics of those in the sample in whom it was detected. As will be detailed later, this was not an exercise in clinical diagnosis but was based on answers provided in a ques-

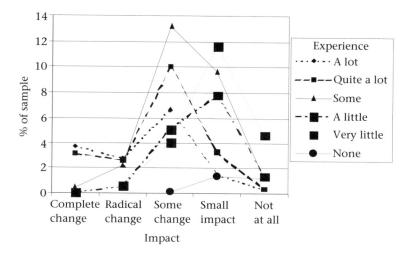

Figure 6.1   Impact of the Troubles by Individuals' Experience

tionnaire. Nevertheless, the task in hand is research rather than treatment and thus there is a value in exploring the issue

2. To develop indicators to identify those who had 'severe' and 'very severe' experiences of the Troubles and those for whom the Troubles had 'severe' and 'very severe' impact (the same cautions apply to these as for the indicator of post-traumatic stress) and to examine their characteristics

3. To test for relationships between the experience and impact variables.

A POST-TRAUMATIC STRESS INDICATOR

A measure was constructed, loosely based on the diagnostic criteria for Post-Traumatic Stress Disorder. Both the International Classification of Diseases (ICD-10) (WHO, 1993) and the Diagnostic and Statistical Manual of Mental Disorders (DSM-IV) (APA, 1994) set out diagnostic criteria for Post-Traumatic Stress Disorder. The latter was used as a basis for this exercise. The criteria set out in the DSM-IV are as follows:

A. The person has been exposed to a traumatic event in which the person experienced, witnessed or was confronted with an event or events that involved actual or threatened death or serious injury or a threat to the physical integrity of self or others, and the person's response involved intense fear, helplessness or horror. B. The traumatic event is persistently re-experienced in one (or more) of the following ways:

1. Recurrent and intrusive distressing recollections of the event, including images thoughts or perceptions
2. Recurrent distressing dreams of the event
3. Acting or feeling as if the traumatic event were recurring (includes dissociative flashback episodes, including those that occur on awakening or when intoxicated
4. Intense psychological distress at exposure to internal or external cues that symbolise or represent an aspect of the traumatic event
5. Physiological reactivity on exposure to internal or external cues that symbolize or resemble an aspect of the traumatic event.

C. Persistent avoidance of stimuli associated with the trauma and numbing of general responsiveness (not present before the trauma) as indicated by three or more of the following:

1. efforts to avoid thoughts, feelings or conversations associated with the trauma
2. efforts to avoid activities, places, or people that arouse recollections of the trauma
3. inability to recall an important aspect of the trauma
4. markedly diminished interest or participation in significant activities
5. feelings of detachment or estrangement from others
6. restricted range of affect (e.g. unable to have loving feelings)
7. sense of a foreshortened future (e.g. does not expect to have a career, marriage, children or a normal life span)

D. Persistent symptoms of increased arousal (not present before the trauma) as indicated by two or more of the following:

1. difficulty falling or staying asleep
2. irritability or outbursts of anger
3. difficulty concentrating
4. hypervigilance
5. exaggerated startle response

E. Duration of the disturbance is more than 1 month

F. The disturbance causes clinically significant distress or impairment in social, occupational or other important areas of functioning. (APA, 1994)

Clearly it is not possible (clinically) to arrive at a diagnosis of Post-Traumatic Stress Disorder without conducting a proper clinical interview. Therefore, this exercise that we have embarked on can only be seen as the loosest of indicators of the stress levels in the sampled population. Our questionnaire did not exactly measure the criteria as set out in the *DSM-IV*, but we constructed a measure of Post-Traumatic Stress based on the following responses to the questionnaire:

Exposure to a traumatic event
Positive response to *one* of the following questions in the questionnaire:

47: *Have you ever had a period of time when you kept having painful memories of your experience/s even when you tried not to think about it?* [frequently/occasionally/rarely/never/don't remember]

48: *Have you ever had a period of time when you had repeated dreams and nightmares about your experience/s?* [frequently/occasionally/rarely/never/don't remember]

49: *Have you ever had a period of time when you found yourself in a situation which made you feel as though it was happening all over again?* [frequently/occasionally/rarely/never/don't remember]

63a: *Do you agree that the Troubles have caused you a great deal of distress and emotional upset?* [strongly agree/agree/neither agree nor disagree/ disagree/strongly disagree]

Re-experiencing the traumatic event
Positive response to *three* of the following questions in the questionnaire:

64j: *Do you agree/disagree that the Troubles have made members of your family and/or you seriously consider emigration?* [strongly agree/agree/neither agree nor disagree/disagree/strongly disagree]

65d: *Do you agree/disagree that the Troubles have restricted the number of areas you are prepared to go into for work?* [strongly agree/agree/neither agree nor disagree/ disagree/strongly disagree]

50: *Have you ever had a period of time when you lost interest in activities that had meant a lot to you before?* [frequently/occasionally/rarely/never/don't remember]

67a: *In general, would you agree/disagree that the Troubles have nothing to do with you?* [strongly agree/agree/neither agree nor disagree/disagree/strongly disagree]

63a: *Do you agree/disagree that the Troubles have caused you a great deal of distress and emotional upset?* [strongly agree/agree/neither agree nor disagree/disagree/strongly disagree]

63f: *Do you agree/disagree that the Troubles have shattered your illusion that the world is a safe place?* [strongly agree/agree/neither agree nor disagree/disagree/strongly disagree]

Persistent symptoms of increased arousal
Positive response to *two* of the following questions in the questionnaire:

52: *Have you ever had a period of difficulty sleeping due to your experiences of the Troubles?* [frequently/occasionally/rarely/never/don't remember]

63e: *Do you agree/disagree that the Troubles have provoked strong feelings of rage in you?* [strongly agree/agree/neither agree nor disagree/disagree/strongly disagree]

29: *During the past 4 weeks have you had any of the following problems with your work or other regular daily activities as a result of any emotional problem (such as feeling depressed or anxious)? – Didn't do work or other activities as carefully as usual?* [Yes/No]

64l: *Do you agree/disagree that the Troubles have made you extremely fearful for your own and your family's safety?* [strongly agree/agree/neither agree nor disagree/disagree/strongly disagree]

51: *Have you ever had a period of time when you were very jumpy or more easily startled than usual or felt that you had to be on your guard all the time?* [frequently/occasionally/rarely/never/don't remember]

53: *Have there been times when you felt ashamed or guilty about surviving events in the Troubles?* [frequently/occasionally/rarely/never/don't remember]

Thus, those who have met these criteria have been exposed to a highly stressful event and report a range of symptoms of traumatic stress, as measured by the specified questions.

When the PTS indicator was constructed, it applied to 390 cases, about 30 per cent of the entire sample. This might seem overly large although the existence of the group of high intensity wards contributed to the high number. It was cross-tabulated with other variables to determine the characteristics of those who 'fitted' the condition. Interestingly, there were only small differences between men (30 per cent) and women (28 per cent) despite the different nature of their experiences of the Troubles. The survey material suggested that men and women tended to have different kinds of experience of the Troubles but that women were much more affected than was indicated by the deaths' database analysis. The PTS Indicator applies a single measure to both genders and the findings indicate that very similar percentages of males and females have been affected by traumatic stress as measured by the indicator (Figure 6.2). Thus, it appears that women are more affected by the Troubles than an analysis simply of deaths in the Troubles would have suggested. The effects of the Troubles on women become more evident in this analysis than in previous analyses.

At the same time, significant differences emerged when the PTS indicator was cross-tabulated with religion and location (Figures 6.3 and 6.4).

A higher percentage of Catholics than Protestants were affected by PTS. This is in keeping with the other survey findings, which point to the greater range and intensity of Catholic experience of the Troubles. This can be explained by the diversity of violence experienced in Catholic areas. Clearly, it can be suggested that the primary axis of the conflict was the Republican campaign for a United Ireland. The source of the conflict was thus Catholic areas, which saw at least four strands of violent activity:

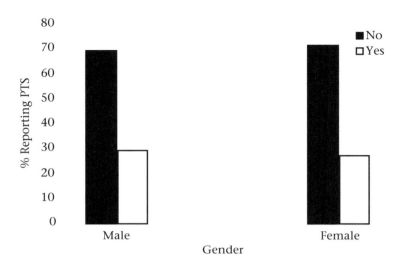

Figure 6.2   Experience of PTS by Gender

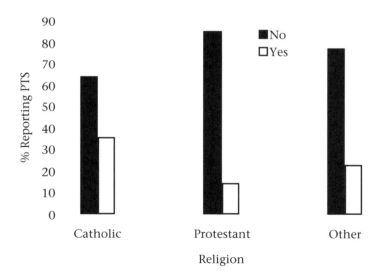

Figure 6.3   Experience of PTS by Religion

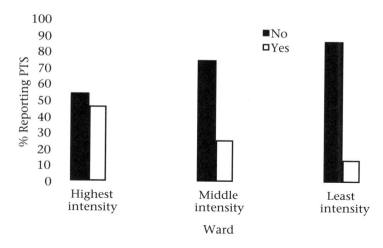

Figure 6.4   Experience of PTS by Ward

- Republican paramilitaries against the security forces and vice versa, including the 'unintended' casualties of both
- In some areas, Catholic victims of Loyalist paramilitaries
- Internal feuds amongst Republican paramilitaries
- Internal 'policing' by Republican paramilitaries.

It is the existence of all four strands that made the Catholic experience of the Troubles that much more extensive. This does not, however, detract from the disproportionate PTS effect. The differences by religion are mirrored in differences amongst areas.

The group of wards selected because they had highest death rates also had the highest incidence of the PTS indicator. Although the variable was constructed without regard to location, almost half (45 per cent) of respondents from such wards showed evidence of PTS.

When the PTS indicator was cross-tabulated with Question 71 ('How much your experiences of the Troubles affected you?'), the pattern shown in Table 6.2 emerged.

Of those who reported a 'complete change' in their lives, just over 90 per cent showed evidence of PTS. Over two-thirds of those reporting 'radical change' also showed evidence of PTS. At the other end of the scale, just over 5 per cent of those whom the Troubles affected 'not at all' indicated PTS. It should be noted that over 15 per cent of the sample reported a 'complete change' or 'radical change' in their lives as a result of the Troubles. The high intensity wards heavily influenced this figure. This, however, could indicate high levels of need. If PTS as measured by our indicator were only one third as prevalent in the general population as it was within our sample, then 75,000 people in Northern Ireland would be affected.

Table 6.2   PTS and Overall Impact of the Troubles

Impact		PTS		
		No	Yes	Total
Complete change	no.	9	90	99
	%	9.1	90.9	100.0
Radical change	no.	52	67	119
	%	43.7	56.3	100.0
Some change	no.	345	176	521
	%	66.2	33.8	100.0
Small impact	no.	426	48	474
	%	89.9	10.1	100.0
Not at all	no.	115	7	122
	%	94.3	5.7	100.0
Total	no.	947	388	1335
	%	70.9	29.1	100.0

We asked about the form of support individuals with evidence of PTS received. Within the statutory sector, GPs seem to bear the main responsibility for support with almost half or those who met the PTS criteria seeking help from this source. Interestingly, non-statutory actors have given support to a higher percentage of the group than any other statutory professional. The important role of the community sector in this regard should also be noted.

In general, there was satisfaction with the support received. Just over half of all respondents who sought help described the help as both 'sympathetic and helpful' with another 15 per cent describing it as adequate. Only six cases described the help as 'harmful'. At the same time, when asked 'Where, if from anywhere, did you receive the best help?', just over two-thirds of respondents indicated a combination of spouse, family and neighbours. From the survey results, it seems that informal welfare systems had the primary role in the provision of help and support. However, provision was by no means comprehensive and 34 cases reported that they had appropriate help from no one.

SEVERE/VERY SEVERE EXPERIENCES AND IMPACT OF THE TROUBLES

Severe and Very Severe Experiences

It was decided to examine those in the sample who had the most intense experience of the Troubles. For that purpose, two new variables were constructed. The first was designed to capture 'severe' experiences; the second, to capture 'very severe' experiences. For the first variable, 'severe' experiences, five key events were identified:

- Being close to a bomb explosion
- Witnessing a shooting
- A neighbour killed
- Seeing people killed or seriously injured
- Having to leave home permanently.

Some of these may have overlapped – for example, a neighbour may have been killed in a bomb explosion. Accordingly, the criterion used to identify 'severe' experiences was having been exposed to at least *three* of these events.

For the second variable, 'very severe' experiences, seven events were prioritised:

- A close friend killed
- Being physically attacked due to the Troubles
- Being injured in a bomb explosion
- Being injured in a shooting
- A member of the immediate family injured
- A member of the immediate family killed
- Another relative killed.

Given the seriousness of these events and the fact that they overlap less than the variable above, the condition specified for 'very severe' experiences of the Troubles was exposure to any *two* of these events.

The variable 'severe experience' affected 123 cases within the sample, just less than 10 per cent of the total. It was more characteristic of men (11.2 per cent) than women (7.3 per cent), of

Catholics (12.3 per cent) than Protestants (2.3 per cent) and of the high intensity wards (19.5 per cent compared to 5.1 per cent and 1.7 per cent respectively within the other two wards).

Almost a third of those who had a severe experience of the Troubles reported that the Troubles had 'completely changed my life' (Figure 6.5). A further 18 per cent claimed a radical change. Thus for around half the group (48 per cent), the Troubles have had significant impact. A further two-fifths reported 'some change' to their lives.

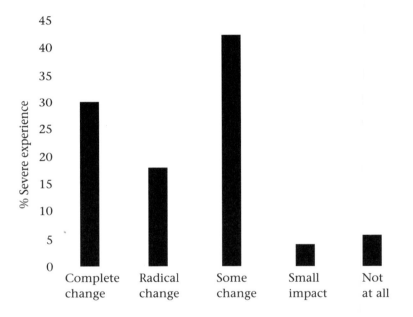

Figure 6.5   Severe Experience of the Troubles by Impact

The group identified as having 'very severe' experiences of the Troubles numbered 208, of which 56 per cent were male and 44 per cent female. The group was 84 per cent Catholic and 62 per cent of them lived in the high intensity wards. About 40 per cent of this group reported a 'complete' or 'radical' change in their lives as a result of the Troubles and another 44 per cent reported some change. Less than 20 per cent suggested that the Troubles had only a 'small' or 'no' impact on their lives.

Severe and Very Severe Impact

Two similar variables were constructed as indicators of the Troubles' impact. The first (severe impact) was based on the following positive responses to questions about the effects of the Troubles:

- Caused me a great deal of distress and emotional upset
- Made violence more a part of my life
- Left me feeling helpless
- Provoked strong feelings of rage in me.

'Severe impact' was said to apply when, on at least *two* conditions, respondents either strongly agreed or agreed.

'Very severe impact' employed a different set of conditions. This category was based on positive responses to questions about the impact of the Troubles, namely that they had:

- Completely ruined my life
- Damaged my health
- Caused me to lose loved ones through death
- Physically damaged me/my family.

Due to the stark nature of these conditions, 'very severe impact' was said to have occurred when respondents either strongly agreed or agreed to *any* of these questions.

The 'severe impact' variable applied to 232 cases. Just over 18 per cent of women (131 cases) compared to 16 per cent of men (100 cases) were identified as suffering 'severe impact'. Over a fifth of Catholics compared to less than a twelfth of Protestants met the criteria, and more than half of those who met the 'severe impact' criteria inhabited wards which had had the highest intensity of violence. Over a quarter of the people living in such wards met the criteria, and over 80 per cent of these individuals also showed evidence of PTS.

There were 252 cases that met the 'very severe impact' criteria. Almost 20 per cent of men and almost 18 per cent of women in the sample and just less than a quarter of Catholics in the sample and less than an eighth of Protestants met the criteria for 'very severe impact'. A third of the population of high intensity wards compared to less than a tenth of the population of least intensity wards also met the criteria.

Almost 45 per cent of those suffering severe impact and 53 per cent of those suffering very severe impact declared that the Troubles had 'completely' or 'radically' changed their lives. In each, roughly 33 per cent indicated 'some change' in their lives due to the Troubles.

Table 6.3 summarises the forms of support received by each group, their respective assessment of the quality of that support and the sources from which they had the 'best' help.

Table 6.3   Summary of Support for Those Reporting Severe Impact and Very Severe Impact of the Troubles on Their Lives

	Severe impact (%)	Very severe impact (%)
Source of support:		
Psychiatrist	15.0	19.8
Clinical psychologist	4.0	4.0
GP	50.3	62.2
Community nurse	22.0	24.6
Social worker	12.0	14.0
Minister/priest	19.2	26.1
Community worker	26.8	28.2
Voluntary organisation	24.3	23.7
Support regarded		
as sympathetic and helpful	51.8	60.1
Source of best help:		
Spouse	24.6	24.8
Parents	17.9	16.2
Other close family	17.4	20.3
Close friends	7.2	9.9
GP/local doctor	2.1	4.1

The pattern of the provision of help is familiar from the analysis of PTS. Doctors are the primary source of support within the statutory system. Other more specialised professionals are substantially less involved. Priests/ministers have been a greater source of support to the very severe rather than the severe category of respondent, presumably because some of the former's defining conditions were associated with death. The significant role of the community sector and the informal welfare systems of family and friends emerges from this analysis.

There are two striking points about the analysis of experience and impact:

- Apparently there are larger percentages of the sample suffering severe impacts than those exposed to severe experiences. However, since all four variables are constructs, perhaps this is a result of decisions about the number and combination of defining conditions
- In stark contrast to the analysis of Troubles-related deaths, gender differences in these data are very minimal indeed. This is particularly true of the impact variables. Thus, this analysis asserts the central position of women as victims of the Troubles.

UNDERSTANDING HOW THE TROUBLES AFFECT INDIVIDUALS AND COMMUNITIES

In attempting to understand how the Troubles affect people, two propositions can be developed. The first is that the intensity of the experience of the Troubles (and its effects) decreases with distance from the event, so the greater the distance from the event, the less intense the experience and the less severe its effects. Second, the greater the distance from a Troubles-related event, the larger the number of people affected (Figure 6.6).

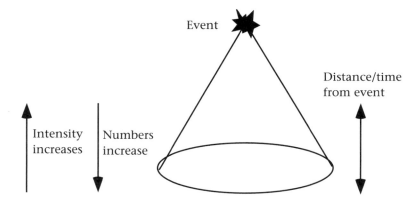

Figure 6.6   Proximity, Intensity and Numbers Affected by a Single Event

Individual Differences

This rather schematic way may help understand the impact of one event in a somewhat simplistic and over-determined way. However, it cannot explain the impact of the Troubles in general. It is too simple for a number of reasons. First, all human beings do not react in the same way to the same event, so allowances must be made for individual differences. Two individuals at the same proximity to an event will be affected differently, for reasons other than their proximity to the said event. Second, part of that individual difference may be related to the individual's previous experience of *other* Troubles events.

Experience of the Troubles as Multiple Events

Over the period of the Troubles, individuals – particularly those living in areas with high Troubles-related death rates – have had multiple experiences of Troubles related trauma, injury and bereavement. So, we can see an event in the Troubles as a 'sun' projecting light (or effects) on to a community. Some communities have one or two such suns, whilst others have a whole constellation, at a variety of distances from them, according to the multiple experiences they have had of loss and trauma in the Troubles. Figure 6.7 illustrates four events and how they might interplay. Many communities – in North and West Belfast, and in the border regions – have seen many more than four incidents on an almost daily basis over a period of decades.

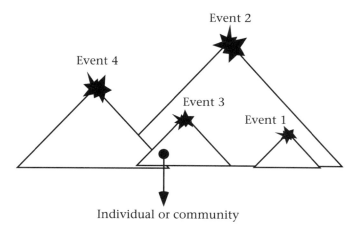

Figure 6.7   Proximity and Impact of Multiple Events

Communities are not simply geographically defined; communities can be communities of interest, such as the small business community, children, and members of local security forces, Unionists or Nationalists.

'Proximity' to an event in the Troubles, too, is not simply a matter of spatial proximity, of being physically close or at the scene when the event occurred. 'Proximity' may be spatial or geographical, or it may be relational – a close relative might be involved, or it might be temporal, close in time or recent. Figure 6.8 is an illustration of these dimensions of proximity.

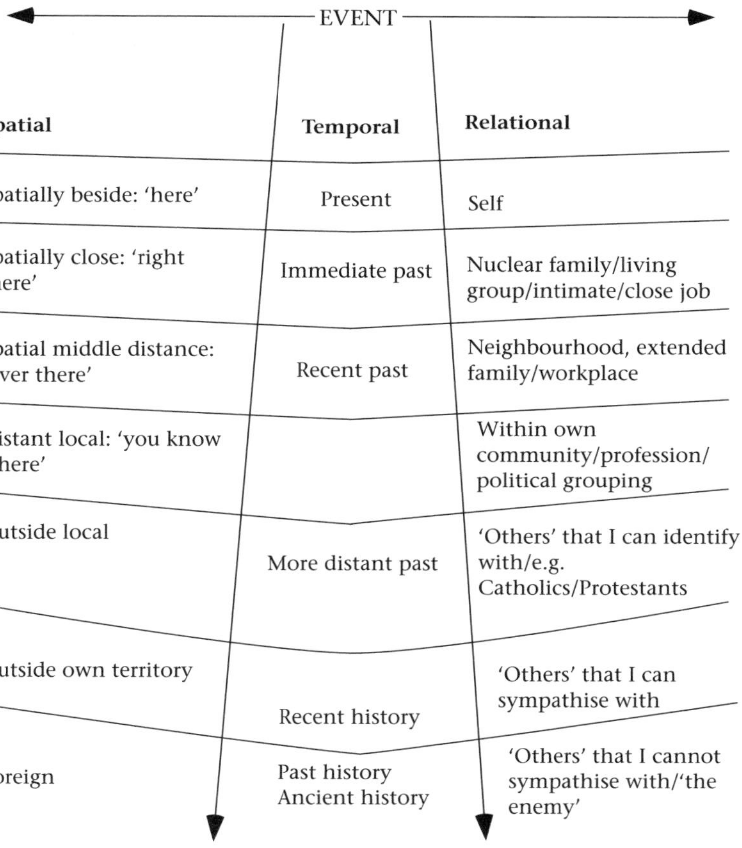

Spatial	Temporal	Relational
◄───────────── EVENT ─────────────►		
Spatially beside: 'here'	Present	Self
Spatially close: 'right there'	Immediate past	Nuclear family/living group/intimate/close job
Spatial middle distance: 'over there'	Recent past	Neighbourhood, extended family/workplace
Distant local: 'you know where'		Within own community/profession/ political grouping
Outside local	More distant past	'Others' that I can identify with/e.g. Catholics/Protestants
Outside own territory	Recent history	'Others' that I can sympathise with
Foreign	Past history Ancient history	'Others' that I cannot sympathise with/'the enemy'

Figure 6.8   Types of Proximity to Troubles-Related Events

Proximity may be temporal in that the event may be recent, or close in time to other events, or an individual may have been alive and remember the event, or may not have been born at the time of the event. Temporal distance can be compensated for by relational proximity. A child who was not born when his or her father was killed will still be impacted by the death because of the relational proximity through the effect on the family, living group or community, even though in temporal terms the child was distant from the event.

Proximity as a Multidimensional Concept

In assessing the impact of any given event in the Troubles, one cannot simply operate in one dimension, spatial, temporal or relational, nor can one assess the impact of the event according to the characteristics of the event alone. This is because the impact of other prior events may have rendered the individual or community vulnerable, and compromised their capacity to cope with crisis or trauma. Therefore the effect of an event may be different because of the wider context, in which the event in question is only one of several impacting on the individual or community. That is not to say, however, that the characteristics of the event are insignificant.

The Characteristics of the Event

The characteristics of a Troubles-related event may have an influence on the impact of the event. Events where there have been high numbers of civilian casualties, such as the Enniskillen bomb in 1987, or events such as the bomb at the La Mon Hotel in 1978 seem to have major impacts on people who are quite distant from the event. In both these events, civilians sustained horrific injuries or stood little or no chance of survival because of insufficient warnings for evacuations. Events that are the first of their kind, or one-offs, such as 'Bloody Sunday' in January 1972 when soldiers opened fire in a riot, or the first death that involved mutilation, may have a greater effect than subsequent events. Indeed, some events are designed to have a widespread effect, such as the Ulster Workers' Council strike in 1974, or the Republican hunger strikes.

SOCIAL CONSTRUCTION OF THE TROUBLES

The Troubles as a Collective Experience; Memory as Communal Property

Some events, for whatever reason have had a widespread effect on large numbers of people who were not directly involved, whether by the images of the event portrayed by the media or by the imagined impact of the event on those bereaved or injured. These events become reference points for the history of the Troubles and as such are public pointers to certain political arguments or positions. They become, at one level, public property. Thousands of people 'see' the event or its aftermath on television and 'know' about it through print and broadcast media coverage. It becomes part of their history, and if the event is intense enough and in proximity to them it is incorporated into their experience of the Troubles. The event becomes known at that public level and incorporated into individual and collective maps of the Troubles. In the absence of any close personal encounter with the effects of the Troubles, this could be described as pseudo-proximity.

The Troubles as 'Communal Property' and Impact on the Identity of Victims

This public appropriation of events in the Troubles has implications for those in close proximity to the event and their sense of identity and social position. Those in close proximity to the event, such as the injured or bereaved, often incorporate the event into their identity. Often, those bereaved or injured will be introduced to others as 'so-and-so whose son was killed in such-and-such event'. This incorporation of traumatic events into identity may have the effect of increasing the social distance between the bereaved or injured person and the 'ordinary' person (who has an average distance from the event and 'knows' about it through the media coverage). This ordinary person has an opinion and feelings (often strong feelings) about the event, and, depending on the proximity of the event to him or her, may well feel that the event also happened to him or her, in that he or she was also affected by the event in some way.

This may explain some of the isolation felt by those who have been in closest proximity to the traumatic events of the Troubles. Their sympathetic neighbour or bystander 'knows' through media coverage often the most intimate details of the loss, and is also affected by it in some way. The private world turned upside down of those closest – composed of grief, fear, anger, hopelessness and loss of trust – is separate and distanced from these collective feelings and experience. Private grief and loss is public property. Those closest to the loss may be reduced in their social world to mere icons of the collective grievance. The private world, in which the worst and long-term effects are experienced, remains hidden, masked by cameo public representations in which blame, condemnation, conspiracy and other public communal concerns are explored.

This isolation is further compounded by other factors. In the dominant discourse over the last three decades of the Troubles, people generally have not talked about their personal experiences of the Troubles. The stoical moral of the dominant world is 'Life must go on', even though patently for some people it has not. This has rendered illegitimate the immediate concerns of those who have been most severely affected. To talk publicly about traumatic loss in the Troubles has tended to unsettle and challenge the unspoken assumption in the dominant discourse, that we will all survive, that we will all get through. In order to maintain a functioning society it was important to avoid facing the reality of the relatively random nature of some violence, which meant that anyone could become a victim at any time. The testimony of those worst affected by the Troubles reminds us of this uncomfortable reality.

Over the period of the Troubles ways of avoiding comprehension of the full impact of the Troubles developed. Practices and rules for maintaining a level of denial and avoidance evolved; rules such as 'Watching the Northern Ireland news is depressing, so don't watch it.' Such rules and practices serve to protect the society from the full emotional impact of the Troubles. These processes are in one sense the psychological equivalent of the 'acceptable level of violence' which has marked Northern Ireland security policy since the 1980s. In order to live with violence, one must find ways of perceiving what is not there – safety and security – in order to maintain an internalised 'acceptable level of fear'. Therefore the task of conducting research can be difficult if not impossible, depending as it must on overcoming these 'ways of not seeing what is there'. In conducting the research we learned more about some of the ways in which our informants dealt with their experiences of the Troubles.

Displacement

In interview, initially individuals would claim to have little experience of the Troubles, and would under-report certain experiences of the Troubles. When the interviewer prompted them with questions, the interviewees would 'remember' other incidents, some of them serious and traumatic, but would only do so when prompted. When this is explored, it appears that other events in the Troubles with greater relational, spatial or temporal proximity and therefore greater impact take precedence in their reported memory. Other (lesser) experiences are 'displaced' out of their account, and are only mentioned if prompted to do so. It is almost as if the individuals have a capacity for retaining a certain number or amount of intense experience. When that capacity is exceeded, they 'forget' or at least no longer spontaneously report earlier events – events that they previously may have regarded as very intense or potent. Less intense events are no longer reported when they are displaced by more intense events. The events that are spontaneously reported are those that tend to represent the most intense experience, unless security considerations prevent the interviewees reporting them. An example of the tendency to 'forget' and to report the most intense experience emerges when interviewees' accounts are compared with those of visitors to Northern Ireland. Very few interviewees in our studies mentioned being stopped and searched by the security forces as an experience of the Troubles *per se*, since residents of Northern Ireland regarded such experiences as commonplace and had for the most part become habituated to them. Yet visitors to Northern Ireland who are stopped at a roadblock and see real guns and battle dress will report such experiences, since they represent their position of greatest proximity and therefore their most intense personal experience of the Troubles. At a wider societal level, a myriad of events have happened to many people in Northern Ireland, and many no longer think spontaneously or even remember them without prompting. They have been displaced in memory and the perceptual field by more intense or closer events. However, all of these events, described or forgotten, affect the social fabric of communities and the society as well as dramatically affecting the individual lives of those in greatest proximity to them.

Stereotyping Victims

Certain myths and stereotypes of those bereaved or injured in the Troubles have developed during the period of the Troubles. Many of these have been developed by the kind of media coverage given to tragic events, and the myths that had developed by the 1994 cease-fires tended to project certain characteristics on to those in close proximity to events: resilience, forgiveness, forbearance, courage, anger at perpetrators, a desire for reconciliation. These stereotypes represent victims as grief-stricken rather than angry, forgiving rather than blaming, passive rather than active, heroic rather than fearful, peace-loving rather than violent, innocent rather than guilty.

Furthermore, their suffering was perceived as short-term, reflecting the soundbite of media coverage that their situation attracted in the immediate aftermath of a Troubles-related event. The proliferation of such events during the Troubles meant that attention and space had to be made for the next tragedy that came along, so the attention span was short. Whatever the myths and public perceptions of those bereaved or injured, the realities of life for those in close proximity to Troubles events were often rather different. The stereotypes through which victims were perceived were based on how the wider society needs victims to be, rather than on any real data about actual victims. These projected characteristics and the public 'pseudo-knowledge' about victims of the Troubles may also contribute to the fragmentation of perception about the Troubles and the situation of victims. Through the existence of stereotypes of how victims ought to be, the variety and diversity of actual feelings and experiences of those who were bereaved or injured are silenced. Where their feelings do not conform to these stereotypes, the bereaved and injured must struggle with the 'illegitimacy' of their non-conforming feelings, thus compounding feelings of isolation. The perception that suffering due to the Troubles is short-term, for example, illegitimises long-term suffering – particularly psychological suffering – pathologising the individual as having some kind of weakness or predisposition to suffering, a lack of resilience or an inability to adjust to loss.

Two Worlds

Whilst conducting this research, a further feature of the social construction of the Troubles emerged whereby perceptions and understandings of the Troubles were segregated into (at least) two worlds. As researchers, prior to engaging in this research we lived largely within the dominant discourse on the Troubles. In that world, knowing or thinking about the Troubles is an option. As researchers, we live in areas that are not too badly affected by the Troubles; we can choose to research something else; we can avoid reading the newspapers or listening to news broadcasts for a period of time. To use the analogy of a television, we can turn the volume up or down – we can even turn the television off. We, as researchers and citizens, have a certain amount of control over how much time and energy we give to thinking and dealing with the Troubles.

When the public hear of an incident in the Troubles, their interpretation, interest and level of understanding of the incident and the situation of those involved in it will be heavily influenced by their own prior experiences of the Troubles and the stereotypes and myths they hold. A form of 'magical thinking' is found, largely in the first world described above, populated by those whose lives have not been deeply affected by the Troubles. Magical thinking is composed of the kind of belief that if you avoid walking on the cracks in the pavement, bad things won't happen. If someone is killed or injured in the Troubles, to this way of thinking, it becomes important to identify ways in which the victim contributed to his or her own fate, to determine that he or she had 'walked on the cracks in the pavement'. This then allows the myth to be perpetuated – that we can, by our own efforts, by avoiding certain things or taking certain measures, successfully avoid being affected by the Troubles. It facilitates the avoidance of the frightening reality that, for example, the majority of fatal victims were ordinary civilians going about their routine daily business.

Since beginning this research, it is as if we have gradually discovered at least one other world. It appears as a world composed of many individual private spaces that are largely silent. In that other world, which we entered by doing this research, things take on a significance that they don't have in the dominant world. Driving to work every day, for example, we notice the bunches of flowers on the roadside that tell us where the relatives of people we have interviewed were killed. We notice when fresh flowers are placed there, and deduce that it is an anniversary of the death. At certain times we remember other anniversaries, and realise that almost every day is an anniversary for someone. In the cities, certain streets, that look just like every other street, are full of memories of death, pain and fear. We now know people who would find it hard to go down that street because a person they loved lay on the street in a pool of blood, or because they themselves were attacked in that place. In this other world, the 'insider's' world, Troubles is not an 'option'. To use the analogy of the television set again, the voice and the picture cannot be turned off. In fact, the voice is an internal voice; the pictures are images in the mind's eye. The dominant discourse, the media coverage and so on, responds in a manner characteristic of the first world where the Troubles are an option, not this second 'insider' world in which the Troubles are a theme running through everything.

Being an insider or an outsider in relation to the Troubles also colours the way in which the Troubles are understood. Listening to the Northern Ireland news, people in Northern Ireland interpret what news stories they hear. They can decode with some reliability from the information given (without being explicitly told) who was responsible for a certain incident, or whether an incident was in response to another incident or event, or whether the victim was 'one of us' or 'one of them'. Our interviews with those severely affected by the Troubles seem to indicate that the 'interpretation' that insiders make of incidents in the Troubles may differ. 'Insider' interviewees have described how, on hearing of, for example, a Troubles-related death, they think about 'what lies in front' for the newly bereaved or injured. Several interviewees related seeing the newly bereaved express their own wish in the wake of their own loss: 'I don't want any other family to go through what we have gone through.' Such responses are based on specialist knowledge of the impact of the Troubles acquired through 'insider' personal experience. For some 'insiders' such incidents are painful reminders, and sometimes act as triggers which re-stimulate feelings associated with their own loss. 'Insider' reactions to Troubles-related events are particular, and often of a different order to those of the general public or the media.

Isolation

Those who have been closest to the events of the Troubles may thus find themselves isolated within this kind of dominant discourse. Those bereaved and injured in the Troubles have described experiencing their social milieu as uncaring and unsupportive after the immediate activities after the event – the funeral, for example – have subsided. In the aftermath of an event, many report discovering that they were 'on their own'. This may partly be a function of the earlier phases of the Troubles where several incidents in one day meant that public attention and sympathy was spread over a larger number of incidents and casualties. However, it is also an artefact of the societal processes that have developed and the way in which popular understanding of the Troubles focused on certain dimensions at the expense of others. The general public 'knew' about the situation of the bereaved or injured because the dominant discourse represented their experience through various (often abridged and truncated) representations. The most common source of information was media coverage. In everyday life, those bereaved and injured encountered embarrassment and incompetence on the part of neighbours who did not know how to behave sensitively in the face of tragedy, and so they said and did nothing. Others feared acknowledging any matter related to the Troubles, such was the level of societal division and suspicion. This communal avoidance accompanied by active disinterest in certain aspects of victim experience, together with censorship of the media in the past, combined to produce a form of pseudo-knowledge about victims. This pseudo-knowledge, combined with other political factors, may – in the past and in the present – militate against the development of a more rounded understanding of the situation of those bereaved or injured. For some, however, the victims' issue is much broader than the situation of those bereaved and injured.

VICTIMS AND PERPETRATORS

Since 1995, and the beginnings of official acknowledgment in the peace process of the situation of those bereaved and injured, various contests have emerged for shares (or monopoly) of that attention. On the one hand, various attempts have been made to include *per se* former paramilitary prisoners in the definition of 'victim'; and, on the other, attempts have been made to define victimhood as exclusively the reserve of those damaged by paramilitary organisations, excluding those injured or bereaved by the security forces. This struggle to draw defining lines between victims and perpetrators fuelled some of the most acrimonious disputes in the peace process. These disputes become intelligible in the light of the significance of victimisation in the Troubles. Close association with a population of victims and public acceptance of their suffering is the means by which all of the armed factions in the Troubles have legitimated their own use of violence. Thus possession of a legitimate cohort of victims whose suffering is widely acknowledged is essential to the moral and thence political credibility of some of the most powerful political and military agents in the peace process. This ensures that the victims issue occupies a central political place in the peace process, but does not necessarily ensure that victims' views or needs are taken into account. Their mere existence is enough to provide political legitimacy. Victims in Northern Ireland have an important iconic role in the political sphere. More often than not, humanitarian provision for victims' needs in the initial phase of the peace process in Northern Ireland was made in the service of this prior set of concerns, rather than in the understanding of humanitarian issues facing victims in Northern Ireland. It was later in the peace process that more systematic assessments of the needs of victims were conducted. Within the array of issues faced within the peace process, issues such as decommissioning, early release of prisoners and paramilitary feuds ensured that more of the attention and resources have been devoted to former combatants and perpetrators than to victims.

Invisibility and Visibility

The relatively low visibility of victims in comparison to perpetrators has never been more apparent than in the post-1994 peace process. The focus on prisoners and their role in the peace process; the visit to the Loyalist prisoners by the then Secretary of State, Mo Mowlam; the early release of paramilitary prisoners – all reinforced the dominance and centrality of the armed factions and perpetrators of violence in the conflict. It was at this stage in the peace process that the subordinance, powerlessness and marginality of the victims were felt most acutely, both by victims themselves and by 'right-minded people'. It has been argued that a more robust humanitarian intervention aimed at victims at this stage in the peace process might have pre-empted some of the later difficulties with the victims issue. Certainly the sense of grievance amongst some of those bereaved and injured ensured that some of the anti-Agreement political parties were able to appropriate their cause with ease, in the service of attacking the Agreement.

Gender and Victimhood

The victims issue in Northern Ireland is gendered. Over 90 per cent of those killed were men, and most members of paramilitary groups and security forces are male. Yet the feminisation of victimhood has been achieved partly by the role that widows have played in the voluntary sector and by media attention to female relatives. This feminisation, in the context of a society with marked gender segregation in public life, has rendered the positions of victim and perpetrator more congruent with existing gender roles. Men are portrayed as 'the paramilitary' or 'the soldier', or occasionally as 'the wounded soldier'. When they are portrayed as victims they are stoical, and often, like the victim of the punishment beating, they can be seen in some sense to have brought it upon themselves. The focus on the policy goal of 'helping and supporting' victims as opposed to the goals of 're-integrating/rehabilitating' prisoners reinforces this role allocation. Politics, and therefore the Troubles, is still very much a male preserve where, stereotypically, men *do* (noisily) and women *suffer* (in silence).

In the early period of the Troubles in particular, men were rarely seen as powerless or long-suffering victims – the single parents struggling to bring up children alone after the death of a spouse, the bereaved parents who can no longer sleep at night, or the eye witnesses who suffer from debilitating panic attacks. Of course, the majority of those rendered single parents by a Troubles-related death have been female, so the representation is grounded in reality. Furthermore, since 1995 and particularly since the Omagh bomb and the coverage of it in the media, the representation of victimhood has diversified and has included a wider range of accounts.

Provision for the needs of victims of the Troubles has also been shaped by a number of perceptual gaps in the past understanding of their situation. A lack of recognition or anticipation of long-term effects of the Troubles springs at least in part from a lack of research interest and evidence on the subject. This, allied with a number of myths such as 'There are services to take care of people', and 'People make money out of compensation and are very comfortably off after big settlements' contributed to a situation where, by 1995, provision was minimal, unfunded, inappropriate and for the most part non-existent. The advent of the Special Support Programme for Peace and Reconciliation (SSPPR) began to stimulate policy-makers to begin to consider the effects of the Troubles. Prior to this, public policy had developed under the direct rule arrangement of policy parity with Britain that ensured that policy in Northern Ireland was in tune with that elsewhere in the United Kingdom. As a result, public policy in most fields in Northern Ireland made little if any mention of the Troubles. Certainly no mention was ever made of victims of the Troubles until well into the peace process. In public policy and in government intervention, social problems in Northern Ireland were construed to be largely economic, with unemployment and social deprivation being the triggers for social intervention by public programmes. Acknowledgement of problematic political divisions took the form of community relations policy and programmes, which were free-standing, largely in the voluntary sector and not integrated into other areas of policy.

Even with the arrival of the SSPPR, the social policy pattern of construing the problem mainly in terms of social deprivation and unemployment tended to continue. Issues of segregation and the dis-economies it causes, or of the impact of the Troubles, were mentioned as goals, but there was little by way of targeting these issues as central concerns. Nor indeed was there the capacity within the voluntary or statutory sector to deliver such programmes had they been central aims. It took until 1997 for an official initiative to specifically address the views and experiences of those worst affected by the Troubles and their families. The government appointed Sir Kenneth Bloomfield as Victims Commissioner and his report was the first official document on the subject. A review of the system for the provision of financial compensation was subsequently instituted.

However, the development of public policy in the field, together with the work of developing strategies for targeting intervention, are at an early stage of development. Both policy and targeting must rely on an understanding of the various factors at work and their inter-relationships. Overall, the analysis suggests the set of relationships depicted in Figure 6.9.

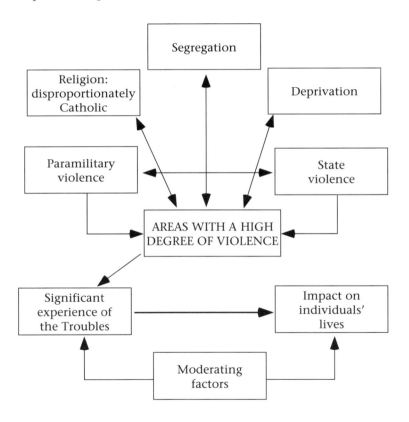

Figure 6.9   Interrelationship of the Various Factors Relevant to Policy and Strategy Development

This should be recognised both in developing and delivering compensatory policies as part of any peace settlement. Moreover, this concentrated experience of violence should figure in the operationalisation of 'New Targeting Social Need'. In certain areas, the experience of violence has been collective and multidimensional (local paramilitaries, paramilitaries from the 'other side' and the security forces have all contributed). Consequently, it makes sense to think in terms of spatially targeted programmes both to alleviate the effects and to emphasise the targeting of social and economic reconstruction.

7 The Troubles: The Experiences and Stories of Young People

The first memory I think I have of the Troubles is when my father got shot ... I was five ... I can't remember anything. I can just remember coming down the stairs the morning after, my mum saying to me ...I can't remember what she said. She was upset ... I think it was the Protestant Action Force [that killed him]. There was a prayer group in the chapel, and he was coming out of it late. He was coming out of the back. I think it was the back door. It was the hall of the church. And I think there were some bushes beside it. When he came out, they grabbed him, and brought him around the side of the church, tied him to the tree, and then shot him. (Young man, North Belfast, The Cost of the Troubles Study, 1997)

My first memory of the Troubles was when I got a petrol bomb put through my window ... It was into my mummy's room, and there was all my wee brothers and that. And we were all in the house, and our house was on fire. And we all had to get out of the house ... See, we live at the back of a 'peace line'. And it was sectarian ... And now we have guards up on the windows. (Young woman, North Belfast, ibid.)

The current conflict in Northern Ireland has lasted from 1969 until the present, decreasing significantly after the ceasefires of 1994. The longevity of the conflict means that only citizens in their fifties and older have any memory of living as adults in Northern Ireland in relative peace. For those who grew up in Northern Ireland, who are in their forties and younger, the Troubles has provided the societal context to their lives as children and as adults. In Chapter 4, it became apparent that young people have been at the highest risk of being killed in the Troubles, with almost 26 per cent of all victims aged 21 or less. The highest death rate for any age group in Northern Ireland is in the 19–20 age group.

Additionally, children in Northern Ireland live in one of the most deprived regions of the United Kingdom with levels of unemployment that have been consistently among the highest in the UK over the past number of decades. Family poverty is a well-known enemy of child welfare (Trew, 1995) and children in Northern Ireland suffer at the hands of this enemy. General childcare provision is not plentiful either. Northern Ireland has the lowest level of nursery provision in the UK, and schooling consistently fails the most deprived and marginalised children (Wilson, 1989). Children of ethnic minority groups such as travelling children, or children in Northern Ireland's Chinese community face marginalisation within the educational system, and this can result in low educational attainment, illiteracy and reduction in life chances (Irwin and Dunn, 1997). Infant mortality and perinatal morbidity in the travelling community in particular is at levels unprecedented in the wider community (Fitzpatrick et al., 1997). Provision for all children with special needs is also poor with very limited or no choice in education provision for such children, resulting in children failing to reach their potential and children being marginalised in unsuitable facilities. It seems educational attainment, as a means to improving life chances, is least accessible to many of those who have most need to improve their life chances.

As was apparent in earlier chapters, the experience and impact of the Troubles occurs against a backdrop of other social and economic issues which also cause some problems and compound others.

RESEARCH APPROACH

In 1999, a survey of 1000 young people in Northern Ireland (the YouthQuest 2000 survey) was undertaken, the findings from which will be explored in this chapter (see Appendix 4 for questionnaire). The survey was conducted according to a number of research principles, namely:

- That any work, research or exploration had to be conducted in partnership with children and young people
- That the work of the project addressed the issues of the effects of the Troubles using an inclusive and humanitarian approach
- That the project would also be conducted in partnership with local grassroots community organisations and individuals within communities who wish to work on these issues with this approach
- That any work should have practical and concrete outcomes and outputs that were of benefit to those children and young people participating in the project and their communities

- That the project should also meet the requirement of compiling good information and reliable data on the level of need and the variety of situations and views of children and young people affected by the Troubles.

The overall aim of the study was to give young people the chance to explore and express their views and opinions on issues surrounding the peace process and the Troubles as a whole. The research involved designing and administering a questionnaire to elicit the views and opinions of young people in Northern Ireland. No existing questionnaire was adequate to this task, and it was necessary to develop an instrument for this purpose. The final questionnaire examined a range of issues, namely the political voice of young people, attitudes to the Good Friday Agreement, the impact of the peace process, the value placed on youth, cross-community attitudes and young people's experiences and stories about the Troubles. Only the last section is reported on here.

This section of the survey aimed to examine the nature, extent and effects of young people's experiences of the Troubles. The questionnaire design drew on the experience of conducting the adult survey described in earlier chapters and on the results of 85 semi-structured interviews with young people throughout Northern Ireland. Questions in the questionnaire were ordered so that they began with relatively common and less distressing experiences of the Troubles and escalated gradually to the more severe and distressing experiences, and took the following form:

- Common experiences
- More direct experiences
- Severe experiences
- Injury or death in the Troubles.

To this section questions were added on two other issues:

- Responsibility for the Troubles
- The impact of events on respondent and their families.

In total, 1000 young people aged 14–17 were interviewed for the survey. It had been originally intended to survey 14–25-year-olds, but this proved to be impractical for the field team due to the difficulty in accessing 18–25-year-olds in a relatively short timeframe for the survey. In any case the young people we worked with felt that since 18–25-year-olds already had the opportunity to express their political opinions through voting at elections, we should concentrate on the disenfranchised young people. Since the young people were to conduct the survey themselves, a practicable way of accessing 14–17-year-olds had to be found. In the end, interviews were undertaken through schools in Northern Ireland and 15 schools were selected through a quota sample based on the following characteristics:

- state schools (predominantly Protestant)
- maintained/controlled schools (predominantly Catholic)
- integrated schools
- single-sex schools
- mixed-sex schools
- rural schools
- urban schools
- secondary schools
- grammar schools.

The schools (Thornhill, Derry; Boy's Model, Belfast; Dungannon Integrated; Ballyclare High; Ballyclare Secondary; Hazelwood Integrated; St Mary's Girls' Secondary; Girls' Model, Coleraine; Drumcree College; Abbey Grammar; Belfast Royal Academy; St Catherine's Girls' Comprehensive; St Mary's and Monkstown Community School) were located throughout Northern Ireland.

The Principal in each school was contacted in order to gain permission to undertake the survey and to outline the objectives of the study. Each survey was administered in the presence of a teacher and a member of the field team, either in a normal classroom environment or in groups of different classes congregated in the assembly hall. The field team comprised members of the Joint Society for a Common Cause (Paul Turley, Judy Cameron, Christopher McArthur, Phillip Weatherhead, Sean Hughes, Carl Graham, Ian Cooke, David Millar, Paul Reid, Tracey Robinson, Ronan Graham, Nial Greenfield and Michael Walsh, led by Leigh Whittley) who were trained by the researchers.

CONTEXTUAL ANALYSIS

An earlier phase of the research involved interviewing children and young people about their experiences of the Troubles. From these interviews and from the earlier studies on adult experience, the experience of children can be contextualised in their wider social world, which can either render children more vulnerable or provide protection for them from the worst risks and effects of the Troubles. Children told us of the reality of danger in their daily lives.

> Her wee brother and sister can't sleep in the back room. They're too afraid, 'cause their back windows been done [petrol bombed, bricked ...] that many times. They're too afraid to sleep in their own room. Her wee sister sleeps between her mummy and her daddy, and her wee brother sleep's upstairs. (Young woman, North Belfast)

Children and young people do not experience conflict and violence in a vacuum, nor is it the only problem they are faced with. Conflict and violence is experienced by children and young people in the context of assets, resources, impediments and handicaps in the child or young person's wider social context. In Northern Ireland this wider social context is characterised by a number of features that help construct and mediate the experience of violence:

- The societal context
- The family context
- Peer relationships and young people's relationship to violence.

The Societal Context

Segregation

Northern Ireland is a deeply divided society in which the two communities are segregated from one another in educational, residential and in some cases, occupational terms. One mechanism which has historically been employed by communities in order to manage these divisions in Northern Ireland is that of residential segregation. Paradoxically, residential segregation can make people feel safer whilst they are among members of their own community; segregation can also mean that certain communities, such as enclaves, are sitting targets.

It was estimated that, following the 1991 Census, 50 per cent of the population in Northern Ireland live in areas that are more than 90 per cent Catholic or Protestant. Segregation is most marked in the larger urban areas, but is also a feature of smaller towns and some rural areas. Residential segregation is more closely associated with public housing areas. Smith and Chambers (1991) estimate that 37 per cent of manual Catholic households living in public housing were in wards where 90 per cent or more of the population were of the same religion. The corresponding figure for privately owned households headed by a manual worker was 19 per cent. The trend towards segregation has been steadily increasing (see McKitterick, 1994; Doherty and Poole, 1995).

Segregation is a feature of almost every aspect of life in Northern Ireland. Residential segregation is the most visible and discussed form of segregation, marked by so-called 'peace lines' (high security fences that separate communities), kerbstone painting, graffiti, flags and other emblems. Areas segregated in this manner are often public housing areas where unemployment and other forms of deprivation are prevalent. Residential segregation also occurs in middle class owner occupied housing areas, but is less visible. Of particular concern are the experiences of residents and their children in enclave areas. These areas, surrounded by the 'other' community, also experience deprivation levels that are the highest in Northern Ireland. It is often residents in enclaves that have experienced the most intense effects of the Troubles. Sectarian attacks are commonplace on the boundary of such areas, and it is young people, particularly males, who are most often involved, both as victims and aggressors.

Education

Children are educated in separate systems in Northern Ireland according to their community of origin, with a small integrated school movement providing the exception to the rule of segregation. The Northern Ireland educational system is not only religiously segregated between the state and maintained schools, but is also streamed according to ability into grammar and secondary schools. Furthermore, gender segregation is also widespread. The educational system also serves children differently depending on their orientation towards education and their location within the system.

Children who do not do well within the education system tend to come from the more deprived areas which are often affected by violence. In some communities in North Belfast that have been worst affected by the Troubles the majority of young people leave school without any educational qualifications, and some leave with significant literacy problems. Those living in segregated areas face a whole range of additional challenges. For example, a survey by

McKeown (1973) of all post-primary schools in Northern Ireland found that over half of those surveyed reported harassment on the way to school. The United Nations Convention on the Rights of the Child purports to protect children from such abuses, so this is an issue that was further probed in this study, with insights into the extent that children experience harassment and bullying within school and on journeys to and from school.

Deprivation and the Troubles

Even a casual observation of the distribution of Troubles-related violence suggests that a correspondence exists between deprivation, on the one hand, and concentration of Troubles-related violence, on the other. A correlation between Robson's (1994) ward index of deprivation and civilian death rates at ward level has been found (Fay et al., 1997). Northern Ireland experiences high levels of deprivation in comparison to other regions of the UK and Europe. Unemployment is high, dependence on social security benefits is heavy, rates of congenital abnormalities and incidence of long-term handicap conditions are high, suicide rates among the young are rising, health is poor and income is relatively low (Jones and McCoy, 1989; Robson et al., 1994; Brown, 1996).

Trew (1995), writing about children in Northern Ireland and their experience of the Troubles, states:

> Poverty is a war against children ... The most economically deprived areas are frequently characterised as regions of high levels of political conflict and violence. The level of violence has varied across the region [of Northern Ireland] and across time ...

In Northern Ireland, the effects of Troubles-related violence augment the effects of deprivation, creating what Smyth (1998) has termed a 'double penalty'. Programmes aimed at targeting social needs have for the most part ignored this double penalty. Intervention programmes and their social policies have operated as if they were dealing with 'simple' socio-economic deprivation rather than deprivation which is interlocked with and compounded by the attritional effect of the violence of the Troubles.

Community Identity and Grievance

Segregation, continuing violence and other factors has served to tighten the networks and the bonds within communities, particularly in enclave communities. This is understandable, even pre-dictable, given that many of these communities perceived themselves to be – and indeed are – under attack. Simplistic assump-tions about the benefits of tight-knit communities overlook the problems that are inherent in many such communities; domestic violence, child sexual abuse, drug and alcohol abuse, poor educa-tional attainment, vandalism, and so on. Another aspect of such cohesion is that outsiders may be regarded with suspicion – partic-ularly outsiders from the 'other community'.

The Troubles has created the fear and suspicion with which the 'other side' – and to some extent all outsiders – are regarded. Furthermore, a sense of grievance and victimhood is felt almost uni-versally. The sense of grievance is often based on real wrongs and injustices, many of which have gone unacknowledged and unad-dressed for many years. In some cases it has appeared as if the political to address grievances is absent. This has been referred to as a 'grievance culture' and children growing up in such a climate inherit these grievances. They often learn at a very early age, either implicitly or explicitly, of the wrongs that have been done to their 'kith and kin'. The tight-knit nature of the community may render young people reluctant to leave the area to seek work or training. The outside world as well as outsiders can seem a menacing and unfriendly place. Young people's religion is often identifiable by items of clothing they wear. These may be *de rigueur* whilst in their own community, but may pose a threat to safety if worn in areas such as city centres, where young people from the other community attack groups from the 'other side' on a regular basis. Clothing, however, is not the only marker of identity. The bus stops or taxi stands used by young people and a myriad of other subtle signs are used to differentiate friends from enemies.

Family Context

Clearly families also live in communities such as those described above where they are fearful for their children's safety. In such com-munities the families' sense of control over their environment may be diminished by a range of problems in the wider community. In the families where the worst impact of the Troubles has been expe-rienced, children are affected in a range of ways, often in spite of the adults' best efforts.

Intergenerational Effects

Communication between parents and children living with armed conflict may be shaped and limited by a suite of protective intentions. Parents raising children in violent and unstable political and social environments deal with a formidable challenge. Faced as they are by impossible choices, few are in a position to realise the full impact of their actions on children, and on subsequent generations. Whether intentionally or not, the effects of the violent experiences of this generation of adults can be passed on to subsequent generations. In addition, individuals within families may live in close proximity to one another, but are frequently unable to discuss openly what has happened to them, using denial and silence as a defence against the horror of their loss (Deane, 1997).

In times of violence and war, the ability of adult caretakers to continue to carry out their care-taking role for the children in their care may be compromised. Adults who have been severely traumatised can be so shocked that they can be rendered virtually incapable of recognising the needs of other people, including the needs of their children. Previous research by The Cost of the Troubles Study (Smyth, 1998) outlines how a number of women who have been violently bereaved in the Troubles have described in interview how, in the total absence of other forms of support, they used alcohol and prescribed and unprescribed medication to self-medicate for long periods after their traumatic bereavement.

Parenting

War and low-intensity conflict appear to create huge obstacles to the discharge of the adult responsibility for protecting children. In situations of armed conflict, physical danger may require the setting aside of normal standards of parenting. Adults may be so preoccupied with crisis management or survival that children's needs are sometimes overlooked. Children and young people may live in families that have been multiply bereaved or traumatised, in which consistent care attention may not always be available, albeit for understandable reasons. Another obstacle to the discharge of the parental responsibility is the fact that due to the nature of violent conflict, parents may be powerless to ensure their children's safety. Clearly parents exercise little control over the level of violence in an area and are therefore relatively powerless over the level of danger that their children are exposed to.

Children of Prisoners

Amongst the most distressing experiences that can befall a child is separation from a parent in times of war and civil conflict (Machel, 1996; Macksound and Aber, 1996). Children who suffer such separations from parents can be among those most severely affected by their experiences. Children who are bereaved suffer a permanent separation, but those whose parents are imprisoned are also affected. Children in families where a parent has been imprisoned suffer the effects of separation from the imprisoned parent, and the added financial and emotional burden that this can place on remaining parent. Where a parent was imprisoned outside Northern Ireland, it may have been virtually impossible for the child to maintain meaningful contact due to the financial and emotional strain imposed by long journeys for visits and disruption caused by the frequent and unpredictable moves to which such prisoners were subjected.

Children of Members of the Security Forces

Another group of children about which little is known is the children of members of the Northern Ireland security forces. The local security forces have been targeted for violent attack since the early Troubles and many have been killed or injured. Quite often officers are attacked whilst at home and off duty, which means that constant vigilance is called for, and not only the officer but also his or her family is vulnerable to attack at any time. Car bombs have been placed under officers' cars; officers have been attacked while travelling to and from work; and some have been attacked whilst socialising off duty, or at home with their families. In some cases children have witnessed these attacks.

Officers and their families have lived with the necessity of secrecy and high levels of personal security over long periods of time. This has had a number of effects. Identity has to be managed in order to protect life. For young children this means that from an early age they learn that they cannot talk at school about certain issues, and they discover early that 'outsiders' can be dangerous and are not to be trusted. In some cases children have grown up unaware of the true nature of their parent's occupation. These factors undoubtedly have implications for their relationship within the family, with other children and for their development and attitude formation.

Peer Relationships and Young People's Relationship to Violence

The Culture of Violence

McVeigh (1994) suggests that over a quarter of young people in Northern Ireland aged between 17 and 19 feel that they have been harassed in some way by the security forces, but few registered complaints and few had confidence in the mechanisms for dealing with complaints. In 1991 there were 8455 joyriding incidents, many of which involve shootings and assaults on joyriders. Some young people report that pressure is put on them by the police to become informers, in order to avoid prosecution as joyriders (Smyth, 1998).

Children who live in a surveillance culture grow up learning to be secretive and to distrust authority (Machel, 1996). Children who have grown up with routine and repeated stopping and questioning in the street under emergency legislation and with house searches, conducted because the police had 'reasonable suspicion', learn to hate the police and security forces. Authority, including the security forces, is often seen to be unfair, not even-handed, and acting against the best interests of the community and of young people. In order to survive the violence and brutality of the Troubles, many people, including many children and young people, have become habituated to violence. Violence is minimised and in the past this has enabled people to survive psychologically.

Set alongside a popular culture that often celebrates and promotes the use of violence, it is difficult to quantify the scale of the damage and brutalisation that has occurred to young people and to children. Everywhere – in the news media, in fiction – violence is presented as thrilling, entertaining, sexy, powerful and exciting. It is not surprising that young adolescents, young men especially, often attach positive values to being tough and aggressive, and negative values to kindness, gentleness and compassion. Children and young people require help to reshape behaviours that were arguably appropriate to the violence, in a context where violence is to be consigned firmly to the past.

Young People's Attitudes and the Reproduction of Sectarian Division

Perhaps partly due to the limited and/or violent contact with members of the other community due to residential and educational segregation, young people often have strong views about the 'other side'. Whilst young people undoubtedly show signs of awareness and openness to the 'other side', there is also evidence of suspicion, anger and at times hatred, directed at the other community (Smyth, 1998). This is in spite of cross-community schemes and positive parental influence. Children and young people's attitudes are formed in the context of the other things that happen to them, and maintenance of open-minded attitudes in the context of violently divided communities is clearly impossible for many young people.

However, it is not only children and young people from highly segregated areas that suffer as a result of the divided nature of this society. All children suffer in terms of the warping and restriction of their education and socialisation. The lack of preparation children receive and the lack of adult models for dealing in healthy, open and mutually respectful ways with different views, aspirations and traditions means that children can grow up without positive models of inclusiveness outside their families. This increases the chances that they will grow into adults who are ill-equipped to deal successfully with the differences contained within the wider political community. Their full capacity for citizenship is not developed (Smyth, 1995a, 1995b). This has far-reaching implications not only for children but also for society at large and for the long-term prospects of peace.

THE SURVEY RESULTS

Having provided the backdrop to the lives of some of the young people worst-affected by the Troubles in Northern Ireland, the survey results are placed in a context. The young people who worked with the researchers hoped that the research would act as a counterbalance to the silence that surrounds young people and the Troubles in Northern Ireland and its political context. The research has thus given an opportunity to 1000 young people in Northern Ireland to express their experiences in Northern Ireland, ranging from daily experiences of harassment and bullying to the most serious consequences of the Troubles, such as bereavement and injury.

Common Experiences of the Troubles

Young people were questioned first in relation to the more common experiences of the Troubles they may have had, which may include being stopped and searched by the security forces, feeling unable to say what they think in front of others, and general safety issues. The results are presented in Table 7.1.

Straying into an area where respondents didn't feel safe was experienced 'very often' by 13.5 per cent of the young people surveyed,

Table 7.1 Experiencing the Troubles

Common experiences	Very often experienced (%)	Occasionally experienced (%)	Seldom experienced (%)	Never experienced (%)	Don't know (%)
Straying into an area where I didn't feel safe	13.5	31.5	29.5	21.5	4.2
Being stopped and searched by security forces	9.2	14.5	18.9	53.5	3.9
Feeling unable to say what I think or being wary in the presence of other people because of safety issues	16.8	30.4	23.1	21.7	8.1
My parents having to take extra safety precautions to secure my home or workplace	7.9	12.9	15.9	55.6	7.8
Having to change my normal routes, routines or habits because of safety	8.1	14.7	16.7	54.6	6.2

and 'occasionally' by a further 31.5 per cent. This represents a significant percentage, 45 per cent, of young people who at some time perceived a danger into straying into the 'wrong area'. The prominence of symbols (flags, emblems, painted kerbstones, and so on) in some areas will sharpen this perception of a threat to safety for those from the 'other community'. A higher percentage of Catholic young people responded that when straying into an area that they 'very often' (15.9 per cent) or 'occasionally' (32.5 per cent) felt unsafe, than Protestant young people – 'very often' (10.5 per cent) and 'occasionally' (30.2 per cent). There was also a higher percentage of males than females who responded that they 'very often' or 'occasionally' felt unsafe with a combined total of 49.3 per cent compared to 40.4 per cent. There was little variation between different age groups and different types of school.

Being stopped and searched by the security forces 'very often' and 'occasionally' was experienced by 9.2 per cent and 14.5 per cent respectively of young people surveyed, resulting in a combined total of 23.7 per cent – almost 25 per cent of the respondents. The overall percentage masks significant differences in religious background and gender of the respondents. A third of Catholic young people surveyed (33.2 per cent) had been 'very often' or 'occasionally' stopped and searched by the security forces, compared to 14.3 per cent of Protestant young people. This may help to provide an explanation as to why Catholics are more likely than Protestants to support the restructuring of the RUC. Males (29.6 per cent) were also more likely to be stopped and searched by the security forces 'very often' and 'occasionally' than females (18.4 per cent).

Feeling unable to say what they think or being wary in the presence of other people because of safety issues was experienced 'very often' by 16.8 per cent of the young people surveyed, and 'occasionally' by 30.4 per cent, almost a half of the sample (47.2 per cent). This figure was higher among Catholics at 51.8 per cent than Protestants at 42.9 per cent, but with consistent levels among males and females.

Almost a fifth of respondents stated that their parents had to take extra safety precautions to secure homes or workplaces, either 'very often' (7.9 per cent) or 'occasionally' (12.9 per cent). This level increased to over a quarter for Catholic young people at 26.3 per cent, compared to 15.7 per cent of Protestants. There were no differences in terms of gender. Having to change their normal route, routines or habits because of safety was experienced 'very often' by

8.1 per cent of the young people surveyed and 'occasionally' by 14.7 per cent (a combined total of 22.8 per cent). Again, this figure for Catholics, at 29.5 per cent, was almost double the combined total for Protestants, at 15.5 per cent. There was little variation between male and female responses.

More Direct Experiences

> My mummy doesn't like me going out of my estate ... As long as she knows exactly where I am, I'm all right, but she wouldn't let me go for a walk or anything, like, unless I was with her. She doesn't like me just going into town on my own or with my friends because she says I'm a far too easy target, you know, if something happens in the town, and I'd have no way of getting home ... (Young woman, North Belfast)

Following the more common experience of the Troubles, young people were then questioned on their more direct experiences. Questions related to events such as ending friendships because of the sectarian divide, having schooling disrupted and experiences of military organisations acting as punishment agencies. The results are shown in Table 7.2.

Interestingly, almost three-quarters of the young people surveyed had 'never' had to end friendships or had relationships disrupted because of the sectarian divide. This percentage is fairly consistent with males and females, but is higher (80.6 per cent) among Protestant young people than Catholic young people (69.5 per cent). Conversely a higher percentage of Catholic young people have 'very often' (4.9 per cent) or 'occasionally' (9.0 per cent) had to end friend-ships or had relationships disrupted because of the sectarian divide, than their Protestant counterparts – 2.7 per cent 'very often' and 5.9 per cent 'occasionally'.

Young people were also questioned on their experience of getting into physical fights about the Troubles. Overall, 8.1 per cent of young people had 'very often' been involved in physical fights with a further 14.2 per cent responding 'occasionally'. The highest response to this question was 'never' with 58.7 per cent. A higher percentage of Catholics responded that they 'very often' (10.4 per cent) or 'occasionally' (17.7 per cent) got into fights compared to Protestants (5.4 per cent and 9.7 per cent respectively). There were also significant location differences, with 10 per cent of urban respondents as opposed to 6 per cent of rural respondents saying

Table 7.2 Direct Experiences of the Troubles

Event/experience	Very often experienced (%)	Occasionally experienced (%)	Seldom experienced (%)	Never experienced (%)	Don't know (%)
Having to end friendships or having relationships disrupted because of the sectarian divides	4.0	7.4	9.4	74.7	4.5
Getting into physical fights about the Troubles	8.1	14.2	16.0	58.7	3.0
Having my schooling disrupted by the Troubles	3.1	9.9	18.7	62.2	6.1
Had experiences of military organisations acting as punishment agencies	4.6	8.0	11.2	61.4	14.8

that they got into fights 'very often'. However, perhaps unsurprisingly, the most significant difference is between the responses for males and females. The combined total of males who 'very often' and 'occasionally' got into physical fights about the Troubles was 31.1 per cent, compared to 13.7 per cent for females. This illustrates that young males are much more likely to become involved in physical fights related to the Troubles, and it would be interesting to investigate if this inclination to violence is reflected in more serious aspects of Troubles-related violence.

Similarly, a higher percentage of male than female young people experienced having their schooling disrupted by the Troubles. Overall, 13.0 per cent experienced schooling disruptions either 'very often' (3.1 per cent) or 'occasionally' (9.9 per cent). Again, there were urban rural differences, with 55 per cent of urban respondents compared to 70 per cent of rural respondents saying that their education had never been disrupted and 4 per cent of urban as compared to 2 per cent of rural respondents saying that their education had been disrupted very often. However, for males this level increases to 16.7 per cent compared to 9.4 per cent of females. Conversely, 68.3 per cent of females had never experienced schooling disruption by the Troubles, compared to 55.3 per cent of males. Percentages experiencing disruption to schooling remained consistent across religious differences.

Overall, 4.6 per cent of the young people surveyed 'very often' and 8.0 per cent 'occasionally' had experiences of military organisations acting as punishment agencies, with 61.4 per cent never having this experience. Catholics are more likely to have had this experience with 6.4 per cent responding 'very often' and 8.3 per cent 'occasionally' (a combined total of 14.7 per cent), compared to Protestants with 3.2 per cent responding 'very often' and 8.3 per cent 'occasionally' (combined total of 11.5 per cent). Urban respondents were more likely to have such experiences with 54 per cent of urban respondents saying they had never had such experiences and 7 per cent saying that they had frequently had them, compared to 70 per cent and 2 per cent correspondingly of rural respondents. Again, a higher percentage of males than females had experienced this more direct aspect of the Troubles. A combined total of 16.9 per cent for 'very often' (7.0 per cent) and 'occasionally' (9.9 per cent) was recorded for males, compared to 9.1 per cent for females (2.4 per cent 'very often' and 6.7 per cent 'occasionally').

Severe Aspects of the Troubles

> My first memory of the Troubles was when my aunt got shot ... It frightened me, so it did. She was only home from visiting my Granny in England, and she was walking around the corner to me aunt's house. She got shot dead ... IRA crossfire ... Well, you're afraid to go out, in case you get shot dead, so you are. (Young woman, North Belfast)

Severe experiences range from having a home attacked or destroyed or witnessing a shooting, to injury or death of an immediate family member. Because of the localisation of the conflict in Northern Ireland, research that takes a representative sample of young people (such as this survey) will tend to overestimate the experiences of children in low-violence areas whilst underestimating the experiences of children in high-violence areas such as North and West Belfast. However, given this limitation, this survey still provides a useful 'snapshot' of today's 14–17-year-olds across Northern Ireland and the affect of the Troubles on their lives. Table 7.3 provides details of the level of severe experience reported.

As would be expected, percentages of those experiencing 'very often' or 'occasionally' these more severe Troubles-related events are lower than the previous section concerned with the more common experiences of young people – however, the figures should not be discounted. Overall, 5.6 per cent of the young people surveyed had 'very often' (2.4 per cent) or 'occasionally' (3.2 per cent) had their home attacked. This figure was higher for Catholic young people than Protestant young people (a combined total of 8.5 per cent, compared to 7.3 per cent respectively). Almost 5.0 per cent had had to leave their home temporarily (either 'very often', 1.0 per cent, or 'occasionally', 3.9 per cent) with a further 1.9 per cent having to leave their home permanently ('very often', 1.2 per cent, and 'occasionally', 0.7 per cent). Of those surveyed, 1.4 per cent 'had their home destroyed' either 'very often' (0.9 per cent) or 'occasionally' (0.5 per cent).

> Well, the age group we're all at, we grew through the Troubles, we all know somebody or have lost somebody very close to us ... Everyone maybe in North Belfast would have, should it be a neighbour or an aunt, an uncle, a son, cousin. You know, everybody's affected, like. Everybody has their own story to tell

Table 7.3 Severe Experiences of the Troubles

Event/experiences	Very often experienced (%)	Occasionally experienced (%)	Seldom experienced (%)	Never experienced (%)	Don't know
Having my home attacked	2.4	3.2	6.9	85.8	1.6
Having to leave my home temporarily	1.0	3.9	6.5	87.1	1.4
Having to leave my home permanently	1.2	0.7	1.6	94.9	1.6
Having my home destroyed	0.9	0.5	2.7	94.1	1.7

... Some people have lost even more than one in one family. (Young man, North Belfast)

Over half (52.5 per cent) of the young people surveyed had been caught up in a riot at least once, with 16.1 per cent 'several times', 16.8 per cent 'more than once' and 19.6 per cent responding 'once'. This percentage increases for both Catholics and males. For Catholics, 61.3 per cent responded that they had been caught up in a riot at least once, with over a fifth stating that this had happened 'several times' (21.1 per cent). This compares to 53.7 per cent of Protestants that had been caught up in a riot more than once, with 10.4 per cent responding 'several times'. A high percentage of males (59.5 per cent) responded that they had been caught up in a riot at least once, compared to 46.7 per cent of females.

Overall, 16.9 per cent of those surveyed had witnessed a shooting with 3.3 per cent responding 'several times', 4.0 per cent 'more than once' and 9.6 per cent 'once'. Again this percentage is higher for Catholics and for males. Exactly a fifth (20 per cent) of Catholics responded that they had witnessed a shooting at least once, 5.2 per cent 'several times', 5.0 per cent 'more than once', and 9.8 per cent 'once'. The corresponding figure for Protestant young people was 12.2 per cent with 0.9 per cent responding 'several times', 2.7 per cent 'more than once' and 8.6 per cent 'once'. For males, 22.4 per cent had witnessed a shooting compared to 10.7 per cent of females. There were also urban–rural differences, with 76 per cent of urban respondents and 87 per cent of rural respondents saying that they had 'never' witnessed a shooting, yet 2 per cent of urban and 4 per cent of rural respondents said that they had witnessed shootings 'several times'.

In general, 17.5 per cent of young people in the survey had stated that a work colleague had been attacked, with 2.6 per cent stating 'several times', 6.7 per cent stating 'more than once' and 8.2 per cent stating 'once'. Consistent with the results recorded above, a higher percentage of Catholics reported this experience. Around a fifth (20.8 per cent) of Catholic young people have had a work colleague attacked, compared to 14.1 per cent of their Protestant counterparts. Again gender differences were noticeable, with 26.7 per cent of males compared to 11.9 per cent of females responding that at least once a work colleague has been attacked. These religious and gender differences are also reflected in the numbers of survey participants who reported that a work colleague had been killed. Overall, 6.0 per cent responded that at least once, a work colleague has been killed. However, this figure increases to 9.0 per cent for Catholics compared to 2.8 per cent of Protestants, and 7.5 per cent of males to 4.5 per cent of females.

A larger percentage of young people recorded that a neighbour had been attacked in the Troubles. Overall, 28.7 per cent of the young people surveyed had experienced this at least once. Similar to previous questions, there was a higher frequency of Catholics (36.8 per cent) than Protestants (19.5 per cent) that had experienced a neighbour being attacked at least once. In this case, male and female responses are fairly consistent. Overall, 14.4 per cent of young people responded that they had had the experience of a neighbour being killed, with 1.9 per cent responding 'very often', 4.0 per cent 'more than once' and 14.4 per cent 'once'. Over twice as many Catholics (19.2 per cent) as Protestants (9.2 per cent) have had the experience of a neighbour being killed in the Troubles. Gender differences were not significant.

Overall, 32.1 per cent, or almost a third, of the young people surveyed had witnessed people being killed or seriously injured at least once: 4.8 per cent 'several times'; 10.8 per cent 'more than once'; and 16.5 per cent 'once'. Consistent with previous Troubles-related events, a higher percentage of Catholics (37.0 per cent) than Protestants (27.2 per cent) responded that this has been experienced at least once. A higher percentage of males (34.9 per cent than females (29.9 per cent) had also been recorded for more than once.

Almost one in ten of the people surveyed (9.8 per cent) had experienced a close being friend killed in Troubles-related violence. However, in contrast to previous severe experiences of the Troubles, similar percentages are recorded across religious differences, with 9.3 per cent of Catholics and 9.8 per cent of Protestants responding that they had had the experience of a close friend being killed. There were also urban rural differences in responses to this question, with 10 per cent of urban dwellers saying that they had 'once' lost a close friend, compared to 5 per cent of rural dwellers; and 85 per cent of urban respondents saying that they had never lost a close friend, compared to 93 per cent of rural dwellers. Overall, 5.1 per cent of those surveyed responded that they had been injured in a bomb explosion at least once, with a higher percentage of Catholics (6.1 per cent) than Protestants (4.2 per cent). There were no significant differences in responses by gender. Being injured in a shooting at least once was recorded by 6.3 per cent of young people in the survey. Religious differences were evident with 8.1 per cent of Catholics, compared to 3.7 per cent of Protestants responding that they have been injured at least once in a shooting incident. Perhaps surprisingly, there was little variation among male and female responses for this experience (6.6 per cent and 6.1 per cent respectively, responding at least once). There were, however, significant urban–rural differences, with 6 per cent of urban and 2 per cent of rural respondents reporting that they had been injured once, and 89 per cent of urban compared with 95 per cent of rural respondents reporting that they had 'never' been injured.

Over a quarter of the sample (25.2 per cent) had experienced a member of their immediate family being injured in Troubles-related violence. This figure decreased to 12.0 per cent for those who have on at least one occasion experienced a member of their immediate family being killed. Responses by gender were fairly consistent; however, Catholic responses were more frequent than Protestant. For injury to an immediate family member, 30.6 per cent of Catholics compared to 19.7 per cent of Protestants responded that this had occurred at least once, and for a family member being killed 14.2 per cent of Catholics responded at least once, relative to 9.0 per cent of Protestants. Again there were urban–rural differences in responses to these two questions: 5 per cent of urban compared with 3 per cent of rural respondents said that they had this experience 'several times' and 8 per cent of urban compared with 6 per cent of rural saying that they had had the experience more than once. A further 18 per cent of urban compared with 11 per cent of rural respondents said that they had had the experience once and 65 per cent of urban compared with 79 per cent of rural said that they had never had the experience.

Young people in the survey were also questioned concerning the extent to which another relative (outside of the immediate family) had been injured or killed. Overall, 29.2 per cent of those surveyed have had a relative injured, with 3.9 per cent responding 'several times', 8.9 per cent 'more than once' and 16.4 per cent 'once'. Furthermore, 14.0 per cent of the young people have had a relative killed in Troubles-related violence, with 2.2 per cent responding 'several times', 3.5 per cent 'more than once' and 8.5 per cent 'once'. Again, it is evident that differences exist depending on the religious background of the respondent. In terms of an injured relative, 37.6 per cent of Catholics have experienced this at least once, compared to 20.2 per cent of Protestants. Similarly, a higher percentage of Catholics (19.1 per cent) have experienced on at least one occasion a relative being killed, compared to their Protestant counterparts (8.0 per cent). Again there were significant urban–rural differences, with 6 per cent of urban compared with 3 per cent of rural respondents saying that they had lost 'several' or 'more than one' family member, and 81 per cent of urban compared with 89 per cent of rural respondents never having had this experience.

> You know, like, you've been brought up in it, and ... to be truthful, like, none of us here know what it's like to live in peace ... We've been living in the war all our lives, and it doesn't seem like it is war to us. It just feels as if it is normal, you know. When somebody gets shot, you go, 'Auch, I feel sorry for them.' But really what you're saying is that you're glad that it wasn't one of your family. That's the way people react nowadays. (Young woman, North Belfast)

Responsibility for the Troubles

Young people were also questioned on the difficult issue of 'responsibility' for the Troubles, with responses that included paramilitary organisations, security forces, politicians and governments, and the general public. Young people were asked to what extent they thought each institution or organisation listed was responsible for the Troubles (see Table 7.4). There are a variety of ways of interpreting the term 'responsibility for the Troubles'. For example, it could mean 'responsibility for beginning the Troubles' or 'responsibility for sustaining the Troubles', 'responsibility for the most violence' or even 'responsibility for violence against a particular community'. The ambiguous nature of this question may help to explain the high percentages of 'don't knows', ranging from 15.6 per cent to 37.5 per cent. Alternatively, this high 'don't know' score could reflect other difficulties that respondents had with the question. They may have been reluctant to attribute blame, or to be seen to do so; or they may have felt that their historical grasp of the Troubles was not sufficient for them to answer the question.

In general, it is clear from the table that few of the organisations and institutions were held to be 'not responsible' for the Troubles by young people. The Church has the highest percentage for 'not responsible' for the Troubles with 42.2 per cent, followed by the 'silent majority for Northern Ireland' with 31.2 per cent. The remaining organisations and institutions were all thought to be 'not responsible' for the Troubles by less than a quarter of the surveyed young people. Only 6.1 per cent and 4.3 per cent of young people perceived that Republican and Loyalist paramilitaries respectively were 'not responsible for the Troubles'.

Conversely, Republican and Loyalist paramilitaries were thought to be 'very responsible' or 'responsible' for the Troubles by 57.8 per cent and 61.6 per cent respectively – which were the highest percentages for responsibility. Following the paramilitaries, 40.1 per cent of young people responded that the RUC was either 'very responsible' or 'responsible' for the Troubles. However, there were some urban–rural differences in responses relating to the RUC, with only 15 per cent of urban compared with 25 per cent of rural respondents allocating no responsibility to the RUC. Males showed a significantly greater tendency to hold the RUC responsible more than females. Eight of the organisations/institutions received similar responses, with young people stating that they were either 'very responsible' or 'responsible', at 30–39 per cent. These include the British Army; Republican, Loyalist and British politicians; the RIR/UDR; and also people living in hard-line areas in Northern Ireland. In all cases, males tended to hold each organisation/institution more responsible than female respondents.

However, as may be expected, there are marked differences of opinion between Catholic and Protestant young people. In general, it appears that Catholic young people are more likely than Protestants to view British institutions and local security forces to be 'very responsible' and 'responsible' for the Troubles. Conversely, Protestant young people are more likely than Catholic young people to perceive Republican and Irish organisations to be 'very responsible' and 'responsible'.

To illustrate this, for Catholic young people the RUC was viewed as 'very responsible' by 49.2 per cent of Catholics, but only 13 per cent of Protestants. A high percentage of Catholics (53.6 per cent) also perceived the British Army to be 'very responsible' or 'responsible' compared to 12.5 per cent of Protestants. Almost twice as many Catholics (41 per cent) as Protestants (22 per cent) thought that the British government was 'very responsible' or 'responsible'.

As further evidence of a polarisation of views, 71.9 per cent of Protestants perceived Republican paramilitaries and 43.3 per cent viewed Republican politicians as 'responsible', compared to 46.0 per cent and 30.2 per cent respectively of Catholics. A higher percentage of Protestants (32.3 per cent) than Catholics (24.9 per cent) also thought that Irish politicians were 'very responsible' or 'responsible'.

Table 7.4   Assignment of Responsibility for the Troubles

	Very responsible (%)	Responsible (%)	Partially responsible (%)	Not responsible (%)	Don't know (%)
Republican paramilitaries	30.8	27.0	18.3	6.1	17.9
Loyalist paramilitaries	29.1	32.5	16.5	4.3	17.6
RUC	20.9	19.2	24.4	19.8	15.6
RIR/UDR	14.1	17.7	16.2	14.5	37.5
British Army	18.0	15.6	19.9	22.8	23.7
Republican politicians	12.5	23.3	27.4	13.7	23.1
Loyalist politicians	13.6	23.5	29.1	10.1	23.7
British politicians	12.9	18.8	27.3	16.4	24.6
Irish politicians	9.2	19.2	28.3	18.8	24.5
All politicians	9.7	21.8	28.3	13.5	26.7
British government	12.1	20.7	24.2	18.1	24.8
Irish government	6.5	17.5	25.4	24.9	25.6
Churches	6.1	10.1	18.6	42.7	22.6
Silent majority in Northern Ireland	6.1	12.9	29.1	31.2	20.8
People living in hard-line areas in Northern Ireland	13.8	23.3	23.2	16.0	23.7

The Impact of the Troubles-Related Experiences

The trouble has to stop sometime, you know. When you're growing up, you just don't want to live in hatred. You want to live in peace with a member of the other community, so you do. And you want to walk down the street with a couple of Protestant friends [and] say, 'How's it going?' Mess about with them. Have a good time. Go about, no fear about you. You can have a good time with anyone you want, you know. And no one can say anything. But if it was like that … it would just be brilliant, so it would! But it's not … (Young man, North Belfast)

Previously we attempted to chart the variety and extent of Troubles-related events that young people experienced. Here, we examine the impact that their experiences may have had, and three factors in particular will be considered:

- Aspects of young people's lives that may have been affected
- How the Troubles have affected young people and their families
- The extent to which young people's lives have been affected by the Troubles.

Aspects of Young People's Lives that May have been Affected

Young people were asked if the Troubles had ever affected a variety of aspects of their lives, which included schooling, home life, social life and leisure.

Overall, 16.6 per cent of the young people surveyed responded 'yes', the Troubles had affected their schooling, education or training, with 78.2 per cent responding 'no'. There was little variation between Catholic and Protestant young people with 16.5 per cent and 15.8 per cent responding 'yes' respectively. There was, however, a larger variation between males (18.4 per cent) and females (14.2 per cent) that had stated 'yes'.

More significant than schooling, 22.6 per cent of young people stated 'yes', their home life, and family relationships had been affected by the troubles, with 72.7 per cent responding 'no'. A higher percentage of Catholic young people than Protestant young people, 29.1 per cent compared to 16.0 per cent, perceived that the Troubles affected this aspect of their lives. Gender did not appear to be significant in responses for this question. There were some small but significant age differences in responses, with respondents under the age of 15 saying that they had experienced no effects or that they 'didn't know'.

In general, 42.3 per cent of young people had stated that their social lives, hobbies and leisure have been affected by the Troubles, the highest percentage for 'yes' in this section of questions. This high response may indicate the importance young people today attach to their social lives and interests outside of school and family life. However, it would also suggest that young people are frustrated with the impact of the Troubles on this aspect of their lives, perhaps with a lack of opportunity for cross-community friendships and relationships or a fear for personal safety in going into certain areas. Similar to family life, a higher percentage of Catholics than Protestants reported that the Troubles affected their social life, with over half of the Catholic young people responding 'yes' (51.3 per cent), compared to around a third of the Protestants surveyed (33.5 per cent). There was little difference in the responses for males and females. Again, there were also significant age differences, with respondents under the age of 15 reporting less disruption to their social lives than older respondents.

Overall, 37.8 per cent of young people surveyed reported that other activities have been affected by the Troubles, although it is unclear what these activities may be. There were different responses by gender and religious background of the young people. A higher percentage of Catholics (46.7 per cent) than Protestants (30.1 per cent) responded 'yes', as did a higher percentage of females (42.5 per cent) than males (32.4 per cent). Some age differences emerged with 15- and 17-year-old respondents reporting more disruption than other age groups.

How the Troubles have Affected Young People and their Families

The survey asked young people to think about *how* the troubles may have affected them and their families. Issues that were considered included health concerns, family safety, life choices such as emigration, and family.

Overall, 4.2 per cent of the young people surveyed reported that the Troubles had completely ruined their lives, with this percentage increasing to 5.1 per cent of Catholic young people compared to 2.7 per cent of Protestants. There were small but significant urban–rural differences with 5 per cent of urban respondents saying that their lives had been ruined compared to just under 4 per cent of rural respondents. Similarly, a relatively low percentage (4.4 per cent) reported that the Troubles had affected their health. This figure was higher for Catholics (4.7 per cent) than for Protestants (3.4 per cent), higher for males (5.9 per cent) than for females (3.3 per cent), and higher for urban respondents (6.5 per cent) than for rural respondents (2.1 per cent). These findings are consistent with those in the adult survey, which also found:

- Significant differences between Catholic and Protestant experience and effects of the Troubles
- Significant differences between locations, with areas with high death rates – almost exclusively urban areas – having more experiences and suffering more effects.

A larger percentage of young people (12.4 per cent) responded in the survey that the Troubles caused them to lose loved ones through death. Again a higher percentage of Catholic young people (14.6 per cent) than their Protestant counterparts (9.5 per cent) responded 'yes' to this question. There were also significant urban–rural differences (16 per cent 'yes' among urban respondents and 8 per cent among rural respondents), but there was little variation between males and females. Related to this issue, 15.5 per cent of the young people stated that the Troubles had physically damaged them or their families. A higher percentage of Catholics (18.3 per cent) than Protestants (12.0 per cent), and males (17.5 per cent) than females (14.0 per cent) responded 'yes' to this question.

Overall, 14.3 per cent of young people in the survey responded that the Troubles had severely altered the path their lives would have taken. This is quite a broad statement, and could have been interpreted, for example, as a lack of opportunities as a result of the Troubles, or the impact on relationships/friendships. Again there were differences in responses by religious background and gender. A higher percentage of Catholics (18.6 per cent) than Protestants (10.0 per cent) and males (16.4 per cent) than females (12.6 per cent) stated 'yes' to this question.

A series of questions then asked whether the Troubles had affected the choice of their families' home location. Overall, 10.5 per cent stated that the Troubles had led to them or their families leaving their home through intimidation or fear of attack (14.2 per cent of Catholics and 6.3 per cent of Protestants). Almost a third

(32.0 per cent) of the respondents stated that the Troubles had influenced where they had chosen to live, with obviously housing segregation a major concern. Again this issue was more prominent amongst Catholic and urban young people, with 38.2 per cent and 34.2 per cent respectively stating that the Troubles had been an influence, compared to 26.6 per cent of Protestants and 29.2 per cent of rural respondents. The Troubles had made members of 21.7 per cent of the young people's families emigrate, with a further 22.7 per cent reporting that they or their families have seriously considered emigration. Emigration appears from the survey to be a more prominent option among Catholics than Protestants, with 38.2 per cent of Catholics stating that the Troubles has made members of their families emigrate and 25.3 per cent stating that they have considered emigration, compared to 26.6 per cent and 17.1 per cent of Protestants respectively. However, it may be difficult to disentangle the impact of the Troubles on emigration from other social and economic factors, such as unemployment.

Overall, 9.6 per cent of the young people surveyed, about one in ten, reported that the Troubles had divided their family and set one member against another, although the specific reasons why this may have happened are not clear. Again this appeared to affect a higher percentage of Catholic young people with 11.0 per cent responding 'yes', compared to 7.5 per cent of Protestants. The responses of males and females were almost identical. The last question in this section considered how the Troubles had affected perceptions of safety. A high percentage of young people, 29.8 per cent, stated in the survey that the Troubles had made them more fearful for their own and their families' safety. Similar to previous responses, a higher percentage of Catholics (37.6 per cent) responded 'yes' to this question compared to Protestants (22.7 per cent). In addition, a higher percentage of females (33.8 per cent) than males (25.6 per cent) responded 'yes'.

The Extent to Which Young People's Lives have been Affected by the Troubles

Young people were then asked to assess the extent to which the Troubles affected their lives, ranging from none at all, to completely changing their lives. Of those surveyed, 5.0 per cent stated that their experience of the Troubles had completely changed their lives, with a further 4.0 per cent stating that their lives had been radically changed. The two most popular responses were that the Troubles had 'made some changes to my life' (30.6 per cent) and that their experiences had 'made a small impact' (34.6 per cent). These responses may on the one hand indicate a remarkable resilience on the part of the young peoples to absorb the affects of the Troubles without changing their perceptions of life. On the other hand, though, it may suggest that the Troubles have become a 'normal' part of everyday life and experiences and are therefore to be accepted. Again, similar to many responses in this section, a higher percentage of Catholics (6.9 per cent) than Protestants (2.5 per cent), and males (7.5 per cent) than females (2.9 per cent) responded that their lives had been completely changed by their experiences. Given the general higher percentages of Catholics and males that reported Troubles-related experiences than Protestants and females, this would appear to be consistent.

CONCLUSION

This chapter has attempted to chart and examine the Troubles-related experiences of young people in Northern Ireland. When common, more direct and severe experiences were considered, it became apparent that a significant percentage of young people have experienced or been witness to a wide range of Troubles-related events. For example, to illustrate this point, over half the young people (52.5 per cent) were caught up in a riot at least once and almost a third (32.1 per cent) witnessed people being killed or severely injured on at least one occasion. It appears in general that Catholics and males, as subgroups, tend to have had more Troubles-related experiences than Protestants and females.

Only 4.2 per cent of the surveyed young people reported that the Troubles had completely ruined their lives and 5.0 per cent stated that they had completely changed their lives. At first glance, given the experiences that have been charted, it may appear that young people are remarkably resilient to Troubles-related events – after all, the Troubles have provided the backcloth to their lives. However, it might also suggest that their experiences of the Troubles has become 'normalised' and accepted as part of young people's lives, or that although young people can talk about their experiences of the Troubles, it is much less straightforward or as simple to talk about the affect of these experiences. Only through further and perhaps longitudinal research will these matters be further elucidated.

Part IV: Conclusions

8 Truth, Justice and Closure

At the outset, this book posed a number of questions concerned with contemporary understandings and evidence about the situation of victims in the Northern Ireland Peace process. We have attempted to address those questions systematically, basing our conclusions on the data gathered and presented here and elsewhere.

The first question we posed was 'How has the victims issue developed within the peace process?' In Chapter 1 we provided the background to the early emergence of the issue in the peace process, the proliferation of groups in the voluntary sector that sprang up to represent the various interests in the field and their role in defining and contesting the definition of victimhood itself. The second question we posed was: 'How do we understand the partial, indeed partisan, narratives of the Troubles that are shaping the politics of victimhood?' Again in Chapter 1, the contest between the various groups and their political allies was set out and the contest defined. However, Chapter 2, which set out the variation in geographical experience of the Troubles, also has a bearing on this question. The partial understanding and the partisan narratives, we argue, may be based on diverse material experiences of the Troubles. The pattern of killing in the Troubles varies enormously from location to location; and local experience – of having neighbours killed, or of heavy militarisation – is formative of strong and passionate beliefs about who is responsible, who is right and who has suffered. However, widely divergent local experiences will lead people to widely divergent conclusions, providing at least part of the basis for contests about the legitimacy of some victims and the scale of suffering of various cohorts.

Our third question, 'Are there special categories of victims?' led on from this. In Chapter 3, we explored sectarian assassination in which victims are chosen solely on the basis of their religion. Our analysis of sectarian assassination provided a quantitative analysis of sectarian killing and pointed to an ideological basis for sectarian killing, challenging the assumption that it is 'mindless' or without political rationale. We concluded that sectarian killing, like racist killing, is supremacist, yet is often explained by the perpetrators in terms of 'defence' or 'reaction' against threat, rather than as terror directed against unsuspecting and defenceless members of the 'target population'. We pointed out that in war situations the combatants on each side target each other, whereas in genocide the target expands to include the entire population on the other side. Targeting civilians, as sectarian killings do, is this kind of strategy, differentiated from genocide elsewhere in the world only by the scale of the operation in Northern Ireland. For this reason it represents one of the most sinister aspects of the conflict and poses real threats in the event of the failure of the peace process. By way of evidence, we pointed to increases in sectarian attacks since the ceasefires together with the increased numbers of sectarian killings prior to the ceasefires. We concluded that a change has taken place in the form of the Northern Ireland conflict, which has become less of a contest about sovereignty and national identity and more an internal ethnic conflict. An analysis of sectarian killings showed that they were predominantly – though not exclusively – carried out by Loyalist paramilitary groups; that the majority of victims were male and Catholic; and that the majority of killings took place in Belfast, with some regions, such as the North West, experiencing very few such killings.

In Chapters 4 and 7 we examined the experiences of young people, asking how have children and young people have experienced the Troubles and if their opinions augur well for a peaceful society. We argued that in areas where violence has been worst, educational achievement also tends to be low, and there is evidence that a culture of violence has developed in the most affected areas. Furthermore, the Troubles seem to have had a negative impact on adult–child relationships; that young people have normalised the Troubles and that their coping strategies include drug and alcohol abuse. Furthermore, services designed to address the needs of young people in the worst-affected areas tend to be inadequate to the scale of need. We also found that a significant percentage of young people have experienced or been witness to a wide range of Troubles-related events. Over a half of the young people (52.5 per cent) we interviewed had been caught up in a riot at least once and almost a third (32.1 per cent) witnessed people being killed or severely injured on at least one occasion. Finally, Catholics and males, as sub-groups, tended to have had more Troubles-related experiences than Protestants and females.

In Chapters 5 and 6, we examined the experience of the Troubles and the effects through the results of a survey of adults in the population. There we asked about the experiences of those who lived through the Troubles, what impact the Troubles had on their lives, and how this could be understood in terms of the areas in which people lived, their religion and their gender. The survey pointed to a highly differentiated experience of the Troubles with some areas experiencing high concentrations of violence and effects; whilst others reported much less, although still significant amounts of experience and effects of the Troubles. Location and religion stand out as the two most significant determinants of the degree of exposure and the amount of effects experienced as a result of the Troubles. Furthermore, spatial polarisation in Northern Ireland means that location and religion are connected. The sampling procedure used was weighted to 'over-represent' those areas where death rates were highest. It was in these areas that the most intensive and pervasive experiences of the Troubles were found.

In Chapter 6 we examined the relationship between exposure to the Troubles and the effects reported. Two main points emerged from this analysis. First, it seems that exposure to severe experiences is not directly related to suffering of severe effects, since larger percentages of the sample suffered severe impacts than those exposed to severe experiences. (However, since the indicators used in this analysis (severe and very severe impact) were our own constructs, it may be that the findings were an artefact of our method.) The other discovery in the analysis was that although the analysis of Troubles-related deaths points to large gender differences in the fatal impact of the Troubles, gender differences in the survey data were found to be minimal, particularly in the impact variables. Thus, it would appear that although men and women may experience the Troubles differently that suffering is more evenly divided between the genders that an analysis of deaths would suggest.

This book has provided more evidence to add depth and breadth to the understanding of the consequences of Northern Ireland's Troubles, in the context of a political process that struggles to establish a more stable and democratic society than has been experienced for three decades. Whether the evidence we offer can be used to inform positive developments depends largely on political issues related to issues of truth, justice and closure; issues that define the state of victim politics in Northern Ireland, as indeed elsewhere.

TRUTH, JUSTICE AND CLOSURE

It has already been asserted that the contemporary cultures of Loyalism and Republicanism in Northern Ireland are cultures of victimhood. Throughout the peace process, various calls for a truth commission have come from those who feel aggrieved at specific armed factions. Although the appetite for truth seems unabated, there is nothing to suggest that any of the armed parties to the conflict would satisfy such appetite that does exist, nor are there available incentives that might persuade them to do so. A 'supply and demand' problem spoils the prospects for a truth commission in Northern Ireland: the demand far outstrips supply. Furthermore, any truth process depends on a political culture that has moved beyond competing claims to victimhood, and has established an atmosphere of political responsibility. The ability to provide incentives such as amnesty to encourage participation of armed individuals and groups in the process is also usually a prerequisite. Whilst a truth commission for Northern Ireland would, no doubt, serve a useful purpose, its political feasibility is in some doubt for these reasons. Although some inquiries, such as the Bloody Sunday Inquiry* announced in 1998, will address individual incidents in the Troubles, a comprehensive truth process does not yet seem feasible.

Various groups and individuals in Northern Ireland experience an acute sense of injustice. This may, in the long run, prove the most serious obstacle to the achievement of peace. Originating in various sources, some of this sense of injustice has been increased by aspects of the peace process itself. The early release of paramilitary prisoners was one part of the Good Friday Agreement that increased anger and disaffection amongst some of those bereaved and injured, although it had always been apparent, even if distasteful to some, that concessions to paramilitary prisoners would form part of any agreement. Both Republican and Loyalist parties had consistently demanded the release of prisoners, and prisoners' views were regularly consulted throughout the negotiations leading to the Good Friday Agreement. The then Secretary of State, Mo Mowlam, met with prisoners in the jails in January 1998 in order to ensure their support for the ceasefires and for the peace process itself. The response of those bereaved and injured to such gestures was anticipated and Mowlam

---

* The events referred to as 'Bloody Sunday' occurred on 27 January 1972 when the British Parachute Regiment fired live rounds into an illegal but otherwise peaceful civil rights march in Derry, killing 13 people instantly (another died later); 17 people were injured. The Tribunal of Inquiry set up after these events under Lord Widgery exonerated the soldiers and was regarded in the Catholic community as a 'whitewash'. More recent calls for a fresh inquiry, together with the publication by the Irish government of *Bloody Sunday and the Report of the Widgery Tribunal* in January 1998 led to the establishment of a full-scale judicial inquiry later in 1998.

apologised to the victims even as she entered the prison, referring, for justification, to the larger goal of peace. Yet some of those bereaved and injured were angry at such gestures and remain unwilling to concede to prisoners or to sacrifice what they considered to be justice – that prisoners should serve their sentences. Early release of prisoners gave rise in some quarters – particularly amongst former members of the security forces and sections of unionism – to a sense of further injustice.

The sense of injustice in other quarters sprang from the lack of legal pursuit of the perpetrators of acts of violence, or the lack of prosecutions. Yet others, mainly in the nationalist community within which the overwhelming majority of deaths by the security forces occurred, felt doubly denied justice: by the original act, by the security forces and then by the lack of redress.

Compromise comes before justice in many political agreements and peace settlements. Where such agreements have been made, justice for the individual may never be achieved. Yet some of these individuals remain reluctant or unwilling to relinquish their individual claim to justice. In other cases, there has been a reopening of legal cases, and the institution of public inquiries where a case has an iconic significance for a community, such as in the case of Bloody Sunday. Whether justice will be achieved to the satisfaction of the victims, their families or supporters is yet to be determined. It does, however, seem apparent that the goal of achieving justice and that of achieving closure or peace of mind can often be at cross purposes. The reopening of the painful events and wrongs of the past through legal or public processes involves the reopening of old wounds, and the re-stimulation of traumatic and painful memories. The choice to forgo their claim to justice in the interests of avoiding the pain of this process must rest with those who have suffered. However, families can be divided on this issue. Some find themselves unable to contemplate the prospect of any kind of closure without justice. In cases such as Bloody Sunday that have an iconic significance to one community, the reopening of cases by public legal processes may serve to achieve both a symbolic and personal resolution of injustice. Other less well-known cases will undoubtedly be left unresolved. Even where a wholesale truth process has been instituted, as in South Africa, resolution remains incomplete and, to many participants and non-participants alike, unsatisfactory.

HEALING

Since the ceasefires of 1994, it has been possible to consider the impact of the violence of the Troubles on the population. Consequently, there has been an upsurge in interest in attending to the damage done by the violence of the past. There is an increasing tendency to pathologise the damage done by the Troubles and to see the issue in exclusively psychological terms. According to this view, counselling, usually on an individual basis, is the solution. However, the main and most effective support directed at those who have suffered in the Troubles has come not from mental health or other professionals, but from their immediate families, close neighbours and communities (Fay et al., 1999b). If any professional is consulted, it is most likely to be the family doctor. In these circumstances, particularly in the past, psychotropic medication was often offered by the general practitioner as a means of coping. Often medication has been the only means of help at the disposal of the family doctor, yet the use of medication has created further problems of addiction to psychotropic mediation, particularly amongst women in communities worst affected by the Troubles.

Some communities – in North and West Belfast, the border counties and elsewhere – have borne a disproportionate amount of loss and suffering as a result of the three decades of violence. The pressure on families and communities in these areas that have seen the worst effects of the Troubles has been enormous, often compounded the pressure of deprivation and other forms of marginalisation. Whilst there is an individual aspect to the issue of healing, it is not an exclusively individual or family issue. Whole communities have been affected and it is not clear how the community dimension can be effectively addressed.

Support services within health and social services have been ill-equipped in the past – and in the post-ceasefire situation – to offer help and support to those affected by the loss and grief caused by the Troubles. On the one hand, a lack of trust between statutory services and the community has impeded access to what services there are. On the other, a culture of silence and denial within the professions – a culture that was once a 'coping mechanism' – continues to operate. This silence and lack of professional guidance disables many who work in existing services from dealing effectively with Troubles-related issues. Since a recent inspection of services to those bereaved and injured in the Troubles, it is generally agreed that retraining of many within professional services is required. It remains to be seen whether the resources to do so will be forthcoming (DHSS/Park, 1998).

Most of the communities that have been worst-affected by the Troubles are also the poorest and most marginalised in the United Kingdom, therefore the availability of resources is a key issue. Poverty not only damages health but also compromises the ability to heal. Recovery and healing requires an environment in which safety, respect and sympathetic listeners are available. In many of the communities worst-affected, ongoing violence, now criminal and drug-related, precludes the achievement of the first condition for healing.

Conducive environments may be available in certain locations outside these communities to those bereaved and injured who are able to avail of the small number of services available in the voluntary sector. However, many return to communities in which the living conditions re-traumatise them by exposure to other forms of violence. From May 1998 to June 2000, the government has spent £5.25 million in this field. No further announcement of funding was imminent at that point. The political will and the fiscal resources are prerequisites to further advances in the welfare of those affected by Troubles-related violence.

There was a period during the announcement of concessions to prisoners when it was politically essential that the government was seen to be proactive in making provision for those bereaved and injured. There has been much anxiety in the voluntary and community sector that substantial political commitment to provide for those who have suffered will not survive that initial period when concessions to paramilitary organisations were seemingly offset by announcements of aid to victims. The record of the Northern Ireland Assembly on these issues will undoubtedly be carefully scrutinised in times to come.

CONCLUSION

Why is the conflict in Northern Ireland so intractable? Because the material experience of Northern Ireland is determined by very particular aspects of identity (and identifications), location (in terms of location and class) and ease of access to weapons. Therefore experience is diverse and fragmented and because of the strength and power of experience or profound danger, it is usually blind to other forms of experience. Those who are dirt-poor and who take up arms against their oppressors end up in Armani suits in the corridors of power. Some others have enriched themselves by using their weaponry in the drugs trade. Much of the power of these political representatives in the past has rested on their ability to deliver the paramilitary organisations. As time goes on and they become more and more involved in constitutional politics, perhaps it is inevitable that this will become harder and harder to do. It is further compounded by the adaptations that they have had to make in order to participate in the formal political world. The embourgeoisement of the working-class representatives is an inevitable process, also witnessed in South Africa where the new black politicians were bitterly resented by some in the townships for their mobile phones, sharp clothes and limousines whilst there was still no proper sanitation in the communities that elected them. It is too facile to see the LVF and the Real and Continuity IRA as the resentful, denim-clad rump of the proletariat. Undoubtedly, however, some of their appeal is rooted in an analysis that argues that participation in the formal political arena is a diversion, and that only force can bring about the required radical change in the situation of the marginalised and oppressed. Whatever the merits of that argument, it is also the marginalised and oppressed who have paid the highest price in the last three decades showing every sign of war-weariness and the desire for an end to the violence.

Within Northern Ireland, preoccupation with the past is perhaps due to a widespread sense of grievance and hurt as a result of the losses sustained in the Troubles. Whilst some advocate 'burying the past' and 'putting it all behind us', others – not always those who have lost most – find themselves unable to do so. In 1905, Santayana wrote:

> Progress, far from consisting in change, depends on retentiveness … Those who cannot remember the past are condemned to repeat it.

Yet the past in a violently divided society such as Northern Ireland is often experienced as unmanageable. Individual and collective histories cannot be rewritten and must be lived with. The desire to avoid the pain of facing the past and to avoid responsibility, shame and guilt are understandable. However, attempting to bury the past is not a reliable strategy, as Augusto Pinochet and others discovered late in life. Things that are buried do not necessarily disappear.

Some take root and grow, only to resurface or be dug up by others in the future.

Whether reconciliation is achievable or even necessary in order to achieve a long-lasting peace is an academic point in Northern Ireland since the prospects for reconciliation seem as distant as ever. Division and feuding within communities has proliferated since the beginning of the peace process, replacing the impetus for reconciliation with concern for the maintenance of the end to hostilities. New problems have replaced the old ones. In the long term, it remains to be seen whether a failure to attend to the management of the past will store up problems for the future. Can people forgive even if they can't forget? Is it just and equitable to expect people to forgive when regret and remorse have not been expressed? Northern Ireland cannot yet answer these questions.

In Northern Ireland, it is now possible to recognise the brink of war. The peace process itself has gone several times to that brink. Most but by no means all of those involved have wished to turn back. That wish to turn back is based on an understanding and recognition of the costs of war. Thus the prospects for peace depend on the past and its losses being remembered painfully and well. This same form of remembering, however, can be used to legitimise a return to war. Perhaps the most important goal in work on victims and victimisation in Northern Ireland is to foster the kind of remembering and understanding that deters from further violence. The achievement of that goal would indeed be a victory for both sides.

Appendix 1:
Constructing a Database on Sectarian Assassination

The Northern Ireland material on sectarian assassination is based on an analysis of a sub-set of data drawn from a database (Fay et al., 1999a) of deaths resulting from political violence. The total database contains data on approximately 3700 deaths that took place from 1969 until the time of writing. In each case the database contains data on the date of death; the first name and surname of the victim; the age at death; gender; religion; affiliation – whether civilian, member of the security forces, or a paramilitary organisation; home address; address at which the death took place and the cause of death.

While death depicts the most extreme manifestation of the conflict, it is also a good surrogate for violence in general. A comparison of the numbers of deaths each year and the number of injuries associated with political violence shows a correlation coefficient of 0.93. Injuries outnumber deaths by just over ten to one but have exactly the same cycle. The combination of deaths and injuries represents the primary human cost of the Northern Ireland Troubles although these do not encompass the trauma of grief, imprisonment and intimidation.

In order to examine deaths due to 'sectarian killing' in Northern Ireland it was necessary to trawl the database and eliminate certain categories of death. Not all deaths in the Trouble can be considered to be as a result of 'sectarian killing'. However, the process of deciding which deaths to exclude and which to include was an exercise in constructing an operational definition of 'sectarian killing'. Like all definitions, it was aimed at delineating and therefore delimiting the phenomenon. Like all definitions it contains borderline categories and grey areas, and, in other circumstances or at other points in the history of the conflict, the definition might have been constructed differently.

Sectarian killing, like hate killing, is distinguished from, for example, the kind of violence associated with drugs or gang warfare in that it targets members of specific racial, national, ethnic or religious groups, and any or all members of that group are potential legitimate targets of attack according to the perpetrators. Since the violence is based on a demonisation of an entire group, it is not personal or dependent on personal knowledge of the individual target. Any member of the target group will meet the criteria for a suitable target. Whilst sectarian killing is often indiscriminate in that it is not targeted at a specific individual, it none the less has a personal dimension. The victim may be abused in personal terms, or may be selected and treated in a manner that manifests the personal and political dominance of the attacker's group over the victim's group. Members of the attacker's group who have associated with or advocated members of the target group may also be the victims of sectarian killing on the grounds of betrayal of their own kind.

The selection made of the data on deaths in Northern Ireland in the light of this understanding of sectarian killing had to take into account all aspects of the definition. Some would argue that all killing in Northern Ireland's Troubles has been sectarian in nature. However, it has emerged during the peace negotiations that there has been some renewed recognition of the political motivations in terms of competing nationalisms of the paramilitary organisations. This has entailed granting some legitimacy to the construction of the conflict as a 'war' fought against an enemy in order to achieve certain political goals. All protagonists, including the security forces, tend to portray themselves as high-minded soldiers who simultaneously waged a ruthless and bloody war against the enemy whilst still helping old ladies across the road. None the less, periodically it becomes apparent in various ways – in courts of inquiry and in the burgeoning memoir industry (of ex-IRA members and the SAS, for example) – that the Northern Ireland Troubles have given rise to, that significant numbers within the ranks of the various protagonists were motivated by hatred rather than high-mindedness. The degree to which this is true has varied between groups and across time.

A series of decisions and steps were taken to select the deaths regarded as sectarian. First, the deaths of those who were not from Northern Ireland were eliminated on the grounds that sectarian killings were related to the dynamic between the two communities in Northern Ireland. Whilst people from outside Northern Ireland have been killed, they cannot be considered to be part of the dynamic of sectarian killing. They have been caught up – some by accident, some by profession – rather than being targets of sectarian killing themselves. Therefore although significant numbers of people, particularly members of the British security forces, have been killed, their deaths are construed as part of a different dynamic and distinct motivation from that of sectarian killing.

Second, deaths of all those from Northern Ireland who were primary protagonists in the conflict were eliminated. All of those whose occupation or paramilitary affiliations involved them directly in the conflict rendered them targets for reasons other than simple membership of a religious or national group. This involved excluding members of local security forces or attributed members of paramilitary organisations (the latter can be detected from death notices in local newspapers).

Fourth, the majority of those who died as the result of explosions were eliminated. In the main, bombs were directed at security or economic targets. Although many civilians died as a result of such acts, they were not the primary victims. Loyalists have frequently claimed that their motivation for joining paramilitary groups was a response to the IRA bombing campaign of the 1970s (see interview with David Irvine in Taylor, 1999). Bombs were perceived as being targeted directly at the Loyalist community. However, civilian victims were both Protestant and Catholic. Accordingly such deaths, no matter how deplorable, cannot be included in the category of sectarian killing. Not all bombing, however, can be excluded. In the late 1990s certain Loyalist groups took to targeting the homes of individual Catholics with pipe bombs and this resulted in a death in Portadown. A family of a 'mixed' marriage inhabited the house targeted and this was the motivation for the attack. Such incidents were retained.

Other bombings were more problematic. Republicans killed ten people with a bomb in a shop on the Shankill Road. Their target was a UFF meeting that was to take place in an upper room. The intended victims were thus members of a paramilitary organisation. However, it is difficult to see how the deaths of civilians below could have been avoided. Were the deaths of ordinary Protestants an acceptable price for dealing a serious blow to a Loyalist paramilitary organisation? The question is particularly pertinent given the fact that the bomb exploded prematurely killing one of the IRA men involved and nine other shoppers. Similarly in the 1970s, a Catholic pub was targeted by Loyalist paramilitaries on the grounds that Republicans were meeting there. Subsequently, it was demonstrated that this was not the case. Was the rationale simply a cover for sectarian killing or a mistaken belief coupled with a disregard for collateral Catholic victims? In such cases, it is almost impossible to make objective decisions or to create the perfect database on sectarian killing. The deaths associated with both of the above events were excluded even though strong arguments could be advanced for their inclusion.

Finally, paramilitary organisations have killed their co-religionists either by mistake or in feuds or other miscellaneous acts. Such deaths were also excluded since they fell outside the scope of what is meant by the term 'sectarian'.

Appendix 2: Background to the Northern Ireland Survey

THE QUESTIONNAIRE

The questionnaire for the survey was designed in five parts, as follows.

1. Cover Sheet and Introduction

This first section contained the date of the interview, questionnaire serial number, ward and interviewer codes, to be used for response rate monitoring and quality control purposes. A written introduction to the survey was also provided for the interviewer to read to each interviewee. This introduction set out the purpose of the survey, conditions of confidentiality, distress and arrangements for further support and help if required.

2. Demographics

This section elicited data on household composition, tenure and type of housing, occupation and work status, benefits and income, and religion and ethnic origin.

3. Health and Well-Being

A standardised measure of health was included in the questionnaire. The General Health Questionnaire was rejected on the ground that it elicited insufficient data on emotional and psychological health. The Short Form 36 (SF36) contained a wider range of data, but comprised 36 questions overall. Since the questionnaire was already lengthy, a shorter version of the SF36 was used. The SF12, comprising only 12 questions, was embedded in the questionnaire. However, one question in the SF12 was worded: 'Have you felt downhearted and blue?' The word 'blue' was altered to 'depressed'. A further question was also added asking respondents to identify causes, including Troubles-related causes, for changes in their health.

4. Experience of the Troubles

The section containing questions that elicited data on respondents' experience of the Troubles was designed as a result of the analysis of the qualitative data, the transcripts of the 85 in-depth interviews. The analysis of the qualitative data involved organising it into categories, and a coding tree was devised by which the interview transcripts were coded. This coding tree formed the structure for questions in the questionnaire on the experience and effects of the Troubles. The main sections on this tree were as shown in Figure A2.1.

At a later stage in the qualitative analysis other nodes were added to the tree, but at the time when the questionnaire was designed, the branches illustrated informed the design of the questionnaire. The two key areas of enquiry were 'Experiences of the Troubles' and 'Effects of the Troubles'.

Using the data collected in interviews, questions in the questionnaire were arranged according to the degree of intensity of experiences, so that they began with relatively common and less distressing experiences of the Troubles and escalated gradually to the more severe and distressing experiences, and took the following form:

- Common experiences (seeing news broadcasts)
- More direct experiences (being stopped at roadblocks)
- Work experiences/intimidation (conflict or threats)
- Severe experiences (injury of friends or family)
- Injury or death in the Troubles (death of close family, personal injury)

To this section three other issues were added:

- Responsibility for Troubles
- Time periods of the Troubles that affected the respondent
- Specific events that affected the respondent

Issues and comments that had recurred in the interviews were used to inform the design of the questions on experience of the Troubles.

5. Effects of Troubles

Similarly, design of the section on effects of the Troubles was partly informed by data collected in interviews with the exception of the first two sections, the first of which examined Post-Traumatic Stress Disorder symptoms, and the second of which examined the recency and onset of these symptoms and disruption to life caused by them. The sections were as follows:

- PTS symptoms
- Recency, onset and disruption to life

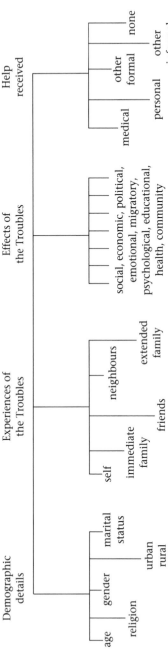

Figure A2.1   Coding Tree for Data

- Medication and self-medication
- Effect on health
- Effect on family
- Effect on education, work, income
- Effect on leisure
- Effect on moral attitudes
- Effect on political attitudes
- Effect on attitude to law and order
- Degree of effect
- Access to and use of help and support
- Compensation
- Legal redress

Again, questions were worded to reflect the range of responses encountered in the interview data. A draft questionnaire was designed and circulated to the advisory group, the Board of Directors and other interested parties for comment. The draft design was amended after each set of suggestions from one source and recirculated. This process was repeated each time substantial amendments were made. Whilst time-consuming and at times frustrating, after approximately 12 drafts a final version of the questionnaire was agreed for piloting.

FIELD FORCE, RECRUITMENT, TRAINING, DEBRIEFING

The administration of the questionnaire was subcontracted to a survey agency, although the research team was involved in setting criteria for recruitment of the field force. The posts for interviewers were advertised in local Training and Employment Agencies and universities. Successful applicants were required to have previous experience in administering questionnaires, the ability to record information clearly and accurately, the ability to deal sympathetically and sensitively with interviewees and an understanding of the importance of confidentiality. Advertisements for posts stated that it was desirable but not essential for candidates to have a university degree. In the main, interviewers selected were graduates, and where possible local interviewees were used to interview within their own community. Interviewers were provided with training on questionnaire administration, on ethical issues involved in the fieldwork, and the range of response likely to be encountered in interviewees. The research team also provided debriefing sessions for interviewers and were available to take referrals from them should the need arise to make a referral to a supportive service. The field force was piloted alongside the questionnaire and any skills or performance issues addressed prior to beginning the main survey.

PILOTING THE QUESTIONNAIRE

Each interviewer was given four questionnaires and four addresses in his or her ward. From the pilot, it emerged that the questionnaire required only minor adjustments to some of the instructions, and to the wording in one or two questions. These adjustments were made. It was also discovered that interviewers were not recording all responses and tended to record only the positive responses. More problematic, however, was the discovery that the electoral list seemed to have a large number of invalid addresses. The response rate was low, partly due to the large number of invalid addresses and partly due to other factors that were not entirely clear. After the necessary amendments were made to the questionnaire and further briefings were given to the field force on question completion, arrangements were complete. The difficulties with the electoral list were beyond the researchers' control. A vigorous publicity campaign on the survey was launched in order to maximise the response rate and to lower levels of suspicion in certain wards. In this way, some of the possible difficulties with response rates were addressed. (A copy of the final questionnaire is included as Appendix 3.)

At one point discussion had taken place about the advisability of using a financial incentive to increase the response rate, but the Board of Directors felt that this was inappropriate given the nature of the survey. Instead, information leaflets on the survey and on The Cost of the Troubles Study were prepared and a mailshot of over 400 community groups throughout Northern Ireland was conducted through the use of Northern Ireland Council for Voluntary Action's circulation of *Scope* magazine. Second, press releases on the survey were prepared and sent to all newspapers and media outlets. Third, a letter was written to all denominations of churches in the target wards, giving information about the survey and asking for co-operation.

SAMPLING

The initial proposal specified 3000 attempted questionnaires or roughly 1 in 500 of the region's population. The challenge was to find a sampling procedure that would adequately reflect the population as a whole whilst simultaneously generating sufficient cases in those areas most affected by the Troubles to make their analysis worth while. In order to do so the following sample procedure was adopted.

From the database of Troubles-related deaths, a calculation was made of the number of residents of each Northern Ireland ward who had died in the Troubles. This was achieved by translating postcodes into ward locations. This procedure ignored the deaths of non-Northern Ireland residents, in order to concentrate exclusively on the regional population. Ideally, an average figure for ward population should have been constructed by taking the average from each of the 1971, 1981 and 1991 Censuses, since the deaths occurred over a 30-year period. However, wards change over time and it was thus impossible to give an average ward population over the two decades. Accordingly, the ward population figures were taken from the 1991 Census throughout. From these two figures a ward 'death rate' was then constructed and all wards in Northern Ireland were ranked in descending order. Three groups of wards were identified:

- Those with the highest death rates (7 or more deaths per 1000 population); there were 10 of these wards
- Those with medium death rates (ranging from 2.0 to 6.9 deaths per 1000); there were 122 of these wards
- Those with low death rates (ranging from 0.0 to 1.9 deaths per 1000); there were 424 of these wards.

All of the wards in the group with the highest death rates were surveyed. From each of the other two groups, 10 wards were selected on a random basis. The sampling fractions were thus 1.0, 0.082 and 0.024. Sampling was thus proportionate to the intensity of politically motivated deaths. The end result was a sample of 30 wards stratified by death rates. The second stage of the sampling procedure involved selecting 1000 cases were randomly selected from the 1997 electoral register from within each group of wards. The number of cases in individual wards was proportionate to the ward's share of its group population.

It was anticipated that the sample would probably survey disproportionate numbers of Catholics, since the wards with the highest death rates were disproportionately Catholic. Initial returns on the survey led to concern about a possible low response rate amongst Protestants. However, it emerged on analysis of the pilot and of the wards sampled, that it was a feature of the sampling frame. None the

Table A2.1 Numbers and Rates of Response by Ward

Ward name	No. attempted	No. ineligibles	No. attempted minus no. ineligibles	No. achieved	Completion rate (%)	Ward population 1991	Achieved as % of Ward population
Wards with high death rates:							
Falls	111	19	92	58	63.0	5215	1.1
Ardoyne	119	15	104	74	71.2	6340	1.2
Clonard	106	32	74	41	55.4	5475	0.7
Waterworks	119	5	114	70	61.4	5742	1.2
Whiterock	102	14	88	74	84.1	5285	1.4
New Lodge	118	8	110	50	45.5	6385	0.8
Valley	66	11	55	24	43.6	2316	1.0
Ballymacarrett	100	3	97	6	6.2	4899	0.1
Upper Springfield	111	14	97	70	72.2	6186	1.1
Newtownhamilton	47	14	33	4	12.1	2336	0.2
High totals	999	135	864	471	54.5	50,179	0.9
Wards with middle-range death rates:							
Charlemont	79	9	70	49	70	2194	2.2
Creggan South	80	19	61	45	73.8	2361	1.9
Killycolpy	69	4	66	50	75.6	2199	2.3

Carrigatuke	72	7	65	36	53.4	2157	1.7
Fortwilliam	169	22	147	56	38.1	5114	1.1
Ballysillan	194	26	168	36	21.4	4857	0.7
Newtownbutler	83	4	79	62	78.5	2285	2.7
Termon	74	2	72	43	59.7	2245	1.9
Annagh	89	11	79	43	54.4	2353	1.8
Corcrain	90	21	69	55	79.7	2961	1.9
Middle totals	999	125	876	475	54.2	28,726	1.7
Wards with low death rates:							
Ballee	80	14	66	27	40.9	2485	1.1
Coalisland South	82	3	79	58	73.4	2023	2.9
Drumgullion	104	11	93	42	45.2	3025	1.4
Fairy Water	69	12	57	31	54.4	1872	1.7
Finaghy	188	48	140	71	50.7	6702	1.1
Gilnahirk	97	1	96	21	21.9	2920	0.7
Glen	104	11	93	56	60.2	3038	1.8
Harmony Hill	113	2	111	24	21.6	3839	0.6
Lawrencetown	77	1	76	49	64.5	1966	2.5
Randalstown	86	10	76	31	40.8	2061	1.5
Low totals	1000	113	887	410	46.2	29,931	1.4
Overall totals	2998	373	2627	1356	51.6	108,836	1.2

less, given the uncertain political climate at the time together with the sensitive nature of the survey, it was considered necessary to disseminate as much information as possible in order to help maximise our response rate. A deterioration in the political situation around Christmas 1997 slowed the fieldwork down and meant an unforeseeably long period in the field. However, the fieldwork eventually concluded and a clean SPSS file was delivered at the end of April 1998.

ADMINISTERING THE QUESTIONNAIRE

After the interviewers began work, they could report any particular difficulties they were encountering at debriefing sessions. In areas least affected by the Troubles interviewers reported lower response rates. An interim report on fieldwork written in December 1997 showed 14 wards with fewer than 10 completed questionnaires. At this stage in the fieldwork management it was necessary to analyse the reasons for low returns in some wards, and rectify any problems. Two hypotheses formed about the low returns for these wards: either conditions in certain wards caused the difficulties, or the problem was the performance of the interviewer in that ward. Reallocations of 'productive' interviewers to wards with low return rates demonstrated that much of the problem was due to interviewers. However, two wards, Newtownhamilton and Ballymacarrett, proved to be too large a challenge for even for the best interviewers. In both these wards, fewer than 10 questionnaires were completed. In the case of Newtownhamilton, we subsequently learned that there was a great deal of strong feeling in the area about the effects of the Troubles, and a local pressure group was formed in the area in mid-1998. In the case of Ballymacarrett, the cause of the low return rate remains unknown.

Table A2.1 identifies the 30 wards, and indicates the attempted number of interviews and the number of questionnaires actually completed.

There was a high level of ineligibles (12.4 per cent) drawn in the sample, although the rate was 25.5 per cent in one ward (Finaghy). The 1997 electoral list was used, which has subsequently been the subject of scrutiny due to doubts about its validity, and this is reflected in our sample. The validity problem with the electoral list immediately reduced the size of our valid sample. Furthermore, within wards, there was significant variation in the numbers of achieved interviews and therefore of completion rates. The very low response rates in Ballymacarrett and Newtownhamilton, are apparent in the table, in spite of redeploying interviewers. The variation in coverage of ward populations in the case of five wards – Clonard, Ballymacarett, Newtownhamilton, Ballysillan and Harmony Hill – falls below 1 per cent of the ward population. Overall coverage of the wards with high death rates (0.9 per cent) was lower than for medium death rates (1.7 per cent) or low death rates (1.4 per cent) wards. However, it should be noted that each questionnaire elicits data on a household so that in all some data was collected on over 4500 individuals. In some wards, completed questionnaires represented over 2.0 per cent of the ward population. In others, however, the figure was closer to 0.2 per cent. Nevertheless, certain questionnaire data relate to a higher proportion of the ward population – around 4.0 per cent.

Arguably, the complications of this sampling procedure undermine the survey's claim to be representative of the Northern Ireland population. However, there is no perfect sampling procedure particularly for a survey in which the aim was to be able to compare those areas where the experience of violence was greatest with those which had no direct experience of it. The end result was 1356 completed questionnaires probing some of the worst experiences of people's lives, with just over a third from those areas where the Troubles were most intense. The selected wards represented about 6 per cent of the region's population.

Appendix 3:
The Cost of the Troubles Study Questionnaire*

Date of interview _|_|_

Questionnaire serial number _____

Ward code _____   Interviewer code _____

Before starting the interview:

'The Cost of the Troubles' wrote to you about taking part in the survey it is carrying out into the effects of the troubles on people right across Northern Ireland.

You will have received a letter from us and a leaflet explaining the aims of our work. You may remember that we aim to establish the extent to which the troubles have affected people in all sections of the community, with a view to improving public understanding and services to people affected in various ways. We believe our work is worthwhile and important, and we hope you agree. We would be grateful for your participation in the survey. It is important that you participate, no matter how much or how little experience you have of the troubles.

All the information you may give me will be treated in strictest confidence, and I will not write down your name or other identifying details.

Some of the questions ask about experiences which are distressing. The questions ask about your experience of the troubles and are not intended to be intrusive. However, you may need to think about whether you wish to go ahead. I will listen sensitively and sympathetically. Some people have found that they felt better after talking about their experiences. If you want, I can also give you an advice leaflet and the names and phone numbers of helping organisations which work in this field, if you wish to get in touch with them. The decision to go ahead is yours and I would greatly appreciate it if you would add your experiences to our study. We wish to have a wide range of views and experiences included in our survey, and we would like you to be part of it.

Complete all items – only leave blank in the event of a refusal or where the respondent is directed away from the item

* This questionnaire includes the SF-12 Health Survey, item numbers 23–34 in this questionnaire. Reproduced with permission of the Medical Outcomes Trust, © The Health Institute 1994; New England Medical Centre.

SECTION A: HOUSEHOLD

		Male	Female	Total
1	How many people, including you, are there in the household? (Complete all cells. If there is no one in a particular category write '0')	___	___	___

2   How many including you are aged:
(Complete all cells)

		Male	Female	Total
(a)	0–4			
(b)	5–9	___	___	___
(c)	10–14	___	___	___
(d)	15–19	___	___	___
(e)	20–24	___	___	___
(f)	25–39	___	___	___
(g)	40–59	___	___	___
(h)	60–64	___	___	___
(i)	65–79	___	___	___
(j)	80+	___	___	___

3   What is your age?   ___

4   Are you:
Male   1
Female   2

5   How many in the household are ... ?
(Complete all cells)

		Male	Female	Total
(a)	Married			
(b)	Single	___	___	___
(c)	Widowed	___	___	___
(d)	Single parents	___	___	___
(e)	Separated/divorced	___	___	___

6   Are you

Married	1	Single parents	4
Single	2	Separated/divorced	5
Widowed	3		

7   How many in the household including you are ... ?
(Complete all cells)

		Male	Female	Total
(a)	In full-time or part-time employment	___	___	___
(b)	On benefits	___	___	___
(c)	At school	___	___	___
(d)	In full-time or part-time continuing/higher education	___	___	___

8   What is the highest level of educational qualifications you have gained?

None	1	Undergraduate degree	5
CSE/NVQ	2	Postgraduate degree	6
O Level/GCSE	3	Professional qualification	7
A Level/ B.Tech	4	Other	8

SECTION B: TENURE AND HOUSING

9   What type of accommodation is occupied by this household?

A caravan or other mobile or temporary structure	1
A whole house or bungalow that is a detached house	2
A whole house or bungalow that is semi-detached	3
A whole house or bungalow that is terraced/include end of terrace	4
The whole of a purpose built flat or maisonette in a commercial building (e.g. in an office building or hotel or over a shop)	5
The whole of a purpose built flat or maisonette in a block of flats	6
Part of a converted or shared house, bungalow or flat with a separate entrance into the building	7
Part of a converted or shared house, bungalow or flat with a shared entrance into the building	8

10   Which of the following best describes your home?

Part of a current or former Housing Executive/public housing estate or development in a town or city setting	1
Part of a current or former Housing Executive/public housing estate or development in a rural setting	2
Part of a sheltered housing development in a town or city setting	3
Rural/isolated setting	4
Publicly owned house/flat in a village	5
In a private development	6
Not part of an estate or development	7
Don't Know/No response	8
Other	9

11   What type of tenure is your home?

Rented	1
Owned	2
Co-ownership	3

12   Housing segregation is widespread in Northern Ireland. Do you see the area you live in as segregated?

Yes   1   No   2

SECTION C: OCCUPATION/WORK

Interviewer instructions: the interviewees definition of work should be accepted, but it must be PAID work. Someone who is retired and sits on a Board or committee and is paid for this work is not regarded as in paid work. Baby sitting, running a mail order club, etc. IS regarded as paid work.

13   Did you do any paid work in the 7 days ending Sunday last, either as an employee or as self-employed?

Yes   1   No   2

14   Which of these descriptions applies to your main activity in the last week, that is the 7 days ending Sunday?

Self-employed (full-time)	1
Self-employed (part-time at least 10 hours per week)	2
Full-time employment	3
Part-time employment (at least 10 hours per week)	4

Employment training	5
Waiting to take up work	6
Registered unemployed	7
Unemployed but not registered	8
Permanently sick or disabled	9
Wholly retired from work	10
Looking after the home	11
At school/full-time education	12
Doing something else	13

Benefits

15 Do you or any member of your household receive at present any of the following state benefits? (Complete all items – if the answer is negative circle 'No')

		Yes	No	Don't Know
(a)	Jobseeker's allowance	1	2	3
(b)	Income support	1	2	3
(c)	One-parent benefit	1	2	3
(d)	Family credit	1	2	3
(e)	Housing benefit (rent rebate)	1	2	3
(f)	Statutory sick pay/sickness benefit	1	2	3
(g)	Incapacity benefit	1	2	3
(h)	Disability living allowance (65+)	1	2	3
(i)	Widow's pension	1	2	3
(j)	Attendance allowance (65+)	1	2	3
(k)	Severe disablement allowance	1	2	3
(l)	Child benefit	1	2	3
(m)	State retirement pension	1	2	3
(n)	Industrial injuries payment	1	2	3
(o)	Invalid care allowance	1	2	3
(p)	Other state benefits	1	2	3
(q)	None of the above	1	2	3

SECTION D: INCOME

16 What is your own personal income before tax and national insurance contributions? Include all income from employment and benefits.

£_____

17 What period does this income relate to:

Yearly	1	Fortnightly	4
Monthly	2	Other (please specify)	5
Weekly	3		

18 What is your total household income before tax and National Insurance contributions? Include all income from employment and benefits.

£_____

19 What period does this income relate to:

Yearly	1	Fortnightly	4
Monthly	2	Other (please specify)	5
Weekly	3		

SECTION E: RELIGION AND ETHNIC ORIGIN

20 In terms of the two communities in Northern Ireland, are you considered
    by others to be:
    A member of the Catholic community   1
    A member of the Protestant community   2
    Other   3

SECTION F: DISABILITY

21 Do you have a long-standing illness disability or infirmity?
    By long-standing I mean anything that has troubled you over a period of time or that
    is likely to affect you over a period of time?
    Yes   1   No   2

22 If yes to Question 21, to what extent does this disability affect your life?
    Severe restriction, e.g. on mobility/unable to work/leave the home 1
    Considerable restriction, e.g. unable to go out unaccompanied   2
    Moderate restriction, e.g. unable to drive   3
    Mild restriction, e.g. need to avoid certain areas/things   4
    Other   5

SECTION G: HEALTH AND WELL-BEING: SF-12

Now I would like to ask you some questions about your health.

23 In general would you say your health is ...
Excellent	Very Good	Good	Fair	Poor
5	4.4	3.4	2	1

The following items are about activities you might do during a typical day. Does
your health now limit you in these activities?

If so, how much?

24 Moderate activities, such as moving a table, pushing a vacuum cleaner,
    bowling or playing golf:
Yes, limited a lot	Yes, limited a little	No, not limited at all
1	2	3

25 Climbing several flights of stairs
Yes, limited a lot	Yes, limited a little	No, not limited at all
1	2	3

During the past 4 weeks, have you had any of the following problems with your
work or other regular daily activities as a result of your physical health?

26 Accomplished less than you would like
    Yes   1   No   2

27 Were limited in the kind of work or other activities
    Yes   1   No   2

During the past 4 weeks, have you had any of the following problems with your work or other regular daily activities as a result of any emotional problems (such as feeling depressed or anxious)?

28 Accomplished less than you would like
    Yes   1   No   2

29 Didn't do work or other activities as carefully as usual
    Yes   1   No   2

30 During the past 4 weeks, how much did pain interfere with your normal work (including both work outside the home and housework)?

Not at all	A little bit	Moderately	Quite a bit	Extremely
6	4.75	3.5	2.25	1

These questions are about how you feel and how things have been with you during the past 4 weeks. For each question, please give one answer that comes closest to the way you have been feeling.

How much of the time during the past 4 weeks:

	All of the time	Most of the time	A good bit of the time	Some of the time	A little of the time	None of the time
31 Have you felt calm and peaceful?	6	5	4	3	2	1
32 Did you have a lot of energy?	6	5	4	3	2	1
33 Have you felt downhearted and depressed?	1	2	3	4	5	6

34 During the past 4 weeks, how much of the time has your physical health or emotional problems interfered with your social activities (like visiting friends, relatives, etc.)?

All of the time	Most of the time	A good bit of the time	Some of the time	A little of the time	None of the time
1	2	3	4	5	

35 How true or false is *each* of the following statements for you?

	Definitely True	Mostly True	Don't Know	Mostly False	Definitely False
I seem to get sick a little easier than other people	1	2	3	4	5
I am as healthy as anybody I know	1	2	3	4	5
I expect my health to get worse	1	2	3	4	5
My health is excellent	1	2	3	4	5

36   If there is a change in your health over the past 5–10 years what, in your opinion, caused this change? (Complete all items – if answer is negative circle 'No')

		Yes	No	No Response
(a)	Troubles-related trauma: e.g. bombings, shootings, intimidation, attacks	1	2	3
(b)	Troubles-related bereavement	1	2	3
(c)	Non-Troubles-related trauma: e.g. road accident, accident in the home	1	2	3
(d)	Non-Troubles-related bereavement	1	2	3
(e)	Occupational factors: stress, chemical pollution	1	2	3
(f)	Environmental factors: poor housing, lead pollution	1	2	3
(g)	Genetic disorder/progressive disease	1	2	3
(h)	Financial worries/shortages	1	2	3
(i)	Loss of job/unemployment	1	2	3
(j)	Isolation	1	2	3
(k)	Street disturbances	1	2	3
(l)	Military presence in my area	1	2	3
(m)	No change in health	1	2	3

SECTION H: EXPERIENCE OF THE TROUBLES

37   How much experience would you say you have of the Troubles?

A lot	Quite a lot	Some	A little	Very little	None
1	2	3	4	5	6

Now, I would like to ask you some questions about specific experiences you may have had of the Troubles. I have a list of experiences that people have had of the troubles, starting with common experiences.

38   Would you tell me how often, if at all, you have had the experience?

Event/experience		Very often	Occasion-ally	Seldom	Never
(a)	Hearing/reading news reports about Troubles-related violence	1	2	3	4
(b)	Getting caught in a bomb scare	1	2	3	4
(c)	Straying into an area where I didn't feel safe	1	2	3	4
(d)	Getting stopped and searched by the security forces	1	2	3	4
(e)	Being stopped in a checkpoint	1	2	3	4
(f)	Feeling unable to say what I think in a situation because of safety issues	1	2	3	4
(g)	Being wary in the presence of people from the other community	1	2	3	4
(h)	Having to take extra safety precautions to secure my home or workplace	1	2	3	4
(i)	Having to change my normal routes, routines or habits because of safety	1	2	3	4

The next question deals with slightly more direct experience of the troubles.

39 Can I ask if you have had any of these experiences, and if so how often?

Event/experience	Very often	Occasion-ally	Seldom	Never
(a) Being called sectarian names *(interviewer: their definition of sectarian)*	1	2	3	4
(b) Having to conceal things about myself – my name or address – because of safety	1	2	3	4
(c) Having to listen to my tradition being criticised or abused	1	2	3	4
(d) Feeling blamed or being blamed for the troubles	1	2	3	4
(e) Having to end friendships or having relationships disrupted because of the sectarian divide	1	2	3	4
(f) Having to turn down work opportunities because of troubles related danger	1	2	3	4
(g) Getting into physical fights about the troubles	1	2	3	4
(h) Having to avoid going into certain areas because of the troubles	1	2	3	4
(i) Having my schooling disrupted by the troubles	1	2	3	4
(j) Being forced to do things against my will	1	2	3	4
(k) Had experience of military organisations acting as punishment agencies	1	2	3	4
(l) Having to pay protection money to a paramilitary	1	2	3	4
(m) Being so afraid that I thought of leaving Northern Ireland	1	2	3	4

Now, I would like to ask about your work experiences.
(For interviewees with no work experience, go to Question 42)

40 Thinking about your current or last job, could you tell me which of the following best describes your workplace?

Mixed 50/50 workplace	1
Mixed, but more of my community	2
Mixed, but less of my community	3
Hardly mixed: very few of the other community	4
Not mixed: all of my community	5
Hardly mixed, very few of my community	6
Not mixed: all of the other community	7
Don't know	8

Intimidation at work

41 Did you have any of the following experiences at work in relation to the Troubles?

	Very often	Occasion-ally	Seldom	Never
(a) Feeling uncomfortable with the attitudes or behaviour of colleagues from my own community	1	2	3	4
(b) Feeling confident that all of us were respected and safe, in spite of our differences	1	2	3	4
(c) Feeling outnumbered	1	2	3	4
(d) Feeling out of place and alienated by the atmosphere at work	1	2	3	4
(e) Feeling unsafe or threatened by some of the attitudes or events at work	1	2	3	4
(f) Feeling unsafe because of direct verbal threats made against me	1	2	3	4
(g) Feeling unsafe because of physical attacks on me or my property	1	2	3	4
(h) Having to leave because of feeling unsafe or because of threats	1	2	3	4

The next question deals with some of the most severe, distressing and direct experience of the Troubles.

42 Can I ask if you have had any of these experiences of the Troubles and if so how often:

	Very often	Occasion-ally	Seldom	Never
(a) Having my work place or business attacked	1	2	3	4
(b) Having my workplace or business destroyed	1	2	3	4
(c) Having my home attacked	1	2	3	4
(d) Having to leave my home temporarily	1	2	3	4
(e) Having to leave my home permanently	1	2	3	4
(f) Having my home destroyed	1	2	3	4
(g) Having my car hijacked/stolen due to the troubles	1	2	3	4
(h) Being close to a bomb explosion	1	2	3	4

The next question deals with situations in the troubles where people have been injured or killed.

43 Can I ask if you have had any of these experiences, and if so how often:

	Several times	More than once	Once	Never
(a) Being caught up in a riot	1	2	3	4
(b) Witnessing a shooting	1	2	3	4
(c) Having a work colleague attacked	1	2	3	4
(d) Having a work colleague killed	1	2	3	4
(e) Having a neighbour attacked	1	2	3	4

(f)	Having a neighbour killed	1	2	3	4
(g)	Seeing people killed or seriously injured	1	2	3	4
(h)	Having a close friend killed	1	2	3	4
(i)	Being physically attacked due to the troubles	1	2	3	4
(j)	Being injured in a bomb explosion	1	2	3	4
(k)	Being injured in a shooting	1	2	3	4
(l)	Having a member of my immediate family injured	1	2	3	4
(m)	Having a member of my immediate family killed	1	2	3	4
(n)	Having another relative injured	1	2	3	4
(o)	Having another relative killed	1	2	3	4

44 How much do you think each of the following are responsible for the troubles?

		Most Responsible	Responsible	Least Responsible	Don't Know
(a)	Republican paramilitaries in general	1	2	3	4
(b)	Loyalist Paramilitaries in general	1	2	3	4
(c)	The RUC	1	2	3	4
(d)	The RIR/UDR	1	2	3	4
(e)	The British Army	1	2	3	4
(f)	Republican politicians	1	2	3	4
(g)	Loyalist politicians	1	2	3	4
(h)	British politicians	1	2	3	4
i)	Irish politicians	1	2	3	4
(j)	All politicians	1	2	3	4
(k)	British government	1	2	3	4
(l)	Irish government	1	2	3	4
(m)	The Churches	1	2	3	4
(n)	The silent majority in Northern Ireland	1	2	3	4
(o)	People living in hard-line areas in NI	1	2	3	4
(p)	Other, please specify	_____			

45 Indicate the extent to which the following periods of the Troubles have affected you.

		Strong effect	Moderate effect	Slight effect	None	Don't remember too young
(a)	1969 and the 1970s	1	2	3	4	5
(b)	The 1980s	1	2	3	4	5
(c)	The early 1990s	1	2	3	4	5
(d)	1994 to present day	1	2	3	4	5

46 To what extent have the following events in the Troubles affected you?

		Affected me strongly	Moderately affected me	Affected me least	Don't remember
(a)	The civil rights campaigns	1	2	3	4
(b)	Internment	1	2	3	4
(c)	The Loyalist general strikes	1	2	3	4

(d)	IRA bombing campaign	1	2	3	4
(e)	Republican targeting of the RUC and security forces	1	2	3	4
(f)	Feuds within Republican paramilitaries	1	2	3	4
(g)	Feuds within Loyalist paramilitaries	1	2	3	4
(h)	The hunger strikes	1	2	3	4
(i)	Sectarian assassinations of Catholics by Loyalist paramilitaries	1	2	3	4
(j)	Sectarian assassinations of Protestants by Republican paramilitaries	1	2	3	4
(k)	Intimidation in housing	1	2	3	4
(l)	Conflicts over parades and marching	1	2	3	4
(m)	Punishment beatings and shootings by Republicans	1	2	3	4
(n)	Punishment beatings and shootings by Loyalists	1	2	3	4
(o)	The Loyalist ceasefire	1	2	3	4
(p)	The Republican ceasefire	1	2	3	4
(q)	Signing of the Anglo-Irish agreement	1	2	3	4
(r)	The alleged shoot-to-kill policy of the RUC	1	2	3	4
(s)	Loyalist bombings in the Republic of Ireland	1	2	3	4

SECTION I: EFFECTS OF THE TROUBLES ON YOU

Some people experience after-effects as a result of their experiences of the Troubles. Can I ask you if you have had after-effects, for example:

		Frequently	Occasion-ally	Rarely	Never	Don't remember
47	Have you ever had a period of time when you kept having painful memories of your experience/s, even when you tried not to think about it?	1	2	3	4	5
48	Have you ever had a period of time when you had repeated dreams and nightmares about your experience/s?	1	2	3	4	5
49	Have you ever had a period of time when you found yourself in a situation which made you feel as though it was all happening over again?	1	2	3	4	5

50 Have you ever had a period   1   2   3   4   5
    of time when you lost interest
    in activities that had meant a
    lot to you before?

51 Have you ever had a period of 1   2   3   4   5
    time when you were very
    jumpy or more easily startled
    than usual or felt that you had
    to be on your guard all the time?

52 Have you ever had a period of 1   2   3   4   5
    time when you had more
    trouble than usual with
    sleeping due to your
    experiences in the troubles?

53 Have there ever been times   1   2   3   4   5
    when you felt ashamed orguilty
    about surviving events in the
    Troubles?

54 How recently have you had the symptoms described in Questions
    47–53?
    Within 6 months   1   5–10 years   4
    6 months–1 year   2   10+ years   5
    1–5 years   3   No symptoms   6

55 Approximately how long after the event/s did the symptoms described
    start?
    Within 6 months   1   10+ years   5
    6 months–1 year   2   No symptoms   6
    1–5 years   3   Don't know   7
    5–10 years   4

56 Have the symptoms interfered in any way with your life?
    Yes, severe interference with my life   1
    Yes, moderate interference with my life   2
    In the past, but not in the present   3
    Sometimes they affect me   4
    No, they do not interfere with my life   5
    No symptoms   6

SECTION J: MEDICATION

57 Have you taken medication from any source – prescribed or non-
    prescribed – for any of these symptoms?
    Yes   1   No   2

If 'No' go to Question 60

58 If yes, for how long have you take medication?
    Taken on one-off occasions/single dose   1
    One day or several days   2

Two weeks or less	3
2 weeks–1 month	4
1 month–1 year	5
1–5 years	6
More than 5 years	7
I am permanently on medication	8

59 Please think only about tablets that you have been given to you because of the effects of the Troubles on you. In your opinion, were these tablets given to you:
(Complete all items)

		Yes	No
(a)	To help you sleep	1	2
(b)	To calm you down	1	2
(c)	To give you a lift in mood	1	2
(d)	To even out your moods	1	2
(e)	To kill pain	1	2
(f)	To keep away the memories	1	2
(g)	To treat a physical condition	1	2
(h)	Other	1	2

Self-Medication with Alcohol/Drugs

60 On balance, do you think your drinking has changed as a result of your experiences of the Troubles?

No, it has stayed the same	1	I have always abstained	4
Yes, it has increased	2	I abstain now	5
Yes, it has decreased	3		

61(a) Has there been a period of time when you drank a lot after a particular experience of the Troubles?
Yes   1   No   2
(b)   If YES, for how long?

Less than 6 months	1	1–5 years	3
6 months–1 year	2	More than 5 years	4

62(i) If you have been taking medication or using alcohol to help with the effects of the Troubles, to what extent has this ever affected you?

Severe interference with my life	1
Moderate interference with my life	2
Mild interference with my life	3
No interference with my life	4
Not applicable	5

62(ii) Has this medication or alcohol ever affected:

	Affected me strongly	Moderately affected me	Affected me little	No Effect
(a) Your schooling, education or training	1	2	3	4
(b) Your home life, family relationships	1	2	3	4
(c) Your social life, hobbies & leisure	1	2	3	4
(d) Your other activities, such as driving	1	2	3	4

Now, I would like to ask about how the Troubles may have affected your health and well-being.

63   Do you agree/disagree that the Troubles have:

		Strongly agree	Agree	Neither agree nor disagree	Disagree	Strongly disagree
(a)	Caused me a great deal of distress and emotional upset	1	2	3	4	5
(b)	Made violence more a part of my life	1	2	3	4	5
(c)	Made it difficult for me to trust people in general	1	2	3	4	5
(d)	Left me feeling helpless	1	2	3	4	5
(e)	Provoked strong feelings of rage in me	1	2	3	4	5
(f)	Shattered my illusion that the world is a safe place	1	2	3	4	5
(g)	Caused me not to want to have anything to do with the other community	1	2	3	4	5

Now I would like to ask how the Troubles may have affected your family.

64   Do you agree/disagree that the troubles have:

		Strongly agree	Agree	Neither agree nor disagree	Disagree	Strongly disagree
(a)	Completely ruined my life	1	2	3	4	5
(b)	Damaged my health	1	2	3	4	5
(c)	Caused me to lose loved ones through death	1	2	3	4	5
(d)	Physically damaged me/my family	1	2	3	4	5
(e)	Severely altered the path my life would have taken	1	2	3	4	5
(f)	Led to me/my family leaving our home through intimidation or fear of attack	1	2	3	4	5
(g)	Influenced where I have chosen to live	1	2	3	4	5
(h)	Caused me to worry a lot about rearing my children	1	2	3	4	5
(i)	Made members of my family and/or me emigrate	1	2	3	4	5
(j)	Made members of my family and/or me seriously consider emigration	1	2	3	4	5
(k)	Divided members of my family against one another	1	2	3	4	5
(l)	Made me extremely fearful for my own and my family's safety	1	2	3	4	5

Now I wish to ask how the Troubles may have affected your life in terms of your education, work and income.

65   Do you agree/disagree that the troubles have:

		Strongly agree	Agree	Neither agree nor disagree	Disagree	Strongly disagree
(a)	Seriously damaged my livelihood/job/business	1	2	3	4	5
(b)	Influenced the kind of work I do	1	2	3	4	5
(c)	Interrupted my educational opportunities	1	2	3	4	5
(d)	Restricted the number of areas I am prepared to go into for work	1	2	3	4	5
(e)	Led me to shop in certain areas/businesses and not in others	1	2	3	4	5
(f)	Have created employment opportunities for me/ members of my family	1	2	3	4	5
(g)	Caused damage or loss to my property	1	2	3	4	5

66   Would you agree or disagree that the Troubles have affected your leisure pursuits in terms of restricting how and where you spend your leisure time?

Strongly agree	1	Disagree	4
Agree	2	Strongly disagree	5
Neither agree nor disagree	3		

67   In general, would you agree/disagree that the Troubles have:

		Strongly agree	Agree	Neither agree nor disagree	Disagree	Strongly disagree
(a)	Nothing to do with me	1	2	3	4	5
(b)	Have not affected me very much at all	1	2	3	4	5
(c)	Caused me a great deal of distress and upset	1	2	3	4	5
(d)	Severely impacted on the area I live in	1	2	3	4	5

Now I wish to ask how the Troubles have affected your life in terms of the kind of person you are and how you present yourself.

68   Would you agree/disagree that the Troubles have:

		Strongly agree	Agree	Neither agree nor disagree	Disagree	Strongly disagree
(a)	Led me to support activities that I would otherwise think wrong	1	2	3	4	5
(b)	Made me ashamed of being from Northern Ireland	1	2	3	4	5
(c)	Made me very careful about expressing an opinion in case I offend someone	1	2	3	4	5
(d)	Made me wary of letting people know details about my life	1	2	3	4	5
(e)	Made me bitter	1	2	3	4	5
(f)	Made me more understanding of other people's difficulties	1	2	3	4	5
(g)	Have taught me the pointlessness and dangers of wanting revenge	1	2	3	4	5
(h)	Led me to stick to the company of those from my own community	1	2	3	4	5
(i)	Caused me to question or lose my faith	1	2	3	4	5
(j)	Made me feel powerless to stop what was happening	1	2	3	4	5
(k)	Strengthened my faith	1	2	3	4	5
(l)	Led me to find a faith or religious beliefs I didn't have before	1	2	3	4	5
(m)	Made me angry with God	1	2	3	4	5

Now I wish to ask how the Troubles may have affected your life in terms of your political attitudes?

69   Would you agree/disagree that the Troubles have:

		Strongly agree	Agree	Neither agree nor disagree	Disagree	Strongly disagree
(a)	Shown those in power to be lacking in the will to sort this conflict out	1	2	3	4	5
(b)	Restricted my opportunities to get to know and understand people from the other community	1	2	3	4	5

(c)	Led to distrust politicians	1	2	3	4	5
(d)	Led me to avoid political discussions, and to keep my opinions to myself	1	2	3	4	5
(e)	Led me to have more negative feelings about the other community	1	2	3	4	5
(f)	Made me more determined to resist being pushed around politically	1	2	3	4	5
(g)	Provoked me to great determination that things have to change and I will make a contribution to bringing about that change	1	2	3	4	5
(h)	Confirmed my belief about the mess made of this country by the older generation	1	2	3	4	5
(i)	Shown dialogue and negotiation to be a dangerous waste of time	1	2	3	4	5

Now I would like to ask how the Troubles have affected your life in terms of how you think about law and order.

70   Would you agree/disagree that the Troubles have:

		Strongly agree	Agree	Neither agree nor disagree	Disagree	Strongly disagree
(a)	Made me more critical of the police	1	2	3	4	5
(b)	Made me believe more in the law and the court system	1	2	3	4	5
(c)	Put paramilitaries in a position of having to police communities	1	2	3	4	5
(d)	Has meant that many people who would not normally go to prison have been or are still in prison	1	2	3	4	5
(e)	Made me feel sympathetic towards the police and the security forces	1	2	3	4	5

71   Overall, how much do you think your experiences of the Troubles have affected you?

Completely changed my life	1
Radically changed my life	2
Made some changes to my life	3
Made a small impact	4
Not at all	5

SECTION K: HELP AND SUPPORT

72 Have you ever seen any of the following trained helpers about the effect of the Troubles on you or on a member of your family?

		Yes	No
(a)	Psychiatrist	1	2
(b)	Clinical psychologist	1	2
(c)	GP and local doctor	1	2
(d)	Community nurse	1	2
(e)	Alternative health practitioner, e.g. reflexologist, acupuncturist	1	2
(f)	Chemist/pharmacist	1	2
(g)	Social worker	1	2
(h)	Child guidance	1	2
(i)	Support through school welfare /educational psychologist	1	2
(j)	Teacher	1	2
(k)	Counsellor	1	2
(l)	Self-help group	1	2
(m)	Marriage/relationship counsellor	1	2
(n)	Social Security agency	1	2
(o)	Citizen's Advice Bureau	1	2
(p)	The Samaritans	1	2
(q)	Minister or priest	1	2
(r)	Faith healer	1	2
(s)	Lawyer or solicitor	1	2
(t)	Personnel department within my employment	1	2
(u)	Accountant	1	2
(v)	Local politician	1	2
(w)	Community worker	1	2
(x)	Other voluntary organisation	1	2

73 Do you think the help available to you was satisfactory? (complete all items)

		Yes	No	Not applicable
(a)	Yes, it was sympathetic & helpful	1	2	3
(b)	It was adequate only	1	2	3
(c)	It was insensitive	1	2	3
(d)	It was harmful	1	2	3
(e)	It was judgemental	1	2	3
(f)	It was critical of me	1	2	3
(g)	I couldn't find help	1	2	3
(h)	Did not need help	1	2	3

74 Where, if from anywhere, did you receive the *best* help? (circle one only)

Spouse	1
My children	2
Parents	3
Other close family	4
Close friends	5
Neighbours	6
Work colleagues	7
Those in a similar position to myself	8

My local doctor	9
Psychiatrist	10
Clinical psychologist	11
Community nurse	12
Alternative health practitioner, e.g. reflexologist, acupuncturist	13
Chemist/pharmacist	14
Social worker	15
Child guidance	16
Support through school welfare/educational psychologist	17
Teacher	18
Counsellor	19
Self-help group	20
Marriage/relationship counsellor	21
Social Security agency	22
Citizen's Advice Bureau	23
The Samaritans	24
Minister or priest	25
Faith healer	26
Lawyer or solicitor	27
Personnel department within my employment	28
Accountant	29
I received appropriate help from no one	30

75 If you found if difficult to get help, was this mainly because ...

I didn't know where to look for help	1
I was unable to find help that met my needs satisfactorily	2
I was not able to look for help	3
I did not believe that anything could help me at that time	4
Other (please specify)	5

SECTION L: COMPENSATION

As you may know, the Northern Ireland Office pays compensation to people injured or who have sustained a loss in the Troubles.

76 Have you ever received such compensation from the Northern Ireland Office?
    Yes   1   No   2
If Yes ...

77 Do you think the compensation was enough?
    Yes   1   No   2

78 What problems, if any, are you aware of with the compensation system?
(a) Doesn't give enough money   1
(b) It is not fair: it gives some people more than others for the
     same injury   2
(c) Delays in payments cause financial problems to businesses   3
(d) There is no appeal against the amount granted   4
(e) I was asked a lot of very intrusive questions   5
(f) Not aware of any problems   6
(g) Other (please specify) _____

SECTION M: LEGAL REDRESS

79 Do you agree/disagree that the law does enough to deal with the
effects of the Troubles on people?

		Strongly agree	Agree	Neither agree nor disagree	Disagree	Strongly disagree
(a)	Yes, the law does enough	1	2	3	4	5
(b)	No, stiffer sentences are required for those who kill and injure people	1	2	3	4	5
(c)	No, not enough effort to catch those responsible	1	2	3	4	5
(d)	No, the law does not protect innocent people	1	2	3	4	5
(e)	No, the law victimises people further	1	2	3	4	5
(f)	No, there are two laws, one for us and one for them	1	2	3	4	5
(g)	I have no faith in the law here	1	2	3	4	5
(h)	The law is not suited to dealing with the troubles – something else is needed	1	2	3	4	5

Interviewer briefing

*I would like to thank you for your time and can assure you that all information will
be treated in total confidence.*

*Would you like information about self-help and support organisations in your
area?*

Thank you for your co-operation.

Appendix 4:
The YouthQuest 2000
Questionnaire

Community Conflict Impact on Children
Formerly known as The Cost of the Troubles Study

Unit 14 North City Business Centre
2 Duncairn Gardens
BELFAST BT15 2GG

Telephone   028 90742682
Fax   028 90 356654
e-mail   cicc@icore.ulst.ac.uk

In co-operation with
JOINT SOCIETY FOR A COMMON CAUSE
Bridge Youth Club, Bridge Road, Monkstown, Newtownabbey.
Tel: 0831 661202 day and evening.

YOUTHQUEST 2000
In co-operation with
CCIC

Date of completing questionnaire _____

Interviewer code _____

Questionnaire serial number _____

Location of interview:		
	School	1
	Youth club	2
	Other recreational	3
	Residential	4
	Own home	5
	Other	6

Location: Urban   1   Rural   2

Postcode   BT _____

Before starting the interview:

YouthQuest 2000 is a project designed to give young people the chance to explore and express their views and opinions on issues surrounding the peace process and the troubles as a whole.

We aim to get good information about the views and experiences of young people, with a view to improving public understanding of the views and wishes of young people. We plan to present out findings to the European Parliament in May 2000, so we will be putting your views to a wider audience. We believe our work is worthwhile and important, and we hope you agree. We would be grateful for your participation in the survey. It is important that you participate, no matter how much or how little you think you have to say about life in Northern Ireland. Your views are important to us.

All the information you may give me will be treated in strictest confidence, and we will not write down your name or other identifying details. We do ask for some personal details but those are for research purposes and do not include your name of address.

The decision to go ahead is yours and I would greatly appreciate it if you would add your experiences to our study. We wish to have a wide range of views and experiences included in our survey, and we would like you to be part of it.

1. How much interest do you generally have in what is going on in politics?

A great deal	1	Not very much	4
Quite a lot	2	None at al	5
Some	3	(Don't Know)	8

2. Thinking about the search for peace in northern Ireland, how helpful do you think the following have been over the last year or so?

	Very helpful	Quite helpful	Neither helpful nor unhelpful	Quite un-helpful	Very un-helpful	(DK)
a. The Irish government	1	2	3	4	5	8
b. The British government	1	2	3	4	5	8
c. The American government	1	2	3	4	5	8
d. Some paramilitary groups	1	2	3	4	5	8
e. Public opinion in general	1	2	3	4	5	8

3. Do you think there are any particular people that stand out as being helpful in the search for peace over the last year or so?

Yes	1	Ask Q5
No	2	
(Don't know)	8	Go to Q6

4. Who do you think stands out as being helpful? Please mark your answers on the table below: anyone else not on the list? write in table below. For Yes, has been helpful, tick box 1, for No, tick box 2, for Don't know, tick box 3.

Local figures			British government			Others		
Gerry Adams	1	2	Tony Blair	1	1	Albert Reynolds	1	2
John Alderdice	1	2	Mo Mowlam	1	2	John Bruton	1	2
David Ervine	1	2	John Major	1	2	Bertie Ahern	1	2
John Hume	1	2	Bill Clinton	1	2			
Robert McCartney	1	2	Senator Mitchell	1	2			
Gary McMichael	1	2						

Monica McWilliams	1	2			
Seamus Mallon	1	2	Other (Write in)	1	2
Ian Paisley	1	2			
David Trimble	1	2			

5. Which particular political party do you usually support?

Alliance	1	UK Unionist Party	9
UDP	2	NI Unionist Party	10
IRSP	3	Women's Coalition	11
PUP	4	Other (please give their name)	12
DUP	5	None	13
SDLP	6	Don't Know	89
UUP	7	NR	98
Sinn Fein	8		

6. Do you think that religion will always make a difference to the way people feel about each other in Northern Ireland?

Yes	1	Other (Write in)	3
No	2	(Don't know)	8

7. Did you read the good friday agreement document?

Yes, I read it all	1	No, I didn't see the document at all	5
Yes, I read parts of it	2	I can't remember	6
I had a quick flick through it	3	I don't know	8
No, I saw the document but didn't read it	4	NR	9

8. If you did read the agreement document, did you understand it?

Yes, I understood it all	1	I understood none of it	6
Yes, I understood most of it	2	I am not interested	7
I understood a bit of it	4	NR	9
I understood very little of it	5		

9. How do you assess the current peace process and the new assembly? Tick one only

I think it will fail soon	1
I think it will fail in February or sometime soon	2
I think it will succeed	3
I am not sure how it will go	4
I haven't really thought about it	5
I don't care	6
NR	9

10. Do you agree with early prisoner releases as part of the peace process? Tick one only

Yes, I agree they should all be released	1
Yes, I agree, but only if the ceasefires last	2
Reluctantly, I agree if it brings peace	3
I don't agree, they should serve their time	4
I don't know	8
NR	9

11. Please say whether you agree with the following statements on decommissioning

	Agree	Disagree	Don't know	NR
Only Republican paramilitaries should decommission				
Only Loyalist paramilitaries should decommission				
None of the paramilitaries should be expected to decommission				
Decommissioning should include the security forces				
Political parties with paramilitary links should be included in government				

12. Do you feel decommissioning should have been a precondition to prisoner release? (Tick one only)

Yes	1	Don't know	8
No	2	NR	9

13. Do you feel young people (of 15 years of age and older) should be able to vote?

Yes	1	Don't know	8
No	2	NR	9

14. If you had had the vote, would you have taken the opportunity to vote on the agreement?

Yes	1	Don't know	8
No	2	NR	9

15. If you said yes to question 10, would you have voted

For	1	Don't know	8
Against	2	NR	9

16. Should paramilitaries have a place in the local community?
Yes, to protect their own communities
Only if the peace process doesn't work
No, they should all be disbanded
No, there are too many violent organisations around
Don't know
NR

17. Should the RUC be restructured? (Tick one)
Yes, restructured and name changed
Yes, restructured without name change
Limited amount of restructuring, with no one losing jobs
No, the RUC are fine as they are
No, the RUC have suffered enough
Don't know
NR

18. Do you think cross-community europe has contributed to the peace process? (Tick one only)
Yes, it has made a big difference

Yes, but some of it was spent on things not related to peace
It made some difference
It made no difference
Don't know
NR

19. Would you mind or not mind if one of your close relatives were to marry
someone of a different religion? (Tick one only)

Would mind a lot	1	Would not mind	3
Would mind a little	2	(Don't know)	8

20. Do you have religious beliefs?
Yes, I am deeply religiously committed
Yes, I regularly practice my religion
Yes, but I am not affiliated to any organised religion
No, but I may change my mind
No
Don't know
NR

21. Do you think cross-community work (that is, projects where people from
both the catholic and protestant communities get together for various
activities) in Northern Ireland is a good idea?
(Tick one only)
Yes, it is very important in order to improve community relations
Yes, but it is not done properly with children and young people
Yes, but there is not enough of it
No, it makes no difference
No, I don't want to mix
No, people should be left to live separately
Don't know
NR

22. Have you ever had the chance to take part in a cross-community project?
(Tick one only)

Yes, and I did	No, but I don't want to
No, but I would like to	Don't know
Yes, and I refused	NR

23. How often do you mix socially with the opposite religion?

I live in a mixed family	Never, on principle
Every day	Never, no opportunity
Every week	Don't know
Every month	NR
Occasionally	

24. Which of these best describes the way you think of yourself?

British	1	Northern Irish	4
Irish	2	Other (Say what it is)	5
Ulster	3	(Don't know)	8

NOW SOME QUESTIONS ABOUT YOUNG PEOPLE IN NORTHERN IRELAND TODAY

25. Please tell me how much you agree or disagree with the following statements

	Strongly agree	Agree	Neither agree nor disagree	Disagree	Strongly disagree	Don't know
These days, schools encourage teenagers to express their views						
Most employers treat young people fairly						
Teenagers are always treated like second-class citizens in shops and cafes						

26. Thinking about politicians, how much do you agree or disagree with the following statements

	Strongly agree	Agree	Neither agree nor disagree	Disagree	Strongly disagree	Don't know
None of our politicians are bothered about the problems facing young people in Northern Ireland today						

27. Have you heard of the UN Convention on the Rights of the Child?
Yes   1   (Don't know)   8
No   2

This is an agreement between the countries of the United Nations that young people should be guaranteed certain rights, among them the right to express their views.

28. One of the things that the UN Convention on the Rights of the Child is concerned about is that young people should have the right to practise their own religion and culture. Have you ever felt that you had to try and hide what religion you were in case other people held it against you? (Tick one only)
Yes   Go to Q29
No   Go to Q30
(Don't have a religion)   Go to Q30
(Don't know)   Go to Q30

29. Has this happened ... (Tick one only)
A lot   Hardly at all?
A little   (Don't know)

30. Have you ever been threatened by other people or verbally abused because of your religion? (Tick one only)
Yes   No
(Don't know)   Go to Q31

31. Where were you the last time it happened?
In the street	Shop
At school	Other (Please state)
Leisure centre	(DK/Can't remember)
Cinema	

32. Do you avoid going to particular places because of the risk of being verbally abused or threatened?
Yes	Can't avoid it
No	(Don't know)

33. Would you say that students at your school get bullied coming to or leaving school by other students because of their religion ...
A lot	Not at all
A little	(Don't know)

34. Have you had any special classes where the problems of sectarianism and bullying because of religion have been talked about? (Tick one only)
    Yes   No
    (Don't know)

35. Thinking about the future, do you think that you yourself will stay in Northern Ireland or do you think that you will leave?
    (CODE 'leave to go to College/University' as LEAVE)
Stay	Go to Q37	
Leave	Ask Q36	
Other	(Write in)	3
(Don't know)	Go to Q36	

36. Why do you think that you will leave? (Tick all that apply)
    Better job prospects elsewhere
    Because of the troubles
    To seek a better future
    Because of a relationship
    To go to college/university
    Other (Write in)
    (Don't know)

37. Housing segregation (i.e. areas with mainly or only Catholics of Protestants living there) is widespread in northern Ireland. do you see the area you live in as segregated? (Tick one only)
    Yes   No

38. How much do you agree or disagree with the following statements regarding the problem of parades?

	Strongly agree	Agree	Neither agree nor disagree	Disagree	Strongly disagree	Don't know
Too many parades						
Unionist/Nationalist insecurity						
Nationalist/Republican impatience						
Unionist/Loyalist desire to show dominance						

Unionist/Loyalist genuine
  fear of losing ground
Nationalist/Republican
  genuine fear of marches
Others (Please specify)

Now some questions about specific experiences that you may have had of
the Troubles. Here is a list of experiences that people have had of the Troubles
starting with common experiences

39. Would you tell me how often, if at all, you have had the experience?

Event/experience	Very often	Occasionally	Seldom	Never	Don't know
Straying into an area where I didn't feel safe					
Getting stopped and searched by the security forces					
Feeling unable to say what I think or being wary in a situation because of safety issues					
My parents having to take extra safety precautions to secure my home or workplace					
Having to change my normal routes, routines or habits because of safety					

The next question deals with slightly more direct experience of the Troubles

40. Can I ask if you have had any of these experiences, and if so how often?

Event/experience	Very often	Occasionally	Seldom	Never
Having to end friendships or having relationships disrupted because of the sectarian divide				
Getting into physical fights about the Troubles				
Having my schooling disrupted by the Troubles				
Had experience of military organisations acting as punishment agencies				

The next question deals with some of the most severe, distressing and direct
experience of the troubles

41. Can I ask if you have had any of these experiences of the Troubles, and
    if so how often?

	Very often	Occasionally	Seldom	Never
Having my home attacked				
Having to leave my home temporarily				
Having to leave my home permanently				
Having my home destroyed				

The next question deals with situations in the troubles where people have been injured or killed

42. Can I ask if you have had any of these experiences and if so how often?

	Several times	More than once	Once	Never
Being caught up in a riot				
Witnessing a shooting				
Having a work colleague attacked				
Having a work colleague killed				
Having a neighbour attacked				
Having a neighbour killed				
Seeing people killed or seriously injured				
Having a close friend killed				
Being physically attacked due to the Troubles				
Being injured in a bomb explosion				
Being injured in a shooting				
Having a member of my immediate family injured				
Having a member of my immediate family killed				
Having another relative injured				
Having another relative killed				

43. How much do you think each of the following are responsible for the Troubles?

	Most responsible	Responsible	Least responsible	Don't Know
Republican paramilitaries in general				
Loyalist paramilitaries in general				
The RUC				
The RIR/UDR				
The British Army				
Republican politicians				
Loyalist politicians				
British politicians				
Irish politicians				
All politicians				
British government				
Irish government				
The Churches				
The silent majority in Northern Ireland				
People living in hard-line areas in NI				
Other, please specify _____				

EFFECTS OF THE TROUBLES ON YOU

Some people experience after-effects as a result of their experiences of the Troubles. Can I ask you if you have had after-effects, for example:

44. Have the Troubles ever affected:

	Affected me strongly	Moderately affected me	Affected me little	No effect
Your schooling, education or training				
Your home life, family relationships				
Your social life, hobbies and leisure				
Your other activities, such as shopping				

Now I would like to ask how the Troubles may have affected your family

45. Do you agree/ disagree that the Troubles have:

	Strongly agree	Agree	Neither agree nor disagree	Disagree	Strongly disagree
Completely ruined my life					
Damaged my health					
Caused me to lose loved ones through death					
Physically damaged me/ my family					
Severely altered the path my life would have taken					
Led to me/my family leaving our home through intimidation or fear of attack					
Influenced where I have chosen to live					
Made members of my family and/or me emigrate					
Made members of my family and/or me seriously consider emigration					
Divided members of my family against one another					
Made me extremely fearful for my own and my family's safety					

46. In general, would you agree/disagree that the Troubles have:

	Strongly agree	Agree	Neither agree nor disagree	Disagree	Strongly disagree
Nothing to do with me					
Have not affected me very much at all					
Caused me a great deal of distress and upset					
Severely impacted on the area I live in					

47. Overall, how much do you think your experiences of the Troubles have affected you?

Completely changed my life
Radically changed my life
Made some changes to my life
Made a small impact
Not at all

RELIGION AND ETHNIC ORIGIN

48. In terms of the two communities in northern Ireland, are you considered
    by others to be:
    A member of the Catholic community
    A member of the Protestant community
    Other

49. How old were you last birthday?_____

50. Gender
    Male   1   Female   2

51. What is the main place you go to for your full-time education?
    School   1
    Sixth Form college   2
    College of Further education   3
    College of Higher Education/Tertiary College   4
    University   5
    Other (Write in)   6
    (Refusal/NA)   7

52. Was there anyone else present apart from the interviewer when you filled
    in this questionnaire?
    Yes, all the time   1
    Yes, sometimes   2
    No   3
    (Don't know)   8

53. Who else was present? (Tick all that apply)
                        Yes   No
    Mother
    Father
    Brother/sister
    Interviewer
    Teacher
    Other (write in)
    Don't know

54. Thinking about your current or last school, could you tell me which of
    the following best describes your school? (Tick one only)
    Mixed 50/50 school
    Mixed but less of my community
    Mixed but more of my community
    Hardly mixed: very few of the other community
    Not mixed all of my community
    Hardly mixed: very few of my community
    Not mixed none of the other community
    Don't know

55. WHAT TYPE OF SCHOOL DO YOU ATTEND?
    Grammar   Other
    Secondary   Don't know

56. What type of house do you live in?
    Rented (Housing Executive)
    Rented (private)
    Owned (outright)
    Owned (with mortgage)

Length of time you took to complete questionnaire

Hours   Mins

Bibliography

American Psychiatric Association (APA) (1994) *Diagnostic and Statistical Manual of Mental Disorders* (fourth edition). Washington, DC: APA.

Bell, P., Kee, G., Loughrey, R., Roddy, R.J. and Curran, P.S. (1988) 'Post-Traumatic Stress in Northern Ireland', *Acta Psychiatrica Scandinavia*, 77: 166–9.

Bloomfield, K. (1998) *We Will Remember Them: Report of the Northern Ireland Victims Commissioner, Sir Kenneth Bloomfield*. Belfast: HMSO.

Brewer, J. (1998) *Anti-Catholicism in Northern Ireland 1600–1998*. London: Macmillan.

Brody, L.R. and Hall, J.A. (1993) 'Gender and Emotion', in M. Lewis and J. Haviland (eds) *Handbook of Emotions*. New York: Guilford Press.

Brown, A. (1996) *An Analysis of Referral for Deliberate Self Harm*. Derry Londonderry: Altnagelvin Hospital Trust.

Burstein, B., Banl, L. and Jarvik, L.F. (1980) 'Sex Differences in Cognitive Functioning: Evidence, Determinants, Implications', *Human Development*, 23: 289–313.

Cadwallader, A. and Wilson, R. (1991) 'A Case of Any Catholic Will Do', *Fortnight: An Independent Review for Northern Ireland*, 295 (May): 6.

Cairns, E. (1998) *Caught in the Crossfire: Children and the Northern Ireland Conflict*. Belfast: Appletree.

Cairns, E. and Wilson, R. (1989) 'Coping with Political Violence in Northern Ireland', *Social Science and Medicine*, 28(6): 621–4.

Community Conflict Impact on Children (CCIC) (2000) *Building the Future: Report of a Conference on Young People and the Troubles*. Belfast: CCIC.

Central Statistical Office (CSO) (1999) *Regional Trends*. London: CSO.

Charny, I. (1991) 'The Psychology of Denial of Known Genocides', in I. Charny (ed.) *Genocide: A Critical Bibliographical Review*. New York: Facts on File.

The Cost of the Troubles Study/Northern Visions (2000) *And Then There Was Silence … .* Colour VHS video, 70 minutes. Belfast: The Cost of the Troubles Study/Northern Visions.

The Cost of the Troubles Study (1999) *Do You Know What Happened?* Touring exhibit in 15 panels. Belfast: The Cost of the Troubles Study.

The Cost of the Troubles Study (1997) *Do You See What I See? Young People's Experience of the Troubles*. Belfast: INCORE/University of Ulster/United Nations University.

Crawford, C. (1999) *Defenders of Criminals? Loyalist Prisoners and Criminalisation*. Belfast: Blackstaff.

Curran, P.S., Bell, P., Murray, A., Loughrey, G., Roddy, R. and Rocke, L.G. (1990) 'Psychological Consequences of the Enniskillen Bombing', *British Journal of Psychiatry*, 156: 479–82.

Deane, S. (1997) *Reading in the Dark*. London: Jonathan Cape.

Department of Health and Social Security (DHSS)/Park, J. (1998) *Living with the Trauma of the 'Troubles': Report on a Developmental Project to Examine and Promote the Further Development of Services to Meet the Social and Psychological Needs of Individuals Affected by the Civil Unrest in Northern Ireland*. Belfast: HMSO.

Doherty, P. and Poole, M.A. (1995) *Ethnic Residential Segregation of Belfast*. Coleraine: University of Ulster, Centre for the Study of Conflict.

Fay, M.T., Morrissey, M. and Smyth, M. (1997) *Mapping Troubles-Related Deaths in Northern Ireland.* Derry Londonderry: INCORE (United Nations University/University of Ulster).

Fay, M.T., Morrissey, M. and Smyth, M. (1999a) *Northern Ireland's Troubles: The Human Costs.* London: Pluto Press.

Fay, M.T., Morrissey, M., Smyth, M. and Wong, T. (1999b) *Report on the Northern Ireland Survey: The Experience and Impact of the Troubles. The Cost of the Troubles Study.* Derry Londonderry: INCORE (United Nations University/University of Ulster).

Feldman, A. (1991) *Formations of Violence: The Narrative of the Body and Political Terror in Northern Ireland.* London: University of Chicago Press.

Finlay, A., Shaw, N., Whittington, D. and McWilliams, M. (1995) *Adolescent Reproductive Behaviour in the Western Health and Social Services Board Area.* Coleraine: University of Ulster/Western Health and Social Services Board.

Finlayson, A. (1999) 'Loyalist Political Identity After Peace', *Capital and Class,* 69 (Autumn).

Fitzpatrick, P., Molloy, B. and Johnson, Z. (1997) 'Community Mothers' Programme: Extension to the Travelling Community in Ireland', *Journal of Epidemiology and Community Health,* 51(3): 299–303.

Flackes, W.D. and Elliott, S. (1989) *Northern Ireland: A Political Dictionary. 1968–1988.* Belfast: Blackstaff.

Frankl, V. (1959) *Man's Search for Meaning.* New York: Washington Square Press/Pocket Books.

Fraser, R.M. (1971) 'The Cost of Commotion: An Analysis of the Psychiatric Sequelae of the 1969 Belfast Riots', *British Journal of Psychiatry,* 11: 237–64.

Fraser, R.M., Overy, R., Russell, J., Dunlap, R. and Bourne, R. (1972) 'Children and Conflict', *Community Forum,* 2. Belfast: Community Relations Commission.

Gaffikin, F. and Morrissey, M. (1996) *A Tale of One City? North and West Belfast: Consultative Document.* Belfast: Urban Institute.

Healey, A. (1996) 'Systemic Therapy in a Culture of Conflict: Developing a Therapeutic Conversation', *Child Care Practice,* 3(1): 68–86.

Hutchinson, J. (1987) *The Dynamics of Cultural Nationalism: The Gaelic Revival and the Creation of the Irish Nation State.* London: Allen and Unwin.

Independent (1998) 'A house in flames, a street in tears', (London) 13 July.

Irwin, G. and Dunn, S. (1997) *Ethnic Minorities in Northern Ireland.* Coleraine: University of Ulster.

Jones, D.R. and McCoy, D.B. (1989) 'Indicators of Health in Northern Ireland's Young', in J. Harbinson (ed.) *Growing Up in Northern Ireland.* Belfast: December Publications.

Kanter, R.M. (1976) 'The Impact of Hierarchical Structures on the Work Behavior of Men and Women', *Social Problems,* 23: 415–30.

Kanter, R.M. (1977) 'Some Effects of Proportions on Group Life: Skewed Sex Ratios and Responses to Token Women', *American Journal of Sociology,* 82(5): 965–90.

Leonard, M. (1992) 'Ourselves Alone: Household Work Strategies in a Deprived Community', *Irish Journal of Sociology,* 2.

Lyons, H.A. (1974) 'Terrorists' Bombing and the Psychological Sequelae', *Journal of the Irish Medical Association,* 67(1) (12 January).

McAuley, J.W. (1994) *The Politics of Identity: A Loyalist Community in Belfast.* Aldershot: Avebury.

McGarry, J. and O'Leary, B. (1995) *Explaining Northern Ireland.* Oxford: Blackwell.

McGinty, R. (1998) 'Hate Crime in Deeply Divided Societies: The Case of Northern Ireland'. Paper presented at the International Conference on

Hate Crime, Brudnick Center for the Study of Conflict and Violence, Northeastern University, Boston, 6–7 November.

Machel, G. (1996) *Impact of Armed Conflict on Children*. Geneva: United Nations Department for Policy Co-ordination and Sustainable Development (DPCSD) (August).

McKeown, M. (1973) 'Civil Unrest: Secondary Schools Survey', *Northern Teacher* (Winter): 39–42.

McKitterick, D. (1994) *Endgame: The Search for Peace in Northern Ireland*. Belfast: Blackstaff.

Macksound, M.S. and Aber, L. (1996) 'The War Experience and Psychological Development of Children in Lebanon', *Child Development*, 67: 70–88.

McVeigh, R. (1994) *It's Part of Life Here ... The Security Forces and Harassment in Northern Ireland*. Belfast: Committee for the Administration of Justice.

Mayhew, O. and Van Dijk, J.J.M. (1997) *Key Findings from the 1996 International Crime Victims Survey*. Wetenschappelijk Onderzoek.

Moloney, E. (1999) 'Simmering feuds near the boil', *Sunday Tribune*, 21 March.

Murtagh, B. (1999) *Community and Conflict in Rural Ulster*. Coleraine: University of Ulster, Centre for the Study of Conflict.

Northern Ireland Office (1998) Press Release, 20 April.

Northern Ireland Statistics and Research Agency (NISRA) (1997) *Northern Ireland Annual Abstract of Statistics*. Belfast: NISRA.

O'Connor, F. (1993) *In Search of a State: Catholics in Northern Ireland*. Belfast: Blackstaff.

O'Mahony, D. (1997) *The Northern Ireland Communities Crime Survey*. Belfast: Queen's University of Belfast, School of Law/Institute of Criminology and Criminal Justice.

Orwell, G. (1949) *Nineteen Eighty-Four*. London: Secker and Warburg.

Pauley, M. (1999) 'Victims "Being Used for Politics"', *Newsletter*, 25 September.

Pollak, A. and Moloney, E. (1986) *Paisley*. Dublin: Poolbeg.

Poole, M. and Doherty, P. (1996) *Ethnic Residential Segregation in Northern Ireland*. Coleraine: University of Ulster, Centre for the Study of Conflict.

Robson, B., Bradford, M. and Deas, I. (1994) *Relative Deprivation in Northern Ireland*. Belfast: Policy, Planning and Research Unit.

Roulston, C. (1999) 'Inclusive Others: The Northern Ireland Women's Coalition in the Peace Process', *Scottish Affairs*, 26 (Winter): 1–13.

Ruane, J. and Todd, J. (1996) *The Dynamics of Conflict in Northern Ireland*. Cambridge: Cambridge University Press.

Santayana, G. (1905) *Life of Reason*, Vol. 1.

Shirlow, P. and McGovern, M. (1997) 'The Political Economy of Ulster Loyalism', in P. Shirlow and M. McGovern (eds) *Who are the People? Unionism, Protestantism and Loyalism in Northern Ireland*. London: Pluto Press.

Smith, D.J. and Chambers, G. (1991) *Inequality in Northern Ireland*. Oxford: Policy Studies Institute.

Smyth, M. (1995a) 'Limitations on the Capacity for Citizenship in Post Ceasefire Northern Ireland', in M. Smyth (ed.) *Three Conference Papers on Aspects of Sectarian Division*. Derry Londonderry: Templegrove Action Research.

Smyth, M. (1995b) 'Borders within Borders: Material and Ideological Segregation as Forms of Resistance and Strategies of Control'. Proceedings of the European Group for the Study of Deviance and Social Control 1995 Annual Conference. Crossmaglen: European Group for the Study of Deviance and Social Control.

Smyth, M. (1995c) *Sectarian Division and Area Planning: A Commentary on the Derry Area Plan 2011*. Derry Londonderry: Templegrove Action Research.

Smyth, M. (1996) *Life in Two Enclave Areas in Northern Ireland. A Field Survey in Derry Londonderry after the Cease-fires*. Derry Londonderry: Templegrove Action Research.

Smyth, M. (1998) 'Remembering in Northern Ireland: Victims, Perpetrators and Hierarchies of Pain and Responsibility', in B. Hamber (ed.) *Past Imperfect: Dealing with the Past in Northern Ireland and Societies in Transition*. Derry Londonderry: INCORE.

Smyth, M. (2000) 'The Human Consequences of Armed Conflict: Constructing "Victim-hood" in the Context of Northern Ireland's Troubles', in M. Cox, A. Guelke and F. Stephen (eds) *A Farewell to Arms? From War to Peace in Northern Ireland*. Manchester: Manchester University Press.

Smyth, M. and Fay, M.T. (2000) *Personal Accounts from Northern Ireland's Troubles: Public Conflict, Private Loss*. London: Pluto Press.

Smyth, M., Hayes, E. and Hayes, P. (1994) 'Post Traumatic Stress Disorder and the Victims of Bloody Sunday: A Preliminary Study'. Paper presented at the International Congress on Violence and Mental Health. Northern Ireland Association for Mental Health/ Ethnic Studies Network. Belfast: Queen's University of Belfast.

Smyth, M. and Moore, R. (1996) 'Researching Sectarianism', in M. Smyth (ed.) *Three Conference Papers on Aspects of Sectarian Division*. Derry Londonderry: Templegrove Action Research.

Smyth, M., Morrissey, M. and Hamilton, J. (2001) *Caring Through the Troubles: Health and Social Services in North and West Belfast*. Belfast: North and West Health and Social Services Trust.

Smyth, M. and Robinson, G. (eds) (2001) *Researching Violently Divided Societies: Ethical and Methodological Issues*. Tokyo and London: United Nations University Press/Pluto Press.

Straker, G., Mendelson, M. and Tudin, P. (1993) 'The Effects of Diverse Forms of Political Violence on the Emotional and Moral Concerns of Youths', in Stiftung fur Kinder (ed.) *Children – War and Persecution*. Osnabruck: Stiftung fur Kinder/UNICEF.

Tannen, D. (1990) 'Gender Differences in Conversational Coherence; Physical Alignment and Topical Cohesion', in B. Dorval (ed.) *Conversational Coherence and its Development*. Norwood, NJ: Ablex.

Taylor, P. (1999) *Loyalists*. London: Bloomsbury.

Templegrove Action Research (1996) *Hemmed In and Hacking It: Words and Images from Two Enclaves in Northern Ireland*. Derry Londonderry: Guildhall Press.

Thomas, L.M. (1999) 'Suffering as a Moral Beacon: Blacks and Jews', in H. Flanzbaum (ed.) *The Americanisation of the Holocaust*. Baltimore, MD: Johns Hopkins University Press.

Trew, K. (1995) 'Psychological and Social Impact of the Troubles on Young People Growing Up in Northern Ireland'. Proceedings of the International Association of Juvenile and Family Court Magistrates Regional Seminar, Belfast.

United Nations (1998) *Protection of Children Affected by Armed Conflict*. New York: United Nations Office of the Special Representative of the Secretary General on Children and Armed Conflict.

Wilson, J. (1989) 'Educational Performance; A Decade of Evidence', in J. Harbinson (ed.) *Growing up in Northern Ireland*. Belfast: December Publications.

World Health Organisation (WHO) (1993) *International Classification of Diseases* (tenth edition). Geneva: WHO.

Index

Compiled by Sue Carlton